Queering SF Comics

Queering SF Comics: Readings

by
Ritch Calvin

Seattle, WA

Aqueduct Press
PO Box 95787
Seattle, Washington 98145-2787
www.aqueductpress.com

Library of Congress Control Number: 2024940176

ISBN: 978-1-61976-264-0
First Edition, First Printing, October 2024

Cover Illustration courtesy Arin Nurius

Book design by Kathryn Wilham

Printed in the USA by Bookmobile

Acknowledgments

Once again, I want to acknowledge my students. They inspire me to continue to learn and to teach. Although I have not yet taught this course, it's the one they want to take. I can't wait to teach it.

Once again, I would like to thank Timmi Duchamp and Kathryn Wilham at Aqueduct. Their input is always incredibly beneficial. All shortcomings remain my own.

My heartfelt gratitude to Arin Nurius for the wonderful cover art.

A huge thank you to my beta reader, Genevieve Ruzicka. Your care and insights were such a huge help.

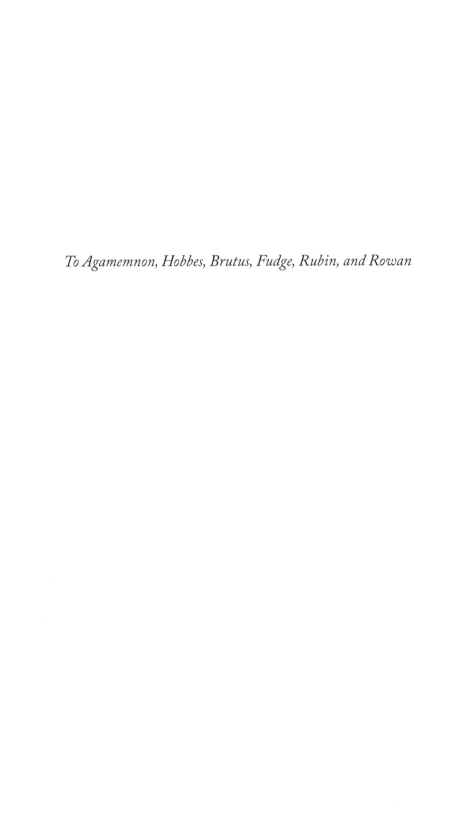

To Agamemnon, Hobbes, Brutus, Fudge, Rubin, and Rowan

Contents

45 Shades of Queer SF Comics: An Introduction

WHERE TO BEGIN? Let's unpack the title first.

What are comics? Arguably, comics—if taken as sequential art and literature—could be one of our oldest modes of narrative. Were the cave paintings an early form of comics? Scott McCloud (he/him)* makes a case for Aztec/Nahuatl origins (10). Will Eisner (he/him), on the other hand, suggests that the first comics appeared "around 1934" (7). Daniel Stein (he/him) and Jan-Noël Thon (he/him), however, note that a schoolteacher from Switzerland, Rodolphe Töpffer (he/him), created the first stories that combined words and images *and* employed a panel border (5). He called these works "stories in etchings" (*histoires en ampes*) (5). Kai Linke (he/him) notes that comics in the United States first appeared in 1895 when Richard Fenton Outcault (he/him) published *The Yellow Kid* in *New York World*. That strip told the story of immigrants in the urban environment of an East Side tenement (22).

---

* A note on pronouns: I have tried to the best of my ability to locate the pronouns for people and characters discussed in the book. I have consulted home pages, references pages, publisher pages, and social media to determine what pronouns a person uses. However, I am aware that, sometimes, the internet does not get things correct. I am also aware that pronouns are not fixed and stable, that they change over time. The pronouns used in mid-2024 may be different in late-2024 or 2050. Nevertheless, I believe that it is important to use desired pronouns whenever possible: (a) it acknowledges the individuals themselves, and (b) it is consistent with the aim and message of the book.

And, wouldn't you know, comics were a huge hit! In the Golden Age of comics—generally taken to be 1938-1945—one out of every three periodicals sold in the US was a comic book. Linke writes that 90% of the nation read comics. Ninety percent! Just take a second and imagine the scope of that. Is any medium that popular these days? Does any form of entertainment capture that large of a market share? In this fractured market, not even close.

But that all changed, didn't it? You can probably guess why.

In 1954, one Fredric Wertham (he/him) single-handedly ended the Golden Age of comics. Every action has an equal and opposite reaction, no? In 1954, Wertham published *Seduction of the Innocent*, a screed against comics that linked the reading of comics to every social ill. To be fair, Wertham was concerned about a number of important social issues. He saw rampant authoritarianism in comics and saw it as a danger. Wertham also railed at the explicit and violent racism in comics. He saw both of these elements as detrimental to the developing mind.

Even so, it was Wertham's focus on sex and sexuality that drew the most attention. He pointed to the scantily clad women, to sexual activity, and to sexual "perversions." The consequence of Wertham's book was the creation of the Comics Magazine Association of America (CMAA), which then produced the Comics Code Authority (CCA). This organization and its code functioned very much like the Hayes Code did regarding film.

The CCA spelled out what could and could not be in a comic in order to get the seal of approval from the CMAA. Only comics that met the guidelines received the seal, and many distributors and retailers would only sell comics that had the seal. The seal was life or death for a comic. The CCA had a lasting impact on the representation of sexuality, in general, and of homosexuality, in particular, within comics (Linke 23).

Well, Sigmund Freud (he/him) has a lot to say about repression. The short version of Freud's take on repression is that one can try to repress something like sexuality or sexual desires, but those desires just return in other ways. That was no less true for the comics industry.

In the 1960s, underground comix began to appear in college towns. Technology had developed enough that college kids could self-produce comic books. These largely white, largely straight, and largely educated men were not beholden to the CCA, and they didn't give a fig about the seal. They also didn't care much about boundaries, except to push against them. All of those things banned by the CCA code returned: rampant racism, authoritarianism, misogyny, and violence. These underground comix flourished until 1973 when a Supreme Court ruling on *Miller v. California* ruled that local jurisdictions could determine obscenity standards for themselves (Linke 24). Now, suddenly, the small shop in the college town was nervous about selling a boundary-pushing comic.

So, queer folx found no representation in mainstream comics under the CCA. Queer folx saw no (positive) representation in underground comix. Well, the old adage goes: if you want something done, you do it yourself.... The time of Stonewall saw a wave of self-produced queer comics. After self-published underground queer comics became successful, a publisher wanted to get in on the act, namely Kitchen Sink Press in Wisconsin. Still, queer comics were largely relegated to indie comics.

However, queer folx did eventually make it into mainstream comics. As Linke points out, a change in the CCA allowed that shift to happen when it did. The CCA was revised in 1989, and in that revision, the clause about "sexual perversion" was dropped. It also stipulated that *some* adult human activities could be represented (32).

And so it was in 1992 that Northstar of the *Alpha Flight* series came out and said, "I am gay" (Linke 32). Nevertheless, it was not until 2010 that the comic *hints* at sexual activity off screen. And it is not until 2011 that Northstar kissed his boyfriend in the comic.

As I noted in my previous book, *Queering SF: Readings* (Aqueduct, 2022), 2010 seemed to be a watershed year for queer representation in SF. This current book will pick up the history there, with readings of queer SF comics published between 2011 and 2022.

The debates about what a comic is are complex and contentious. At their most fundamental, the definitions of a comic boil down to form versus function. Some histories of comics, such as Will Eisner's *Comic and Sequential Art*, focus on the elements of a comic. That is, the things on the page (the panels, the images, the words, the order) are what define it as sequential art, or a comic. Other histories, such as Darrieck Scott (he/him) and Ramzi Fawaz's (he/him) introduction to *American Literature*, focus on what those things on the page *do*. They argue that comics formally and necessarily queer the reader's perceptions of the world because they "direct[] readers toward deviant bodies that refuse to be fixed in one image or frame" (203).

Even so, we can employ a basic definition of what a comic is. A **comic** can consist of a single frame, a single panel that employs some combination of images (or icons) and words. That comic can also take the form of a **comic strip**, a short, often three- or four-panel strip, that runs in daily newspapers— or on web-based platforms, in which case it is a **webcomic**. A comic book is generally a short booklet with a series of strips. Comics run from 2-32 pages. An **omnibus**, as the name suggests, is a longer work that collects 3 to 6 comic books into a single volume—presumably for convenience, but also to sell additional copies. Finally, the most recent iteration of sequential art is the **graphic novel**, which is generally not conceptualized as a serial but rather as a whole and constructed as a single unit.

In this collection of readings, I will consider all these forms. In other words, the "comics" in the title is an umbrella term for all forms of sequential pictorial and narrative art. However, I will offer the caveat that I will not spend a lot of time on the formal elements of the comics, except where I think they queer the comic.[†]

To further unpack the title, let's look at the term "science fiction." Writer, editor, and critic Damon Knight (he/him) quite (in)famously said that "[Science fiction] is what we point to when we say it" (Clute and Nicholls *Encyclopedia,* 314). In other words, it's whatever we say it is. Flippant though that definition may be, it is more or less the definition I have used in collecting these works. If an author calls their work science fiction, fantasy, or speculative fiction, I take them at their word. I have no interest in policing whether or not a particular piece is or is not SF.

However, I focus on SF comics for a reason. After all, the field of comics is *vast,* and I am only discussing those comics that are SF. Why? Well, first and foremost, I enjoy SF as a mode of narrative. If science fiction is a literature of ideas, then I'm there for it. Secondly, I think that SF is ineluctably connected to the queer. As I wrote in *Queering SF: Readings,* queer writing and SF writing tend to engage in a similar project—imagining and bringing a new reality into being, both science fiction and queer writing imagine societies in which social structures are differently constructed. Everything can be called into question and redefined: the family, government, relationships (personal, sexual, romantic, business), commerce,

[†] A note on spoilers: A number of my readings will contain spoilers. Reader beware.

the law, and so many other elements that have historically marginalized queer folx. Third, writers and artists are creating some magnificent SF comics right now. If 1938-1945 was the Golden Age of comics, then 2010-2022 just might be a Golden Age of queer SF comics.

Finally, let's unpack the final term from the title, "queer." Though historically deployed as an insult, *queer* has been recuperated to signify something positive and generative. In its positive senses, queer can signify an identity. Philosophically and ideologically, some who took up the term *queer* did *not* want it to be an identity, like woman or man, gay or lesbian. All of those terms of identity have fraught histories; all of those terms have limitations; all of those terms are part and parcel of the very heteronormative patriarchy they seek to dismantle (or at least live outside of). Nevertheless, intentions are things with wings, and no one can lock down the meanings and uses of any word. In 2022, when I was researching and writing these essays, many queer folx did, indeed, use queer as a category of identity. In this sense, queer can refer to sex, gender, or sexuality.

Queer can also refer to a state of being. Perhaps one does not identify as woman or man but identifies with some other term. In the past decade, the number of gender terms available and in circulation has increased rapidly. Some online social media sites offer as many as 100 gender options when setting up a profile. An individual can use fairly specific terms, such as agender, bigender, neutrois, pangender, or two-spirit, all of which reject the binary of woman and man. They can also use more amorphous categories such as genderqueer or, simply, queer. In this sense, queer signifies something outside the historically given norms.

Similarly, queer can also be taken to refer to sexuality or sexual practices. Historically given terms really define sexuality in terms of objects of desire (e.g., same-sex desire or opposite-sex desire). Some terms, such as asexual or aromantic, suggest a complete rejection of that sexual paradigm. Some terms still rest upon objects of desire, but they add to the possibilities, such as bicurious, pansexual, or omnisexual. At the same time, some terms reject the object strategy altogether and use queer to signify a much more open and fluid "zone of possibilities" (Jagose 2).

Speaking of possibilities, throughout the book I will make a point of the importance of representation. For example, if a child has never seen, never heard of, or never read about a nurse, that child is unlikely to grow up and want to *be* a nurse, or to think that being a nurse is a possibility. Visibility matters! Even so, that comparison is limited. After all (not to degrade the nursing profession in any way), nursing is a profession, a trade, a job. It is not the core of that person's being (again, I am quite certain that some in the nursing profession see nursing as the core of their being). Even so, that person *can* walk away from being a nurse. Queer folx cannot walk away from being queer. And so, seeing queer folx in comics is crucial. Seeing a range of kinds of queer folx is crucial, both for someone struggling with their own identity, and for those who are already quite confident in their queer identity.

Furthermore, the range of representation is important. What makes a comic queer? What are the criteria? Again, I tend to take the artist's word. If they call it queer, I accept that. You will see a wide range of *kinds* of queer texts. Some comics here are marginally queer. Perhaps the comic features a single queer character. Other comics will be more fully queer, featuring multiple queer characters. Others are not limited to queer characters but will also represent sex, sexuality, and relationships. And finally, some comics here are radically queer, by which I mean that they fundamentally challenge and reimagine the comic form. I believe that it is important to include all of these variations of queer. Too often, marginalized narratives are reduced to a single type. What I hope to show is that queer SF comics cannot be reduced to a single type. I hope to show a wide and dynamic range of kinds of queer comics.

Even so, I do not use "queer" in the title but "queering." This specific use of the term is connected to the fourth definition of queer. Queer can also be used as an analytical or critical approach. To queer something, in this sense, is to make it strange or different, to look at it from a novel perspective, to use something in a nonconventional manner. As I argued in *Queering SF*, both queer and SF seek to make the familiar strange and to make the strange familiar. Both of these strategies play with and challenge our expectations. Both of them seek to bring about newly imagined futures. Scott and Fawaz argue that comics are queer by their very nature. They suggest that "comics do not need to be queered, comics themselves 'queer' the archive of US culture" (199). Even so, I am suggesting that artists can queer the content of SF comics and the form of SF comics (all the while being cognizant of the notion that those two are *not* separable).

In this sense, queering SF comics means challenging the very form of comics: what they represent, what they take as subject matter, how they represent it, what they aim to achieve. Queering SF comics means making them new. Queering comics means reimagining what they can do. Queering comics means imagining a new reality.

Let's begin.

Shade 1 — *A Quick and Easy Guide to They/Them Pronouns* (2018)

Welcome to the Future

> "We are living in a science fiction world."
> (George Takei [he/him] in Topel, 2013)

EVEN THOUGH THIS particular comic does not really fit the criteria of the book, I nevertheless begin here for a set of reasons.

For one, *A Quick and Easy Guide* is written in the form of a comic. Archie Bongiovanni (they/them) has been writing and drawing comics for a long time, including for *Autostraddle*, *The Nib*, and *Everyday Feminism*. Co-author Tristan Jimerson (he/him) has worked on various zines, for *The Moth*, and for NPR.

For another, *A Quick and Easy Guide* addresses queer issues and concerns.

Finally, as Lt. Sulu (actually, George Takei) noted, we are all living in a science fiction world right now. Many of the devices, gadgets, and technologies that once appeared only in SF stories and shows are now realities. When Dick Tracy (he/him) wore his amazing watch in the 1940s that sent and received video calls, many thought that that idea was preposterous. Now, we have the iWatch (and other smart watches). When Arthur C. Clarke (he/him) wrote about geosynchronous satellites for communications in 1945, it was the stuff of magic. Now, we all rely on those same satellites for our cars, GPS systems, weather forecasts, TV and cable broadcasts, smart phones, and smart watches.

So, as Bongiovanni and Jimerson write: "It's the future, we don't have time for that nonsense" (6).

This *Quick and Easy Guide* is set up in a first-person address. Long-time friends Bongiovanni and Jimerson tell the reader what they hope the book will accomplish. Bongiovanni is nonbinary, and Jimerson is cisgender and straight. They hope that two people from two different backgrounds with two different sets of experiences can demonstrate the need for and relevance of using non-gendered pronouns.

What does it matter that this book is presented in the form of a comic? For one, the publisher, Limerance Press, is an imprint of Oni Press. Oni is a significant publisher of comics and graphic novels, including *Rick and Morty*, *Black Metal*, *Helheim*, *Letter 44*, *Merry Men*, and *Kim Reaper*. I suspect they hope to tap into their usual reading audience.

For another, I suspect they see the social need. Social mores and practices change *fast*. A lot of people have had no exposure to they/them and gender-neutral pronouns. They simply do not know what to do, even if they are well intentioned. Additionally, Archie makes the point that many individuals who are nonbinary also may not be sure what the appropriate convention or practice might be. Everyone, they argue, can use a guide.

What Bongiovanni and Jimerson offer might seem basic for someone who reads a lot of queer and nonbinary literature. It might seem a tad introductory for someone who *is* queer or nonbinary. However, as they note, the book has a range of intended readers. One, they write for someone who is working through their own identity and pronouns. Two, they write for someone who actively wants to be an ally and engage in best practices. And three, they write for someone who may not know a whole lot about non-gendered pronouns and is open to learning. Four, they also suggest that you can throw the book at the head of someone who stubbornly resists changing and persists in misgendering people. I'm pretty sure that was said in jest. No book throwing!

Instead, buy extra copies. Give them to friends, family, and colleagues. Buy copies and leave them on coffee tables worldwide. Buy copies and bring them to work so that HR and your bosses can begin to institute changes in their policies and practices.

The *Guide* correctly notes that all languages change over time. Sometimes slowly. Sometimes quickly. Right now, we are in a moment of rapid change, leaving many people uncertain of how to address family members, friends, and co-workers. The *Guide* also argues that no one owes anyone else an explanation as to why they would want to be addressed with they/them pronouns. If they share that explanation, fine. If they do not, also fine. The bottom line assumption here is that every person deserves to be recognized, acknowledged, and addressed as they please. It is basic human decency to do so.

The *Guide* also offers a "Practical Guide" to they/them pronouns. It reminds us not to make assumptions based on appearances—despite the fact that we were long taught that that was exactly what we should do. Things change. It reminds us not to ask about "preferences"—another recent change in practice. For a while we were always encouraged to ask about "preferred pronouns" at the beginning of a class or meeting. However, "preference" suggests everyone has a choice about identity and pronouns and that someone is just choosing the pronoun for, perhaps, frivolous reasons. The *Guide* then provides some scripts for how to introduce pronouns into the conversation and how to respond when meeting an individual.

The "Professional Guide" section recommends talking about nonbinary identities and practices early and often. It's important to do so whether or not nonbinary folx work in the office (or whatever the work space is). Making changes in language, terminology, forms, titles, and paperwork, can make the work space more comfortable for enby (nonbinary) and queer folx who work there. Nevertheless, even if no enby and queer folx work there, those conversations still need to happen. For one, those conversations make everyone a more receptive and empathetic human being. For another, those conversations make the workspace more desirable for anyone who might even think of working there. And, finally, those conversations make working with clients and customers better. Win, win, win.

So, pick up a copy of the guide and join us in George Takei's science fiction future.

Plus, it'll come in handy for the rest of this book....

Shade 2 — *Gingerbread Girl* (2011)
You Can't Catch Me, I'm the Genderbread Person

IN LATE MARCH 2022, Florida governor and then presidential hopeful Ron DeSantis (he/him) held a press conference to announce the "Don't Say Gay Bill" (he has a different, euphemistic name for it). In order to illustrate his point for the need for a "Don't Say Gay Bill," he displayed his printed out version of "The Genderbread Man." He suggests that the Genderbread Man is being used to indoctrinate children into changing their gender identity. What is he talking about?

Well, The Genderbread *Person* does exist (just not gendered in the way deSantis talks about it). Sam Killermann (he/him) created a simple gingerbread figure in 2011 in order to break down and discuss the elements of gender/sexual identity. Since that time, the edugraphic has been revised and is now in its fourth iteration and available for free on the web. According to the drawing, identity resides in the brain; gender expression resides in the body; biological sex resides in the genitals; and attraction lives in the heart. The first iteration relied fairly heavily on continua — that is, every aspect of identity could be found along a continuum between two binary opposites. The continua have now been replaced, though the edugraphic does still rest upon a number of binary choices.

By chance (or not), also in 2011 Paul Tobin (he/him) and Colleen Coover (she/her) published the graphic novel, *Gingerbread Girl*. Tobin has worked for Marvel Comics, and Coover writes lesbian-themed erotic comics. Between the two of them, they have been nominated for seven Eisner Awards (the top awards given annually in the field of comics), with three wins. *Gingerbread Girl* was written by Tobin and illustrated by Coover.

The graphic novel centers around Annahnette "Annah" Billips (she/her), a young woman who may or may not suffer from a neurological disease, or who may or may not have had her Penfield Homunculus removed by her father. (The cortical homunculus is a real thing, first mapped out by Dr. Wilder Penfield [he/him] and his team.) Annah believes (or so she would have *us* believe) that she has been split into two. She calls this extracted double the Gingerbread Girl because young Annah liked to eat gingerbread men cookies, make them playfight, and sometimes make them have sex (19). She, Annah, is devoid of feeling, and her double, the Gingerbread Girl, feels all the feels. For example, Annah tells us that she has had sex while the Gingerbread Girl hid in the closet. Only the Gingerbread Girl felt anything in the experience.

The razor's edge that Tobin and Coover walk is the epistemological verification of what has happened to Annah. Did her father experiment on her? Has she been divided into two beings? Or is the Gingerbread Girl a psychological cushion used to handle her parents' divorce? That divorce happened when Annah was nine, right before the Gingerbread Girl appeared. In any event, Annah can be a bit cruel, and she seems to not fully understand—or not to play by—social norms.

The novel uses several techniques to dump information on the reader. *Gingerbread Girl* begins with pages from Annah's yearbook. Annah often breaks the fourth wall and addresses the reader. For example, she faces the reader and says, "My name is Annah Billips, and as you can see, I'm currently in my panties. This is because I'm a *tease*" (9). Other characters do the same. When Annah's date arrives, she, too, directly addresses the reader. Chili Brandals (she/her) lets us know that they work together, that she is smitten with Annah, and that Annah is confused about her sexuality. They have been on eight dates and slept together twice (97). Chili is also the one who informs the reader of the Gingerbread Girl. In other words, we get the information at third-hand.

Gingerbread Girl employs a Virginia Woolf-like (she/her) style of connecting narratives. Take *Mrs. Dalloway*, for example. Woolf shifts the narrative perspective from Clarissa Dalloway (she/her) as she looks up and sees an airplane passing overhead to Septimus Smith as he sees the same plane overhead. I would suggest that this connection is more than passing. Woolf's own sexuality is up for debate, though many have suggested that she was bisexual. Clarissa Dalloway may, at first, seem to be the quintessential upper-middle class heterosexual woman, but she tells us about that time with Sally (32). Further, Septimus Smith is a young man back from the Great War, suffering from PTSD. He tells us, however, about that time on the rug with his sergeant (86). And, keep in mind that Dante damns homosexuals to the seventh (septima) circle of hell for a "sin against God" (homosexuality).

In *Gingerbread Girl*, Tobin and Coover use a number of similar techniques to shift the narrative voice. From the pages of yearbooks, to Annah's direct addresses, to Chili's voice, to the pigeon outside the apartment window, to some random dude walking past Annah and Chili, to Dr. Spectra who has insights into Annah's motivations, and many others. Some of these pieces of information could have come from Annah herself. Some of them could have been thought bubbles or flashbacks. Some of them could have been conversations with other characters. In this case, however, Tobin has other people besides Annah provide Annah's thoughts, her past, and her motivations. An interesting choice for a character who already believes that a portion of her self is separate from her body.

In some ways, however, the graphic novel is fairly conventional. The black and white drawings are precise and provide enough detail to locate the reader in the action. The characters are cartoons, with most detail stripped away, yet Coover provides facial and expression detail to convey mood and thought. The panels on each page follow standard conventions. However, a number of things in the content challenge the conventions of a graphic novel.

For one, a bisexual woman as the protagonist is fairly rare (even if Chili tells us that Annah is confused about that). We will find far more lesbians and gay men in these comics than bisexuals. Second, the narrative is putatively about The Gingerbread Girl/Annah, and yet a great deal of that tale is in the voices of others. Toni Morrison (she/her) employs this technique of decentering the protagonist in her first novel, *The Bluest Eye*. In this case, Tobin decenters the narrator so that the reader cannot be certain of Annah's "real" (whatever that might mean) condition. Finally, the novel offers no resolution. We are no closer to understanding whether the Gingerbread Girl is a psychological construct or a physical manifestation. We have no idea whether Annah *really* believes in the Gingerbread Girl or if the Gingerbread Girl construct is an excuse for her lack of feeling—and occasional cruelty. We have no idea if Chili and Annah will remain together (Chili thinks not), or if she'll end up with Jerry (which also seems unlikely). In these three ways, then, Tobin and Coover queer the graphic novel narrative. They do not provide any certainty or resolution. They do not resolve Annah into a coherent unified subject. In fact, the last 14 pages of the comic are merely a summation, a list of things that Chili knows about Annah, things she likes and things she dislikes. And, yes, they are frequently inconsistent or contradictory. That's us. We are not consistent beings. Science does not provide an answer here. Psychology does not provide an answer here. The closest we come to any answer is the subjective data provided by Chili. "That's all I really know about Annah" (104).

Well, what does any of this have to do with Ron DeSantis and Sam Killermann? Killermann's Genderbread Person suggests that "Identity ≠ Expression ≠ Sex" and that "Gender ≠ Sexual Orientation" (Killermann). In other words, one's identity is separate from one's body. The self is located in the mind, but that mental map, that self is not bound to the body one is born with. Furthermore, one can express that identity in different ways at different times in different contexts. Ron DeSantis's Gingerbread Man, or what he envisions instead of Killermann's model, is quite static. One is born with a (binary) sexed body, and that body will necessarily express the corresponding masculine or feminine identity.

Tobin and Coover's *Gingerbread Girl* is much closer to Killermann's model, and the underlying philosophy is the same. We are not unified and consistent people; gender and sexual identity are something outside the sexed body.

Maybe if Ron DeSantis runs, runs, runs, he can catch up with the times....

Shade 3 — *Decrypting Rita* (2011-2015)
Sound and Fury

> "…it is a tale
> Told by an idiot, full of sound and fury,
> Signifying nothing."
> (William Shakespeare, *Macbeth*, Act 5, Scene 5)

THE US FICTION writer William Faulkner (he/him) had big plans for the publication of *The Sound and the Fury* (1929). Because the novel is focalized through four different narrators, and because the narrative jumps back and forth in time, Faulkner wanted the publisher to print the novel using different colors. Fourteen of them, in fact (Golden). The colors would guide the reader, would allow the reader to know which narrator was narrating and which moment in time any section was set in. The idea did not fly with his original publisher, though a new edition using Faulkner's color scheme was published in 2012 (for a mere $345). US comic writer Margaret Trauth (she/her) has tapped into this Faulknerian strategy.

Decrypting Rita is one of the most dynamic and fascinating comics I've read in a while. The series began as a webcomic (http://egypt.urnash.com/rita). As of spring 2024, it still lives there. It was then edited, modified, and published in book form (Collapsar Press) via two Kickstarter campaigns. The first Kickstarter resulted in the Omnibus, which collects Books 1 and 2 of the webcomic, and the second campaign resulted in Book 3, which was published as a separate volume. The books are oversized, vibrant, and lovely. The print versions *try* (not wholly successfully) to replicate some of the formal fluidity available as a webcomic (more in a bit). The chapters are arranged as follows: 1, 2, 3, 4, 5 (Book 1), VI, VII, VIII, IX, X, 23, XI, 19 (Book 2), and 12, $0E, 16, 21, 13, 20, 1110, 23, 24, 14, א (Book 3) (more on this in a bit).

A short précis: Rita (she/her) is a posthuman robot who is a spy for an organization that intends to enforce a hivemind upon all of Earth. In a timeline resembling our own, Rita is also a burlesque dancer whose best friend has killed herself because she believed we are living in a simulation. Rita is also a ship captain who may be immortal, and Rita is also a shape-shifting, polyamorous dragon. Rita is surrounded by a core of friends, lovers, and acquaintances. However, the four worlds all begin to merge and blur together.

In part because *Decrypting Rita* is a webcomic, and in part because it deals with multiple, simultaneous timelines, Trauth renders the comic as a continuous, horizontal scroll. The reader can drag the comic across the screen as a continuous image, or can click the javascript arrows to advance the page. In either case, the horizontal orientation alters the reading process. In this sense, Trauth makes a formal choice based on content (timelines) and on technology (online interface). The reader cannot read along in real time with the events as they happen. This is the case for every form of narrative. So, how does the writer address the narrative passage of time? How does the reader maintain a willful suspension of disbelief? As Scott McCloud (he/him) points out in *Understanding Comics*, the frame on a page in a comic book represents the "present— in the narrative and for the reader. The subsequent frame will represent some point in the future" (104)—perhaps a millisecond later, perhaps a week later. In *Decrypting Rita*, Trauth challenges that model, though she cannot escape it entirely.

Nevertheless, the multiple timelines complicate the new reading strategy. Trauth visually represents two, three, or four timelines on the same page, but the reader cannot read them simultaneously. The reader is again forced to make a choice— read all the timelines on the screen, or read one timeline and then go back and read another timeline. In either case, the verisimilitude of multiple, simultaneous timelines is ruptured.

The story tracks six individuals, (Rita, Barrett [he/him], Carol [she/her], Tom [he/him], Kim [she/her and he/him], and Gary [he/him]) across four parallel timelines. In Trauth's Faulknerian move, each of the 4 timelines is rendered with a different color palate. The comic picks up, *en media res*, in the Blue timeline (B). These pages are drawn entirely in dark blue, light blue, and white, with no gradations and no transparency. The second timeline introduced is drawn with yellow, brown, and white. The third timeline is composed in orange, brown, and white. The color palates in the second and third timelines (Y/B and O/B) are very similar. The yellow and orange differ only slightly, which adds to the confusion, though that is precisely the point. Finally, the fourth timeline is rendered in dark green, light green, and white (G). An update in September 20, 2012, was the first to include purple. The webcomic does not have a purple timeline; however, at several places, purple creeps in, suggesting that the conflation of timelines are at play. In the hashtags that run along the bottom of the webcomic, Trauth identifies the characters as Rita1 (B), Rita2 (Y/B), Rita3 (O/B), and Rita4 (G). All six characters are identified with this nomenclature.

The story begins with Rita1 as a stylized robot who is breaking into a building in order to assassinate Barrett1, a company exec. As Rita moves through space, she receives constant feed from an external handler. Carol1 provides her pathways, probability data, and other useful info. Along the way, she runs into an unexpected person in the stairwell (Kim1) and knocks her unconscious. But the mission is compromised. The video feeds are fake, and Barrett is not there. When Carol attempts to recall Rita, Rita refuses, fearing she might be compromised. She says "goodbye" and runs off. At that moment, Rita2 awakens from a dream. She tells Barrett2 that in the dream she wanted to kill him and that she knocked out Kim2. However, in between and behind the frames of the Y/B world, we can see tiny bits of the Blue world. The Blue timeline has begun to creep into the Yellow/Brown timeline. It only gets more complicated from that point on. As Trauth notes, "I had to teach you to read in the first volume! I made myself hold back and introduce the whole parallel worlds thing slowly, to give readers time to make senses of it" (Morris).

To this point, however, only one timeline has been preset on the page at a time. The June 23, 2011, update‡ begins with a tiny speech bubble in white, "I can't." That thought then leads to parallel statements by Carol1 and Kim2. The two scenes in two different timelines then appear simultaneously on the page: Blue world on top, Y/B world on the bottom. Book 1, Chapter 4 (November 15, 2011) introduces the O/B and Green worlds. On November 17, we see a glimpse of a third simultaneous timeline, and on November 22, Trauth draws three simultaneous timelines on the page. In the final frames of the February 1, 2012, update, Trauth renders four timelines on one page, with Rita appearing in all four. The figures of Rita2, Rita3, and Rita4 appear as one vertical figure, rendered in three different color palates. In the background, Rita1 looks bewildered. Fragments of the words "what's happening" appear in the gutter between frames. What's happening, indeed?

As I noted above, Rita1 is a posthuman spy. Rita1 shuts down, gets erased, gets respawned, and downloads the memories

---

‡   A note on citations: The book pages are unnumbered. The webcomic does not follow the standard convention in designating pages. See Shade 6, *Crossed Wires*. Since this webcomic does not exist as pages but, rather, as a continuous horizontal scroll, Trauth indicates each update according to the date it was posted. I will use the dates from the webcomic to cite quotations.

of the others in the hivemind. So, is Rita a trans woman? Trauth is a trans woman and suggests that Rita's tale is a trans tale, but not in the way that one might imagine. According to Trauth, Rita1 is quite comfortable in her body. She loves her abilities; she loves her skills and agility; and she loves (or certainly flirts with) Carol. Similarly, the other three Ritas are not wish fulfillment for the Rita1. Whether a posthuman cyborg, a human, a wizard, or a dragon, they are each exactly where and who they want to be. They do not represent the desire to be in a different body. No, instead, Trauth suggests that this transgendered tale is "not About The Transition" [sic] but "when the transition is *over*" (Morris).

In addition, many of the characters are queer. Rita1 and Carol1 have dinner, flirt, and arrange a date. Rita2 and Barrett2 are in an "open relationship." Rita2 had been considering adding Kim2 to their relationship prior to Kim2's suicide. Trauth herself has spoken of her poly relationships, and we see a number of poly relationships. As Wisp writes in *Yes Homo*, "It's a damn good thing these people seem to be poly in every universe, otherwise who's-dating-who would get really hard to keep track of. That's a joke: it's still basically impossible."

What does it all mean? Is it sound and fury signifying nothing? In a word, "No." *Decrypting Rita* gets more and more convoluted, reflecting a general belief in the epistemological uncertainty of life. None of the Ritas can tell with any certainty if they are real or a dream. None of them can tell if the in-breaking of other memories is reality or an illusion. Instead, *Decrypting Rita* argues for a more fluid understanding of identity, of relationships, and of the universe. The universe is poly, with multiple versions, multiple arrangements, and multiple outcomes. Trauth says, "At the end of the story, you probably won't have a definite idea of What Really Happened, but if I've done things right, you'll have two or three very compelling theories of that" (Morris).

And that's not nothing.

Shade 4—*The Pride* (2014)
"Now Go Change the World"

THE IMAGES WERE all-too stark and -too clear. An angry group of protestors held signs at the funeral of Matthew Sheppard (he/him), a young, gay man from Laramie, Wyoming, who was murdered by two men, precisely because Sheppard was gay—signs saying that God hates all queer folx and other hateful things. Although it was not their first protest, it was the one that catapulted the Westboro Baptist Church (WBC) into the limelight. Their leader, Fred Phelps (he/him), argued that homosexuality and sodomy have ruined the world, that every bad thing that happens in the world is retribution for homosexuality. After the Matthew Sheppard protest, the WBC protested at the funerals of many others, including celebrities and victims of mass violence or natural disaster. Phelps used the Bible and his own version of Calvinism (yes, a very distant relative of mine) to justify his group's actions ("Fred Phelps"). I have no idea whether or not writer Joe Glass (he/him) was thinking of Fred Phelps when he created the character of Reverend Franklin Phillips (he/him), but the comparison seems apt. The Sheppard protest was held in 1998. The WBC held protests throughout the early aughts. *The Pride* was written in 2011 and published in 2014, and it is, I would argue, a response to the negative perceptions of queer folx, offered as an antidote to those sentiments.

The Pride was initially published as a limited-run comic by Queer Comix. The 6-issue run is copyrighted 2011, with the collected Season 1 published in graphic novel form in 2016.

Subsequent comics were all collected in an Omnibus edition in 2021 (for Pride Month). The original comics consisted of six stories along with a one-page backstory for each of the members of The Pride. All of these were written by Joe Glass (sometimes credited as Joseph Glass), who has worked as a "comics news reporter and critic" ("Who Is Joe Glass?"). He has also written *Acceptable Losses* (2020), *Glitter Vipers* (2020), and *The Miracles* (Kickstarter goal has been met!). The artwork in *The Pride* is handled by nearly a dozen individuals, leading to a mix of styles, sometimes within the same issue.

Issue 1 begins:

> "Welcome to the Pride.
>
> "Have you ever felt like you didn't matter? Have you ever felt misrepresented? Have you ever felt there's no one out there to fight for you? Have you ever felt alone?
>
> "You are not alone.
>
> "There are people who will fight for you. There are people who will fight for everyone."

We are introduced to our protagonist, Fabman (he/him), via a news story about the "gay vigilante" stopping an out-of-control subway train in New York City. However, the newscasters make a joke about the "flamboyant-crusader" flying off with a "hot new trick" before he could be interviewed. Instead, Fabman comforts a young boy, Billy, who is ridiculed for playing with his Fabman action figure. And so, Fabman decides to create a league of queer superheroes. The Justice Division, another league of superheroes, has a "don't ask, don't tell" policy about queer members (a clear reference to the Clinton-era policy for the US military). In this world, public perception of queer superheroes is negative, but Fabman believes that an entire superhero team, all of whom are queer, would help counteract that public perception. So, one by one, he gathers his team: Angel (she/her), a "New York Super Drag Artist" whose superpower is confusion fields; Queen Sapphire of Labrysia (she/her), who has superhuman strength and stamina; White Trash (he/him), who also has superhuman strength; Mistress Evangeline Isabella Ryder III (she/her), who can freeze things; Twink (he/him), who has metal plating; The Bear (he/him), who is a giant bear with augmented senses and strength; and Wolf (he/him), who has no superpower but is really smart and an excellent tactician.

The superheroes here have their powers by virtue of several different phenomena. Many of the superheroes are X-Cel positive, a clever play on and reversal of the stigma of HIV positive. No explanation is given for the origin of the X-Cel, but we sure do have a lot of superheroes running around. This particular virus allows the host to "excel." The virus can remain dormant for an extended period and activate at any time. In addition, The Bear is both X-Cel positive and HIV positive, which provides a space to talk about HIV treatment protocols and transmission.

Frost, on the other hand, has acquired her superpowers through medical enhancements. She has undergone a series of operations to augment her abilities. Because she does not have the X-Cel virus, she is immune to Phillips's later attacks.

With his new team, The Pride, assembled, the team members discover that they need to learn to work *as* a team. Each member has fought primarily as an individual, and at first they cannot coordinate the use of their individual talents and powers. But, as luck or nature would have it, they never really get the chance, as one calamity after another befalls them. No sooner have they assembled than the homophobic, white nationalist Firebomb sets a gay bar on fire, trapping many of the patrons. However, the real villain here is the Reverend Franklin Phillips. He is on a mission from God (or his own ego) to rid the world of all evil, starting with homosexuality. Phillips, like Phelps, attributes world strife to homosexuality. Phillips sends his henchman, Basher, to capture one of the Pride members. He uses The Bear's son as bait and draws him to an isolated spot. Fortunately, the Pride Team has placed a tracking device on The Bear, and the Pride soon follows. But, because they have not gelled as a team, they are collectively defeated, and Basher flies off with The Bear.

Interestingly, Phillips himself is X-Cel positive. He, too, has a super ability. In his case, he can use his voice to convince people to act against their own best interests. Further, Phillips has built a machine that amplifies his superpower and, through the body of The Bear, the machine broadcasts his voice to all X-Cel positive individuals. So now, the Reverend has an entire army of superheroes working for him. They are under his command. That seems a bit like Phelps, as well. After Sheppard's funeral, Phelps's voice was amplified, and he swayed a number of people to his homophobic ways. In the comic, however, goodness wins. The team coheres; the Reverend is defeated; and public opinion of queer superheroes shifts.

The comic borders on stereotype at times. Five of the members are white men (at least, Bear was before his transformation). They're all pretty buff, too. Angel is Black and a drag queen. Sapphire hails from a remote island of strong womyn, though she has an accent that seems Southern US. And Frost is an icy-cold, stiff-upper lip British woman. So, although it is a diverse cast, the white, gay male is over-represented. Still, in his review of the series, Matt Santori (he/him) writes:

> But when I pick up a book like *The Pride*, or *Secret Six*, or *Midnighter*, or *Catwoman*, I get something powerful that resonates like heroes did to me as a child. It's more than recognition, more than celebration. It's seeing my value as a human being amplified on the page. That's damn important stuff to me. And I'm not alone. (Santoni, "Review")

Without a doubt, *The Pride* offers a positive anodyne for negative public perceptions. The Pride members may all be queer, but they will not exclude someone who is not queer. They rescue queer bar patrons but make it clear that they will aid and assist anyone who needs help. They risk their families and their own lives to defeat a megalomaniac who would rule the world.

In the final frames of the comic, Fabman returns to little Billy, whom we met in the opening pages. Billy feels alone and unrepresented. He just wishes that everyone could see how fabulous Fabman is. Fabman responds, "Maybe someday they will…." After the Reverend has been defeated, Billy is proud of Fabman. Through his new superhero team, and through his own actions, Fabman has changed the minds of Billy's mean friends.

Billy gives Fabman his action figure and says, "Now go change the world."

Shade 5 — *Strong Female Protagonist* (2012)
Another Superhero I Can Love

IN *QSF*, I wrote about a short story titled "Je me souviens" by Su J. Sokol (xie/xir). The story centers on a man who has escaped the torture he faced as a gay man in Latin America. In the story, he lives in Canada with his wife and child. He sees himself as a kind of superhero. In my commentary on that story, I noted that I wasn't much of a fan of superhero stories, though occasionally one hits the mark for me. At the end of my discussion, I noted, "He is a superhero I can believe in" (Calvin 106). I feel the same way about *Strong Female Protagonist*.

What writer Brennan Lee Mulligan (he/him) and illustrator Molly Ostertag (she/her) have done with *Strong Female Protagonist* is to take the superhero trope from romance to realism. In romance, the characters are generally two-dimensional and flat. They don't have a lot of development or complexity. They are either good or bad — think early Superman (all good) and early Lex Luthor (all bad). Furthermore, their actions take place outside of realistic social relations. For example, Superman lives in Metropolis (a nonexistent place), and we see none of the political, social, and cultural complexity of a recognizable city.

In realism, the characters tend to be three-dimensional and round. They tend to be much more complex as people. Think of Mark Twain's (he/him) *Huckleberry Finn*, in which the titular character grows and changes over time. Realism also tends to be rooted in a particular place and time that is central to the story. Consider, for example, the way in which the culture and society of New York City figure prominently in the works of Edith Wharton (she/her) or Henry James (he/him). In a realist tale, gender, race, class, and other elements of identity play a role in the story and in the development of the character.

To be fair, Mulligan and Ostertag are not the first to do this. The *Dark Knight* series, for example, fundamentally complicated the Batman franchise. Films such as *Hancock* also offer a superhero who is not uniformly good and who is psychologically complex. Nevertheless, I suppose that, as an academic, I really enjoy the way Mulligan and Ostertag undermine and redefine the superhero figure. Their black-and-white webcomic uses a realist approach to argue for systemic change.

In *Strong Female Protagonist*, our superhero is Alison Green (she/her), a 20-year-old from Westchester, New York. Her father was a social worker and her mother a teacher. She was a good student and excellent (if not always team-oriented) soccer player. When Alison was still in utero, however, a bizarre weather phenomenon blanketed the globe. Fourteen years later, everyone saw the result. Thousands of children were discovered to be "chromosomally dynamic individuals." In other words, they developed superpowers. Those powers differed widely, and while many of the mutations made little difference, some were quite significant. Some people used their new-found powers for evil, and some used them for good.

Alison developed super strength and invulnerability. As superhero Mega Girl, she joined a group of superheroes called The Guardians. The Guardians emerged shortly after the supervillain The Maniac (he/him) declared his intent to dismantle the government and take over. Together with the Guardians, Mega Girl saved the world at least seven different times (or so we're told). But that kind of responsibility and maturity takes a toll on a teenager.

When the supervillain Maniac is finally captured, Alison is supposed to deliver him for imprisonment. But as she zeroes in on him, Maniac rejects his role as supervillain and reveals himself to her as Patrick, an intelligent and idealistic telepath. Maniac hands Alison a set of dossiers. All of the superheroes who might have made a difference have been killed. He suspects that those superheroes were all part of a government project. The deck is stacked, and he wants out. Alison recognizes his disillusionment. Consequently, she lets him go, an act that causes fury.

The problem is, Alison fundamentally does not believe in superheroes. She agonizes over her role and her complicity. Mostly she is distraught over her uselessness. She throws down her mask, rejects her identity, and enrolls in The New School in Manhattan. For Alison, the problem with superheroes is that they treat symptoms and not causes. The problem is that, "If saving the world means preserving it just how it is, then saving the world is not for me" (136). She has realized that only a few people are trying to save the world. And for what? The rest just want to maintain the status quo. For Alison, the status quo is precisely the problem.

Alison has another superhero friend: Tara/Feral (she/her). Her superpower is regeneration. If she gets a cut, it heals quickly. If she loses a limb, it grows back—though the process makes her violently ill. When Alison goes back to college to improve herself (and perhaps find some insight into human nature), Feral feels inadequate. So, Feral devises a plan to help save the world. She will donate organs to chromosomally static individuals (i.e., those who are not mutated). But the thing is, she can donate her heart eight or ten times in one day. She can donate all her organs with astonishing frequency. It will be painful, and it will make her violently ill, but she sees it as her only way to save the world. Consider all the lives she can save. Consider all the good those harvested organs can do in the world.

Tara and Alison have a romantic past. When working on a mission together, Tara kissed Alison. Tara is a lesbian, but Alison is not. Still, Tara remains in love with Alison all these years later. But, now, Tara has made up her mind—this act of self-sacrifice is how she can contribute. Alison tries to argue her out of it, arguing that it changes nothing. Tara can save 100,000 lives, but the world will remain unjust and unequal.

The world of *Strong Female Protagonist* is a familiar one. Much of it takes place in New York City. Alison attends The New School. When biodynamic individuals are discovered, George W. Bush makes the announcement on air. People quickly protest the biodynamic, much as they do LGBTQ people. Tara is the target of both sets of prejudices. The idea that her organs would be placed into static individuals is abhorrent to these bigots. They protest outside the hospital, and one of them—with the help of a hospital staffer—takes a flamethrower and torches Feral. But, of course, Feral is biodynamic, and she regenerates.

Alison, however, loses her cool. She destroys stuff. She threatens to kill every single one of the protestors. Patrick tries to talk her down, but it is Feral who emerges from the hospital—regenerating even as she crawls out—who begs Alison to stand down. Alison/Mega Girl, the world crusader, the world peace maker, the philosophical superhero, thinks about killing people. She confesses to a friend that she has homicidal thoughts all the time, even though she almost never acts on them.

Is *Strong Female Protagonist* queer? Sort of. For one, a secondary character (Tara) is a lesbian. Her identity is presented in a neutral way—i.e., it's just who she is. Further, Tara is presented positively. She works with the good superheroes, and she genuinely wants to make the world a better place. And, as is to be expected in a realist work, we see the political and social consequences of her queer identity. The protestors literally want to kill her for her marginalized identities. Tara is willing to give her entire self to help others. While the comic skirts dangerously close to the "bury your gays" trope, Tara cannot die. Even so, her plan to donate organs is a form of self-abnegation.

What makes the comic queer is its approach. It asks the reader to think about the superhero trope in a new way. It asks the reader to fundamentally question the mode of the superhero. "Truth, justice, and the American way" (a legendary phrase, quoted within these pages) just does not cut it. Superman and Batman (at least in early iterations) offer a liberal critique of social and political issues. They can make the world a more equitable place by removing the (few) bad actors. Alison Green understands, however, that the only way to make things more equitable is to make systemic change and to build new foundations.

The real questions is, can she find a way to do so?

Shade 6 — *Crossed Wires* (2014-2021)

"Let's Get Diverse Like We F**king Mean It"
(Iris Jay, *Kickstarter*)

IMAGINE THE ENTIRE internet all up in arms, motivated by the same outrage. Imagine a collective action so large that the entire internet shuts down. Imagine users collectively stifling multinational corporations and national governments. Can you see it?

Yeah, me neither.

That was the premise of Caitlin Sullivan (she/her) and Kate Bornstein (they/them)'s *Nearly Roadkill: An Infobahn Erotic Adventure* (1996), which chronicles the online and IRL adventures of two gender outlaws. They take a stand against mandatory—and binary—gendering on the internet. For them, the net is a space of radical possibility. The net is a space to rupture the body-identity matrix (see Shade 2). For Winc (ze/hir) and Scratch (ze/hir), the requirement to pin down one's gender is a hill too far. They take a stand. They start an uprising.

While the novel *Nearly Roadkill* takes place in the days when the web was entirely textual, Iris Jay's (she/her) webcomic *Crossed Wires* (2014-2021) takes place in a near future, where web interactions are in virtual spaces. Even with Jay's homage to *Nearly Roadkill* on page 00.34, *Crossed Wires* borrows heavily from the iconography of William Gibson's (he/him) 1984 novel, *Neuromancer*, which also gets a shoutout (03.125). For example, the very first page of the comic begins with the word "Cyberspace." That word is accompanied by what appear to be large ice crystals, both references to one of the key images in *Neuromancer*.

Crossed Wires ran as a "post-cyberpunk" (Christianson, "Upgrading") webcomic with four chapters totaling 489 pages. (Quotes here are indicated as 00.00, the first set of digits the chapter number, and the second set the page published online in that chapter.) The first page appeared on May 1, 2014, and it has continued to be updated into early 2024. Writer/illustrator Iris Jay describes herself as "an NB trans femme." For the comic, Jay was determined to tell a story that represented her and her friends' own experiences—in college and in the gaming world. To that end, she worked to make representation a central issue. She writes: "Nearly all of the main cast are queer in some way, shape or form! Alan and Theresa are both trans, and we've got secondary characters of all sorts of genders and orientations" (Jay, *Kickstarter*).

Crossed Wires centers around 5 friends/colleagues/exes. Alan (Alejandro Xavier Winter) (he/him) is a trans man of Latinx [sic] descent and a huge fan of The Dark Spectrum book series, all of which feature hackers and cyberspace. Alan is a would-be hacker who uses the avatar Ultra Drakken (also from the book series). While sitting in Creative Writing class, he notices that one of his classmates is reading the series, too. He tries to strike up a conversation, but she's pretty guarded. It turns out that his classmate is Theresa Petrosky (she/her), an immigrant trans woman who just happens to be a super-successful and super-secret hacker, Vrrmn. I mean, she is a *ghost* on the web. This casual conversation sets off a chain of misadventures over the next seven years (realtime).

Alan does manage to learn that Vrrmn is a hacktivist who primarily hits corporate targets. For example, she once targeted a major bank in order to wipe out student loans. In another operation, they hit a major pharmaceutical corporation. In the final chapter, Alan and Theresa's team takes on an Elon

Musk-like figure, here named Tucker Todd (he/him), who runs a company of public hackers called Zanzibar. In order to promote Zanzibar's new division, Haqr, and in order to rip off the goods and skills of small-time hackers, Zanzibar hosts a giant Hack-off. They recruit and fly in all the best hacking prospects for the chance at an internship and a cash prize.

Other teammates include Cassandra Holt (she/her), aka The Magpie Queen aka CS-One. Cassandra is a 23-year-old computer science student, who also quite conveniently works for university administration and has access to student records. She and Theresa dated previously, but that had ended badly. So, when Alan pops by to ask for access to Theresa's student records, she warns Alan off in no uncertain terms. "Then *forget* her. She's bad news" (00.24). You see, Cassandra had been the mighty Magpie Queen, and Vrrmn/Theresa blew her cover. She could never be the Magpie Queen again. All her work and a major part of her identity were just—gone. Cassandra was *pissed*.

Another team member is Adanya Nwosu-Harris (she/her), aka Anakonda. Adanya has two fathers, one of whom is African and the other African American. The two make up the infamous team of Asp & Adder. Apparently, Adanya has inherited her fathers' flare for all things virtual. She is the team's "gearhead." Though her fathers are legends, they were also mixed up in some serious research. They worked on a project called Amphibaena—a project so feared that no one will even speak its name. Rest assured that Amphibaena rears its head before we're finished.

Alan also relies a lot on his roommate, Niko Lizarazo (they/them), aka Orbit, who is a 21-year-old nonbinary computer science major and avatar designer. Orbit has a virtual shop and designs and sells avatars.

In her iconic essay "Alien Cryptographies," Wendy Pearson (they/them) sets out four categories of types of queer SF.

Her third category is of texts that are "coded" as queer, with clues and references hidden in plain sight (5). I would suggest that *Crossed Wires* is an "overtly queer" text (5). After all, Alan stands up and shouts "I'm Ultra Drakken, I'm gay as hell, and I'm an elite hacker" (03.76). Even so, *Crossed Wires* leaves coded breadcrumbs for the initiated. Jay hides queer references in plain sight. For example, in his youth, Alan played *Kingdom Hearts* via Instant Messenger. *Kingdom Hearts* was a role-playing game first released in 2002, and many fans followed it for the queer storyline.

Throughout the comic, Jay is attuned to social justice issues in general and queer issues in particular. Jay, though, takes a subtle approach, much like Octavia E. Butler, who would not introduce characters according to their physical or identity characteristics but would allow that information to appear in an organic fashion, dropping breadcrumbs hinting at an identity. Jay follows a similar principle. Jay leaves hints, for example, that Theresa is of Russian descent. Instead of introducing Theresa as "the Russian Theresa," Jay provides clues to Theresa's Russian identity throughout the comic.

Similarly, she hints that Alan is a transman. For example, in Chapter 2, we see a flashback to Alan's quinceañera—a coming-of-age party for a Latina. Alan's mother simply refuses to accept Alan's identity and presses forward with the charade of holding a quinceañera for Alan. His uncle, though, supports Alan. Here (and in other places) Jay uses a specific technique to handle deadnames. The deadname is written out in the speech bubble, but that name is scribbled over and illegible. The effect is that we see someone deadnaming Alan, but we never see the deadname.

The deadnaming gets a little trickier in Chapter 2. At the end of Chapter 1, the crew get ambushed by Alan's ex. When he and Alan dated, his ex went by the name "Mickee." However, his ex now uses the handle Monsieur Michael Mayhem (he/him). When they dated, Alan used the handle Drakonik, which his ex continues to use to refer to Alan. In other words, Michael uses the avatar associated with Alan's deadname.

We saw that, for Cassandra, her online persona was integral to her own identity and sense of self. She was devastated by the loss of Magpie. So, what about for Alan? His shift from Drakonik to Ultra Drakken seems to coincide with his transition. Michael's use of Drakonik is deliberate and meant to be hurtful. He goes so far as to say that he preferred Alan when he was a girl (02.141).

But Alan, too, strategically calls Michael "Mickee." Has Alan committed the same offense? The stakes here seem to be different. It is not at all clear that Michael has transitioned, but rather taken on a new online persona, unrelated to his IRL identity (which I say being fully aware of how intertwined those two can be).

Apart from queer representation and politics, Jay also addresses other social justice issues. As noted above, nearly everyone on the team is a person of color, an immigrant, and queer. I think it's fair to say that the perception is that gaming and hacking are white-dominated. Here, though, Anakonda's two fathers put the lie to that truism. Even so, when Zanzibar holds its huge recruiting event, the recruitees notice that Zanzibar is pretty homogeneously white.

The potential interns see all the perks of Zanzibar: cafeteria, aquatic park, haptic VR arena, and more (03.85). But as Jay notes: "There were a lot of queer people into cyberpunk back then, too—we've always been sci-fi fans, computer innovators, early adapters, stuff like that. But as with all nerd culture, it was a product of its time, and it had its share of really cringe-worthy content, too—stuff like crummy gender politics, broad cultural appropriation, and a conflicted love-hate relationship with unchecked capitalism" (Christianson).

So, yes, Zanzibar has a Trans@Zans Chat group, and the Zanzibar team has members from across the LGBTQIA spectrum (03.88). Nevertheless, the wretched Tucker Todd is outing employees and revealing details he *should not* (03.88). After Alan notices that the Zanzibar workforce is "monochromatic," he asks a loud question about Latine programmers. (They have none.) Theresa asks about a Black engineer. (They have none.) And then the other recruits pile on. Someone asks about Native Americans. Someone asks about disabled people. Questions about sick leave, about recruiting practices, about warehouse workers. Todd looks like a deer caught in the headlights.

So, *Crossed Wires* offers a diverse cast, but much like *Strong Female Protagonist*, it simultaneously makes the point that structural (and personal) barriers remain for marginalized folx to succeed. Jay's queer post-cyberpunk webcomic pays tribute to antecedents, even as it updates and transcends them. Jay does diversity like she means it! She offers a diverse representation of the participation and innovation of marginalized people in cyberspace, even as she demonstrates both the reality and the consequences of cyberpunk's more traditional take on gender, race, and capitalism.

Here's hoping that Jay finds the time and wherewithal to pick the story up again. It remains as relevant as it ever was.

Shade 7 — *Galanthus* (A Space Fantasy Webcomic) (2015-2018)

Space Is Gay

THIS READING TAKES its title from a cloth patch that I saw on Ashanti Fortson's (they/them) webpage, presumably something that they designed. It's a circular patch, embroidered in brown and orange and maroon. The wake of a comet or a rocket divides the patch. In bold white letters, the patch reads: "Space Is Gay." Well, that's a lot to unpack.

Author and illustrator Ashanti Fortson lives in Baltimore, Maryland, with a spouse, a cat, and three rats. Their work focuses on interpersonal relations and is centered through a "tenderhearted lens" ("About"). Fortson has worked on a number of comics, including *Leaf Lace* (2021, winner of Ignatz Award for Outstanding Comic), *Song of the Court*, *Capturing Comfort* (2020, for *Bitch* magazine), *Through Whose Eyes* (2019, about the erasure of autistic personhood), and *I'm Not a Robot* (2017). The latter comic is an autobiographical depiction of Fortson coming to terms with themself as a person with autism. Their project *Cress & Petra*, a YA graphic novel, was released in 2023.

Fortson has also written a number of nonfiction pieces, including *Constructs* (2017, a comic-form analysis of *The Matrix*, which examines trans themes in the 1999 film). Fortson has illustrated both stories and book covers, including Ursula K. Le Guin's *Tehanu*.

The ideas for my comics are often inspired by emotions I'm experiencing, concepts I'm thinking about, story nuggets that pop into my head, moments or places I observe, the feeling of certain things, something someone says to me, etc. Art can be borne from anything and exists in the context of everything, so I just live my life and jot down what's impactful. (Fortson, "Artist Interview")

I'll say upfront that the webcomic is incomplete. Fortson completed and posted two chapters of Book 1 between 2015 and 2018. Despite the explicit promise of another chapter to soon follow, that next chapter has never materialized. Consequently, a lot of things in the narrative remain unexplained and unresolved. I suspect that Fortson has redirected efforts to jobs that pay real money.

The comic centers on Farah Sarki (she/her), a 15-year-old Muslim girl who labors in a factory on the space station *Resilience* (no doubt ironically named). In common parlance, she is a "factory rat." In other words, she is a captive who is compelled to work in a factory. She dreams of finding a way off the station. Her grandmother had told her it was possible and that she should not give up hope. And now, even though her grandmother is dead, Farah holds onto the hope that she might get out of the factory. Her friend Lera (she/her) is more pessimistic about it. Nevertheless, due to some good fortune and her incredible technological skills, Farah finds an opportunity to dismantle a keypad and make a break for it.

Farah, however, has never known anything except the factory. She does not understand the basics of station life, of commerce, or of money. She takes refuge in a crate of fruit awaiting transfer to a ship. In that way, she finds herself aboard the *Galanthus*, a ship with a good-hearted captain and some very sketchy business practices. (Galanthus is also the scientific name for the genus of snowdrop flowers.) When Farah is discovered in the crate, and everyone is trying to figure out who she is, they stop in the midst of their agitation to make sure they have the correct pronouns. That insistence signals an awareness of, and the importance of, not misgendering anyone. The captain says, "You may be a stowaway on my ship, but I'll get your pronouns right!" Because of her excellent technological skills, she's hired onto the ship as a Tech Assistant. Once hired, she's given a tour of the ship. Though the crew is made up of many different species, everyone on this ship seems to be acutely aware of pronouns. When they meet Farah, they also seem attentive to pronouns, and they default to "they." She corrects them, and that's that.

Nevertheless, the comic demonstrates a bit of an English bias. When Farah escapes the factory and walks along the dock, all the signs at kiosks (that we see) are in English. We learn that humans are despised, so why are the signs in English? Could it really have become the universal language? The aliens (and they appear quite alien), also use English pronouns—or we are provided the English translation of whatever pronouns they would use in their own languages?

In the background, an existential, even cosmic crisis is underway. Even as the very space-time fabric unravels and planets disappear, the members of the Galactic Assembly bicker and fight. Even as certain factions seek a mythological artifact that may hold the key to controlling (or destroying) the universe, Farah wants nothing more than a community and a family, which she finds aboard the *Galanthus*.

We know from the opening scenes that the Imperator (pronouns unknown) wants the artifact, probably for revenge. We know from the closing scenes that a nefarious drug cartel wants the artifact, too. They've hired the crew of the *Galanthus* to locate it and return it in order to solidify their market.

None of this really matters to Farah. She wants her grandmother. She wants liberty. She wants family.

Her new onboard family is diverse. Captain Seo (she/her) is human, as is the low-ranking José de los Rios (he/him). The very large, very intimidating engineer Nur Eyom (they/them) is Utaran. Ariniam Chrast (she/her) is a Rakachak, a very tall, green, lizard-like being. The medic on the ship, Doc (they/them), is Scemarian and resembles a large jellyfish. Finally, the brains of the operation is Enkh (they/them), a disembodied, floating device called a Mechanica, who is addicted to social media. In one of the final panels of the series, we see Farah sitting at a meal, and looking at her new-found family. She smiles broadly and lovingly. She has found what she has been looking for.

Fortson has described *Galanthus* as a "queer space fantasy." In what ways is it queer?

So far, *Galanthus* does not seem to be queer in the sense of sexual identities or practices. For example, Nur hints at a relationship with Seo. They kiss her on the cheek once, and they say, "I'll leave you," another time. That threat, however, could be about a personal or a professional relationship. Maybe they're saying they'd leave the ship. Furthermore, the 15-year-old Farah makes no statements about her desires or practices.

So, if it's not queer regarding sex, sexuality, and sexual practices, then is it queer in some other way? For one, the characters challenge some of our expectations. Farah is no comic-book cover babe, complete with the stereotypical floatation-device breasts. No, she is a demure Muslim girl. Her body is fully covered. Farah is also represented as full-bodied. She is not the slender sexual siren of so many comics. In addition, Capt. Seo uses she/her pronouns, but is drawn as gender-nonconforming or, perhaps, gender ambiguous. The usual cues of clothing, body type, hair style, and so on do not clearly indicate a gender (see Shade 1). For another, the nonhuman characters rupture the body-gender relation. Ariniam, a very tall green lizard with four eyes, is actually anything but intimidating. She is sweet, caring, and astutely attuned to others' emotional needs. Her choice of clothing, often being stereo-typically (in the human sense) feminine, signals her femininity, and disrupts the correlation between size and gender. At the same time, Nur is tall and burly and stereotypically brusque and threatening. Even so, despite that correlation, they do not see themselves as male or masculine.

So, let's go back to where we began: Fortson's "Space Is Gay" patch. As noted in the Introduction, Scott and Fawaz argue that comics, as a medium, are queer because the comic form is "expansive" (201). It can represent all things, and it has the formal pliability to do anything. And they suggest that that pliability is formally like sexuality. Human sexuality is pliable and can assume any form. In *Galanthus*, we see a wide range of sentient beings—though far from the entire possible range. We see a variety of gender expressions—think of Kill-ermann's Genderbread Person in Shade 2. Fortson calls this webcomic a "Gay Space Fantasy." But which of the possible readings does she mean? Is it a Gay Space-Fantasy? A space fantasy that is gay? Is it a Gay-Space Fantasy? A fantasy of a space that is gay? Is it a Gay Fantasy of Space? Or, and per-haps this one lends itself to Scott and Fawaz's reading, Fortson imagines a space in which all things are possible and nothing is predictable (202).

Indeed, this 15-year-old Muslim technician who escaped enslaved labor has found something even beyond her own imagination: a queer family.

Shade 8 — *Always Human* (2015-2017)
Somewhere Over the Rainbow

I READ SCIENCE fiction when I was a child. Tons of it. I read and reread everything I had. I read everything in the library (it was a small-town library) and then read more via interlibrary loan. I would argue that that was a formative experience for me. Through reading SF, I was exposed to new kinds of societies, new kinds of beings, and new kinds of sexualities. To be perfectly honest, I read less of the last variety. When I was that 12-16-year-old, I just did not read a lot of SF that dealt openly with sexuality. Even so, some did. And it had an effect, for me, specifically, but almost certainly for other young SF readers, as well. But the youth of today, those 12-16-year-olds who are reading SF and SF comics, have a whole rainbow's worth of comics to read.

Ari North's (she/her) book *Always Human* is marketed to readers "12 and up." North is a queer comic writer from Australia (where the comic is set). The webcomic ran on the online platform Webtoon from 2015-2017. Subsequently, via a partnership with GLAAD, the comic was published in book form by Yellow Jacket (an imprint of Little Bee Books). According to the back cover, "A portion of the proceeds from the sale of this book will be donated to accelerating LGBTQ+ acceptance." The comic features two young, queer women in a romantic relationship, an agender friend, a gender nonconforming sister, and an asexual best friend.

The story centers on two young women, one 18 years old and another who has just turned 22. They live in a technologically advanced future society in which people use nano-modifications (mods) for almost everything. They alter their bodies with mods to fix hay fever and cancer. They use mods to enhance their ability to learn and "fashion mods" to alter their appearance. They do this a *lot*. Via these fashion mods, they can modify their skin color, hair color, eye color, hair style, and so on. With these mods, the body has become malleable.

The older protagonist, Sunati (she/her), modifies her appearance a lot until she meets our other protagonist, Austen (she/her). Austen lives with Egan's Syndrome, an immune response that rejects nano-modifications. Consequently, she uses no fashion mods. Sunati marvels when she sees this young woman who maintains a natural look that never changes. Sunati thinks that Austen is brave. Little does she know.

After they meet, they work their way through all the cringey moments of first love. Sunati, though, becomes hyperconscious of her own use of mods. Would using fashion mods around Austen be insensitive? Cruel? Mocking? Would not using mods be overly sensitive? Eventually, a visit from Austen's younger sibling, Yasel (they/them), convinces Sunati that Austen would consider such self-imposed limitations condescending and would not appreciate it. At the same time, Sunati also worries that her current body mod, her current look, is what Austen fell in love with. Would changing her look alter the way Austen feels about her?

In the penultimate chapter, Sunati and Austen sit together in front of some computerized simulators in order to find a new look for Sunati. She selects a radically different look, which Austen finds "radiant."

At its most basic level, *Always Human* is about two young women who negotiate all the pitfalls and thrills of a first romance. They have their meet-cute story; they have an awkward first date; they have an uncomfortable second date; they nearly break up over school pressures; they nearly break up because of a secret. And yet they continue their inexorable march toward coupledom. As a couple, they are adorbs, and they complement one another well. In the context of the story, however, they face none of the uncertainties nor hostilities of being a same-sex couple. It's unremarked upon. The techies don't take notice; the naturalists (who reject the modifications) don't seem to care; their friends and families are perfectly accepting of the relationship. Austen's two dads don't seem to object. That may be the biggest modification of all.

The comic is also about the effects of certain technologies. What would happen if we could modify our appearance at will? Would the connection between bodies and race disappear? Would the concept of marginalization be altered? Or abandoned? Would self-image be radically transformed? Would the nature of attraction be fundamentally altered? In this particular vision of the future, the answer seems to be "not much." As Sunati prepares to make her new modifications, she says that she promised her mother that she would not alter her skin color, which, throughout the comic is dark. That seems to suggest some racial or ethnic consciousness that Sunati does not want to abandon. Furthermore, Austen and her sibling speak Spanish. The suggestion is that it is a familiar and perhaps cultural trait that they hold onto. So, in the face of so much change, for these two individuals, racial, ethnic, and linguistic identity seem to persist.

Even so, the possibilities are endless, and they seem to offer a way to end the body=gender equation. The historic argument was that our body determined our gender. In this particular future, that practice simply cannot hold. When a person can alter the body at will, do they remain the same person? When the person radically alters the form of the body, how would that shape that person's gender? And while *Always Human* does not show radical bodily alteration, it would be a possibility. And it would be a way to reconfigure and reconsider gender.

One of Sunati's greatest fears is that Austen would no longer be interested in her if she modified her appearance. Austen saw and was attracted to a particular version of Sunati. Is Sunati's concern a superficial one? Perhaps, but she and her peers are hyper-conscious about appearance. While we have *long* been concerned about appearance, the fashion mods seem to have heightened that awareness. The nanobots have exaggerated all the things we used to do with fashion—alter our hair, highlight our eyes, emphasize our bone structures, etc. Now, they can actually change those things, and that ability has made them very conscious of them. And, yet, Sunati's fears are unfounded. Yasel tells her that Austen will not change her feelings. Austen tells Sunati that she was attracted to the person (whom she also called "hot" earlier in the comic) and not just the body. She would still be attracted to the person Sunati is. And she would never want her family or Sunati to limit themselves to the wonders of technology on her account.

What does all of this say to the young audience? For one, it illustrates a "zone of possibilities" of queer identity (Jagose 2). Sunati pursues Austen without a single consideration of sexuality, of familial repercussions, or of social stigma. As I noted in the Introduction, visibility matters. It's crucial for young readers to see a world they would like to bring into being. *Always Human* also says that relationships can be hard. The complications that Sunati and Austen face, despite all the technological changes, are all-too-familiar—having the courage to act upon attraction; getting to know the real person, who is not the fantasy version we have created in our heads; persevering through adversity. Although they begin in a whirlwind, they eventually realize that they have to slow down and really get to know one another.

A good message at any age....

Shade 9 — *ODY-C: Off to Far Ithicaa* (2015)

"If some god strike me on the wine-dark sea..."
Wilson, trans., Homer, *The Odyssey*, 187

GENDER-SWAPPING IS NOT a new thing in literature. Indeed, gender-swapped fairy tales abound. For example, Karrie Fransman (she/her) and Jonathan Plackett (he/him) released *Gender Swapped Fairy Tales* (2021), in which they have swapped out gendered words such as "he" and "she," and "son" and "daughter," but have left the fairy tale itself intact. Or, Leslie Vedder's (she/her) *The Bone Spindle* (2022) retells the Sleeping Beauty fairy tale in which a female treasure hunter and a warrior seek a sleeping prince to awaken. And, of course, the ever-popular gender-swapped retelling of Cinderella by Marissa Meyer (she/her) in *The Lunar Chronicles* (2012-) is under contract for a TV series.

Quite a few writers have re-written myths, as well. In some cases, they update the myth and retell it in a modern setting. For example, Sarah McCarry's (she/her) Metamorphoses series (3 volumes, 2013-2015) reimagines Orpheus and Eurydice in the contemporary US northwest with two young women in the lead roles. In other cases, authors retell the myth from a different perspective. For example, Margaret Atwood's (she/her) *The Penelopiad* (2006) retells *The Odyssey* from the perspective of Penelope. As you might guess, she sees things a bit differently than Homer (he/him) did. Others still reimagine gender roles. For example, Fransman and Plackett's *Gender-Swapped Greek Myths* (2022) doesn't re-write the myths but rather swaps the gender of the characters, which in and of itself creates a very different understanding of the myths and the times.

In *ODY-C: Off to Far Ithicaa* (2015), Matt Fraction (he/him) and Christian Ward (he/him) offer a gender-bent retelling of Homer's *The Odyssey*. It is also one of the most dynamically illustrated comics I have read. The illustrations and the colors splash all over the pages. The 5-issue limited series was released in early 2015, with the omnibus version released in June 2015.

Homer's original tale is steeped in ancient Grecian gendered and sexual norms. To begin with, the Trojan War is launched over a possession—Helen (she/her). Two men fighting over the possession-who-is-Helen kill off a generation of warriors. Away from their wives, the men have field slaves or field concubines. As Odysseus (he/him) tries to get back home, he's lured away by the sirens. Those pesky women will always distract you from your mission! Meanwhile, back home, his long-suffering wife, Penelope (she/her), must fend off male suitors. A desirable woman cannot just be sitting around. She's up for grabs! Oh, but Penelope is clever, and she is true. Odysseus returns and all is right with the world.

In this new version, however, (nearly) all of the characters are female. Why tell a gender-bent version of a classic? Why tell it now? As Ursula K. Le Guin (she/her) reminds us, myths can be living or dead. For her, simple retellings of old myths make little sense. Although I cannot say for certain, I have to believe that she was not much moved by Kevin Sorbo's (he/him) *Hercules* (1995-1999). Le Guin argues that myths must be alive, must speak to us, and must be relevant and in a form we can relate to. So, does the myth of Odysseus contain something that remains relevant for us today?

In this first volume (a second volume appeared in 2016), the graphic novel narrowly focuses on Book Nine and Book Ten from *The Odyssey*. Much of the first eight books of *The*

Odyssey center around Penelope and Telemachus. In Book Nine, though, "clever" Odysseus begins to tell his own tale. Odysseus claims that Zeus blew them off course, and they landed at Cicones. After they kill the men and "took their wives and shared their riches equally among us," they drink to excess. They leave when they are attacked, but again Zeus sends them off course, and they end up in the land of the Lotus Eaters. When his crew members are given lotus flowers, they forget home and lose their will to continue. Odysseus must tie up his crew so that they will stay aboard the ship. (In this summary I am using Emily Wilson's [she/her] translation.)

ODY-C begins with the sack of Troiia-VII, a remote "siege-world," by "cunning" Odyssia (she/her), our female Odysseus (7). The three female warriors, Odyssia, Gamem (she/her), and Ene (she/her) celebrate. They take the male leader of Troiia, and they humiliate him. "No one could want him again" (9). Then, Odyssia and her female warriors board the ship *ODY-C* and leave for far Ithicaa. That ship, though, is no rocket, no hurtling phallus. Instead, it is in the form of a C, a half-circle. She leaves behind the "killer and thief" Paris (pronouns unknown) (11).

In *The Odyssey*, Odysseus and his crew travel to the land of the Cyclopes. They find the Cyclops Polyphemus's (he/him) cave and marvel at his elaborate pens for raising and harvesting sheep. Polyphemus returns from a day in the pastures, but when he enters the cave to find strangers, he grabs two, dashes their heads on the floor and eats "them like a mountain lion on the mountains" (Book Nine, line 292). The clever Odysseus, though, devises a means to attack the giant. He gets the giant drunk with wine and deceives him about his name. He tells Polyphemus that his name is "Noman." The crewmen attack Polyphemus with carved sticks and gouge out his eye. When he screams out for help, he says that "Noman is hurting me." The other Cyclopes leave. Odysseus and his crew escape by clinging to Polyphemus's sheep as he drives the sheep out of the cave the next day. Odysseus's remaining crew members cry at the loss of friends, but Odysseus orders them to "stop their crying" (line 469). Odysseus tells Polyphemus that Zeus has punished him for his failure to treat guests properly. In a final taunt, he says tell anyone who asks that "Odysseus, the city-sacker, Laertes's son, who lives in Ithaca, destroyed your sight" (lines 504-506). Polyphemus calls on his father, Poseidon (he/him), to make sure that Odysseus never gets home. Odysseus takes the ram he stole and sacrifices him to Zeus. Odysseus claims that the god ignored his prayers and "planned to ruin all of my ships and all my loyal men" (lines 554-555).

In *ODY-C*, the Olympians gather and discuss next steps. Whatever will they do for entertainment now that the war is over? Poseidon (she/her) is jealous that Odyssia made a sacrifice to Amphtrite (she/her) and not to Poseidon herself. The gods sitting in the circle are petty and jealous and downright mean. Poseidon says they cannot make things easy for the puny humans. And, so, Poseidon blows Odyssia off course again. Some of the crew members are not too happy that Odyssia has raised the gods' ire. The disharmony throws them out of sync; they are lost, somewhere in Cicone space (17). Odyssia orders her crew to kill all the "code-less barbarian junkers" (18). After they prevail, Odyssia is in bed with her lover Sebex Ero (she/her). The Sebex is a manufactured being, nonbinary, not-woman, not-man. The Sebex can bear children, but only other sebex or females. Sebex Ero asks Odyssia about mothering, about her daughter Telem (she/her).

Zeus (she/her), first daughter of Cronus (she/her), murderer of Cronus, tells us that she has no use for children. In a full-page image, a large, angry Zeus holds what appears to be the head of Cronus. Zeus is covered with spattered blood and viscera. In Zeus's genital region, a bloody hole. Zeus toys with humans; Zeus murders her father; Zeus fears children. They—like she—become powerful and a threat. Zeus, with her rainbow

inflected collar of ice shards, matters most to Zeus. So that
no children could ever again be a threat, the mighty Zeus has
destroyed all men. The universe may have wailed, but Zeus
says, "and I slept like a baby" (35). Her daughter Promethene
(she/her), great friend to man, does not take that lying down.
Promethene, in an image in which she manipulates the double helix, creates a new kind of being, the Sebex. "Of course,
I cannot touch Promethene and still be righteous all-mother
Zeus" (38).

Odyssia and her crew come ashore in the land of Lotus
Blossoms. There, as in Homer's tale, the crew members suc-
cumb to the drug. They forget themselves; they forget the war;
they forget their home. But like Dante's concentric circles of
hell, the Land of the Lotus has many layers, filled with avarice
and lust and more. Odyssia and Sebex Ero find their way to
the circle beneath all other circles. There, under the influence
of the lotus bloom, Sebex Ero asks to be the mother of Odyssia's child. Odyssia, though, wants only Penelope, and Telem,
and far Ithicaa (45).

Rainbow-encircled Zeus and Poseidon argue over Odyssia. Does she forget her place? Will she come for the throne?
As accusations fly, the two Olympians lock in an ardent kiss,
colors bleeding together on the page. Odyssia gathers "every
last" member of the *ODY-C*, save Sebex Ero who languishes
in the pool of deep forgetting, and leaves the Lotus behind.
Neither Zeus nor Poseidon are finished with them.

In another gender-bending scene, we see a woman giving birth. A very male-looking and bearded Zeus claims the
child. Hera comforts her and torments Zeus. Hera reminds
the woman that no god may remain in disguise if a mortal asks
them to reveal themselves. And, so, Zeus splits open the mask
and steps forward. The woman explodes into a kaleidoscope of
viscera. Zeus cradles the tiny form in her hand and says, "Behold your mother-father. Behold your god" (56). Child now

grown, the bearded Hera reminds Apollo that she protected and nurtured her, not Zeus. Apollo, annoying Zeus, gives a blessing and casks of wine to aid Odyssia.

Poseidon damns them once again. The *ODY-C* is forced down onto Kylos, "that fetid dank jungle star, searing of atmosphere, deadly of ground" (62). There they find the cave door for the giant Cyclops. Inside, they find pens of animals of all stripes. Poseidon's abandoned daughter, the Cyclops of Kylos (she/her), enters the cave and begins eating the women. Though they battle, the women are thrown into the pens with the carnage, the offal, the guts. Odyssia tricks the Cyclops and says "Call me 'All-men'" (74). As in Homer's version, the Cyclops gets drunk with Apollo's wine and belches into the pits. As in Homer's version, they blind the Cyclops and make their way out. In this version, though, the pages drip in blood. When they escape and the Cyclops is blind and defeated, she calls upon her mother Poseidon to, once again, foil Odyssia's plans and to avenge "All-men's grim crimes" (90).

The *ODY-C* is damaged and seeks a port in the storm. They find the land of Aeolia. In Homer's version, Book Ten begins with Odysseus arriving in Aeolus. As one must treat guests, Aeolus hosts Odysseus for a month, bestows on him food and wine and then provides Odysseus with a bag of wind to see him home. But the rumor mill grinds, the jealousies mount, and the crew members open the bag of wind, thinking Odysseus had been given riches. They end up back in Aeolus, no closer to home. This time, though, Aeolus sends them packing.

In our gender-bent version, the world of Aeolia is high-tech. Countless nymphets operate machines. The nymphets ask their god, the four-handed Aeolus (he/him), what to do about the *ODY-C*. He has a use for them. Aeolus has constructed a machine that allows near-instantaneous travel. Odyssia could be home in a flash. He would like to install the machine on the *ODY-C*, and he would like to travel with them. Odyssia, though, has an uneasy feeling. Something about the man is "off" (112). Clever Odyssia selects six of her soldiers to remain behind. They will fuck him; they will sate him; they will bear his children. But they will distract him so that the *ODY-C* can make one more escape.

I must say, the artwork here is some of the most interesting and striking I have seen. It is deep in color and rich in detail. The details fill the foreground and the background. Each page, each frame holds layers of details, symbolic and literal. The images bear reading and re-reading. They bear consideration. They bear the refracting light of a magnifying glass. The colors contribute to the retelling of the wine-dark sea. The details lend significance to the overwhelming tale of creation and destruction. Further, the comic often destroys panel conventions, with many scenes that spill across the page in a kind of visual and narrative excess.

Even so, what matters all this? The male Olympians fuck with human beings, literally and figuratively, for sport. The female Olympians do so, as well. The male Zeus imprisons his son for fear that he would overthrow him; the female Zeus does as well. The male Odysseus wages war to regain a possession (Helen); Odyssia does, as well. On the battlefield, Odysseus commits atrocities; Odyssia does, as well.

In what way, then, does the gender swap queer the tale?

Well, apart from the stunning visuals, the queer impact is limited. ODY-C does not fundamentally challenge the logic of the mythic tale. The characters are generally doing similar things for similar reasons. Does that meet the Le Guin test for updating a dead myth? Probably not. It may be set in a spacefaring future, but only the scale of travel has changed. The gods behave in very similar ways. Does it alter, then, the reader's takeaway, the mythical lessons learned? Probably not. The gods are cruel, be kind to your guests, fear being usurped, sex is a weapon. Does it alter sexual desire and relationships?

Yes. We see women in relationships, and we see Odyssia with the enby Sebex. Even so, the relations don't seem all that much different—or all that healthy.

"This is absurd // that mortals blame the gods…." (Wilson 106)

Shade 10 — *Inhibit* (2015-2022)

Pulling Back the Curtain

I REMEMBER BEING scared to death by *The Wizard of Oz*. When I was younger, the movie was broadcast once a year. The family would gather around and watch. I would be fine until the scene where Dorothy (she/her) goes to see the wicked witch. The witch's "little pretties" gave me nightmares. But Dorothy plods along and finds her way to the Emerald City, where she eventually gets an audience with the "great and powerful Oz" (he/him). Of course, he is anything but. The Wizard of Oz has built up the machinery of a powerful domain. He has built up the image of a powerful wizard. But, in the end, it is all show, all manipulation. When Dorothy pulls back the curtain and reveals the man behind the mystique, the power shifts from him to her. The knowledge that the machinery is merely a front empowers Dorothy. *Inhibit* offers a similar hope.

Scotland's Eve Greenwood (they/them) wrote and published the webcomic *Inhibit* starting in January 2015 and continuing through the present. Greenwood is the writer, illustrator, *and* publisher of the comic. The first 5 chapters have been packaged as a graphic novel and sold by Greenwood's own publishing house (Quindre Press). The webcomic continues to be updated online. (Page citations here are taken from the webcomic.)

The comic takes place in a near-future, alternate Great Britain. It would appear that in this future *most* people have one of eight "variants," aka superpowers. Several items in the comic suggest that these variants are widespread (more on that in a bit). Some children are chosen to attend the Urquhart Clinic for Variational Research and Training. The assumption is that these individuals will then become "Britain's protectors" (05.01). We see young Vic's eyes light up at the idea of being one of the chosen ones. After all, he's seen the TV adverts his whole life. Of course, not everyone accepted into Urquhart makes it through the training. Some people just can't fully master the self-control and discipline needed. Enter our heroes....

The Earl Estate is one of several residences where dropouts are housed. In these facilities, they get minimal training and minimal education. Every once in a while, one of them will demonstrate sufficient control so that they can get a "domestic license" that allows them to be out in the world unsupervised. More often than not, they go "dormant." That is, they lose their powers altogether. In either case, they only have until age 18, at which point they are sent home.

In Unit 3 of the Earl Estate, we find young Victor "Vic" Allen (he/him), a young man capable of electromanipulation, though his control of it is very, very bad. He is just weeks from his 18th birthday. His roommates include Julia "Jules" Blue (she/her), a young woman capable of cryomanipulation, and David (he/him), a young man with hypersense. Jules can freeze things, including herself. In an accident, she froze the tip of a finger and froze her legs. She lost one of those limbs and now uses a prosthetic and/or crutches. David has super senses, though he uses hearing aids and frequently speaks in sign language. His senses sometimes gets overloaded, and he shuts down completely (02.07-08).

It's not all fun and games on the Earl campus, though. They are locked in their rooms at night, locked on campus at all times. Contact with home is limited. And, despite the fact that they are there as a (potential) national resource, their family foots a portion of the expense. They undergo regular check-ups and tests. They know that they have one hope—to control their power and get a license.

Of course, the system does not go unchallenged. The revolutionary group Chalice fights against the entire variants mechanism. They protest the conscription and confinement of people with variants. They attack training facilities (01.25). When the anomalous Paulina (she/her) appears, she drops the big plot bombs. She claims that "dormancy" is not a real thing. The trainees had all been told that, sometimes, people naturally lose their power. They are tested regularly to see if they are going dormant. When they test dormant, they are sent home. Paulina claims that dormancy is, in fact, manufactured. The authorities can counteract and nullify the variants at will. The search for evidence of this conspiracy becomes the center of the story. Paulina's claim is that it is all about control. Having the power to enforce dormancy allows the government and its institutions to control its variants.

On the "About" page for the webcomic, Greenwood, who describes themself as a "queer artist," notes that "99% of the cast is queer." As the comic begins, Julia is dating another Earl member, Cameron (he/him). Much later we discover that prior to Cameron, Julia had been dating Joanne (she/her). In one rant, Cameron notes that Julia defines herself as "ace" (aka asexual). David is horribly shy, but has a thing for Sid (they/them) and wants to ask them out. Although he never quite gets up his courage, Sid saves the day and kisses David. In addition, Greenwood provides a hint that Masha might be trans. When they first arrived at Urquhart, at about age 9, Vic made fun of Masha's name. She defends her name, saying she picked it out herself. According to Masha, her parents had given her a boy's name, "but they were wrong" (05.06). That fact, of course, could mean any number of things, though it certainly could be a breadcrumb about Masha's identity. Finally, three of the secondary characters are identified as nonbinary: Sid, Nirav, and Rosalyn are all enby and use "they" pronouns.

Unsurprisingly, then, the residents of this world tend to be attuned to pronouns. They do not make assumptions and generally ask about pronouns. For example, when the "terrorist" Paulina (she/her) crashes a mission, all the members of the team default to "they" when they refer to Paulina (not that they even know her name at that point). Later, when she is with Vic and Julia, they continue the use of "they" until Paulina corrects them. Much later, Vic meets one of Nate's (he/him) team, Bronwyn (she/her). She notes that Nate never informed her of Vic's pronouns. Vic's answer: "Oh, um. Anything's fine."

Unlike other comics, such as, say, *The Pride* (see Shade 4), *Inhibit* does not exactly announce its queerness. The hint about Masha appears in Chapter 5. Sid kisses David, but not until Chapter 8. In other words, Greenwood introduces these pieces of information in organic ways. In Chapter 8, we see a shot of a hallway at the residence. Cameron is walking toward Julia. However, he passes in front of a banner hanging in the hallway. Although some of the letters are obscured, it appears to read: Ear Pride. However, the letter L is folded over, which means it should read: Earl Pride. Apparently, the Urquhart rejects at Earl Estate have a Pride group. Is the body in front of the letters deliberate? Of course it is. But why? Is the curled letter L on purpose? Of course it is. But why? Just a little word play: Ear/Earl? It's another of the references to queerness that Greenwood leaves throughout the comic.

So, what's the connection between *Inhibit*'s variants and queer folx? For one, by having "99% of the cast" being queer, Greenwood clearly links variance and queerness. True, the variants here have only eight forms, but we learn that that is probably also a lie. Paulina seems to defy that rule. Maybe others do, too. Perhaps variations have other forms, as well. Perhaps, variants come in all shapes and colors. For another, the government tries to inhibit the variants. The variants in Urquhart and Earl must wear physical inhibitors that quell their variant power. And when those inhibitors do not work, they force dormancy. It does not require much of a leap of faith to read that as a form of government-compelled conversion therapy. Of course, another way to read the variants is that being a variant is a superpower, therefore, being queer is a superpower. They just cannot let the government quash it.

Most importantly, I think, Greenwood queers the superpower trope. They ask us to think about superpowers in a different way. For one, we see no examples of the variants out there fending off bad guys. In fact, *Inhibit* takes place in the dorm of those who have failed as superheroes. Instead, we see the bureaucratic side of it, the maintenance side of it, and the failure side of it. Vic is absolutely not the typical superhero. He's a teen. He's miserable and moody. He cannot control his emotions. He is disillusioned by the system. And much of that discontent stems from the fact that they have been inhibiting him. He cannot be his true self. None of the kids at Earl can. For Vic and the others, being inhibited is hell.

But now they have pulled back the curtain, and they have seen that the machinery is a front. It's no wonder that they just might want to pick up the Chalice and challenge the status quo.

Shade 11 — *Angela: Asgard's Assassin* (2015)
"Everything Has a Price"

So, JUST WHAT do we mean to each other? What does one person mean to another? What should the foundation of our relations and our interactions be? Since the 1940s, one particular take on this question has been pushed by Ayn Rand (she/her). For Rand, we are nothing to one another. For Rand, the height of evolution is that we have superseded our basic instincts to help one another (as in an animal pack). The pinnacle of humanity is to be ruthlessly self-centered and individualistic. The bottom line is that each person should pursue their own self-interests — regardless of how that affects anyone else. The most recent exemplar is, of course, Donald Trump. For him, all human relations should be treated as transactions. In what can be called Trumpian transactionalism, any other person is only worth what value Trump thinks he can extract from that person. Once he can no longer extract something from that person, they are persona non grata. I was reminded of this sort of a relationship as I read *Angela: Asgard's Assassin*.

The pathway for Angela of Asgard (she/her) to be the lead of a comic series is a bit circuitous. Her character was created in 1993 by Neil Gaiman (he/him) when Todd MacFarlane (he/him) contracted Gaiman to write an issue of *Spawn*. In that franchise, Angela was a Hellspawn slayer created when five mortal souls were merged together ("Angela"). The character, however, was acquired by Marvel Comics (2013). According to the Marvel Fandom Wiki (as of mid-2022), Angela has made 83 appearances in Marvel comics, including *Age of*

Ultron (01.10), *Guardians of the Galaxy* (03), *All-New X-Men* (01), *Original Sin* (01), and *Thor* (several volumes). Apart from these (and others), she has been the lead characters in two 6-part series: *Asgard's Assassin* (2015) and its direct sequel *Queen of Hel* (2015-2016). In the Marvel Universe, Angela is the daughter of Odin (he/him) and Freyja (she/her), and her name is Aldrif Odinsdottir (she/her) ("Aldrif Odinsdottir" [Earth-616]).

When the kingdom of Heven wages war against Asgard, the Queen of Angels (she/her) kidnaps Aldrif, hoping to use the infant as leverage against Odin. When Odin does not capitulate, the Queen of Angels vows to kill the child. In a classic mythological move, the baby is saved by a handmaiden and is raised among the Angels, now with the name Angela. Raised in the Tenth Realm, Angela *hates* all things Asgardian. When Angela learns that she really is an Asgardian, she threatens to kill Odin. At the same time, when her true identity as an Asgardian is revealed, Heven exiles her. At that point, Angela is a woman without a home, but she is also a woman who settles her debts. At the beginning of *Asgard's Assassin*, written by Kieron Gillen (he/him), however, Odin and Freyja have a new baby daughter. In an apparent squaring of the circle, Angela kidnaps the child and threatens to destroy her.

What makes *Angela* a queer comic? Well, for one, the implication is that Angela herself is queer and has a girlfriend. Furthermore, her girlfriend, Sera (she/her), is a transwoman. To be fair, the series is a pretty straightforward (pun intended) action comic. Angela and Sera bounce from realm to realm, running ahead of the Asgardians who chase them relentlessly. The narrative center of the story is whether or not Angela will destroy her baby sister, and whether or not she can save her sister from Surtur (he/him). The fight sequences are prominent and vivid, rendered in stunning color, but the relationship between Angela and Sera is secondary.

Even so, in those moments between the chases and the battles, we do learn something of Angela and Sera's past. Sera had been an Anchorite, one of the rare males born in Heven. The Anchorites are protected and sheltered in a temple, where they study and pray. Sera, however, had a desire for forbidden knowledge, which, of course, had negative consequences. When monsters attack the temple, Angela the Hunter tracks them. In that attack, Sera helps Angela defeat the monsters. In payment of her debt, Angela agrees to take Sera away and allows Sera to become "her true self." Angela vows to never allow Sera to step back into the "hell" of the temple and presumably into a place and time where and when Sera could not be her true self.

Outside the arc of this series, Sera is killed, but at the opening of *Asgard's Assassin*, Sera is back. How can that be? As we all know, dead characters have ways of coming back to life, don't they? Angela suspects foul play, suspects deception, but Sera passes all her tests. Sera knows all of their personal details. Through these questions, we relive some of their past together. Nevertheless, in this series, Sera is really relegated to the margins. Their relationship is tangential. Sera's identity and lived experience as a trans woman are irrelevant to the story at hand.

Well, if the queer relationship is minimal, and if the transwoman is marginal, why include the comic here? As I noted in the Introduction, I want to examine a wide range of queer comics, from those in which queerness is marginal to those in which queerness is central. For another, I hope to show a wide range of publishers, and I do think that it's significant that Marvel features a queer character so prominently. However, I am even more interested in missed opportunities. I am no expert in the Marvel Universe, but I do know that Marvel's authors work under the constraint of keeping storylines consistent with canon (except, you know, when they throw canon out the window). Even so, writers must keep the story of Angela somewhat consistent across story arcs and multiple appearances. Indeed, a *lot* of this comic reads like a history lesson in Marvel lore.

However, I am not suggesting a rewriting of canon. I'm not suggesting they ignore Angela's past. Instead, I'm wondering what the comic might have been like if the love between Angela and Sera had played a role in the story. Yes, it is true that a major reason that Sera wants to leave the temple is because of her identity. She could not be herself there. Yes, Sera helps Angela escape, but *not* because they are lovers. But what if their escape had depended on their trust? Or, what if their escape depended upon the strength of their love and commitment? Or, what if Sera's identity as a trans woman made a difference in their escape? Perhaps Sera becoming her true self was precisely what made their defeat of the monster possible. What if becoming her true self enabled their mutual escape? Angela is a person caught between two worlds—Heven and Asgard. She is rejected by both. She exacts revenge on both. However, Sera is caught between two worlds as well. Perhaps Sera could mirror Angela's liminality. Perhaps Sera might offer insight to Angela in negotiating the two realms. Perhaps they could instruct one another on the dangers of living a lie in one realm, or on the benefits of living one's own life.

Instead, Angela is motivated by a very strict code of honor and ethics. For Angela, no debt can go unpaid; she will not consciously take on a debt unless she believes she can repay it. Failure to repay a debt is a capital crime. In the end, Angela believes that she has repaid two debts. Asgard brought her into being, and being an Asgardian has shaped who she is. In purifying and returning her sister, she has repaid her debt to Asgard (despite the fact that she stole her sister in the first place). Since Heven took Angela in and raised her, she owed a debt to Heven. She has restored their failing furnace and allows them to continue to exist.

But just perhaps, Angela—through Sera—could have been changed in her outlook, in her rigidity, in her simplistic binary view of the world and interpersonal relations. Angela's motto is: "Nothing for nothing—everything for a price. Balance is kept." Is that the same as Trumpian transactionalism? Not quite. One way to read Angela is that no one has intrinsic value, but rather that one is worth only what can be extracted. Even so, whereas Trumpian transactionalism focuses on the excess gotten from the relationship, Angela's transactionalism looks for a balance. Sera helps Angela slay a monster; Angela helps Sera escape her personal hell. But here I see another missed opportunity. What would a queered version of transactionalism look like? Or, better still, how would a queer relationship eliminate transactionalism?

So many missed chances.

Shade 12 — *The Infinite Loop* (2015)
The Malleability of Time

ON FEBRUARY 28, 2022, the US House of Representatives passed the Emmett Till Antilynching Act. The vote was 422-3. The US Senate then passed the bill on March 7, 2022. The bill passed via unanimous consent. On March 29, 2022, President Biden (he/him) signed it into law. Under the new Act, lynching becomes explicitly defined as a federal hate crime.

The Act is named, of course, for the 14-year-old Emmett Till (he/him), a Black boy who was murdered after a white woman falsely accused him of either flirting with or whistling at her in Mississippi in 1955. Several days after the incident, the woman's husband and his brother took Emmett Till, beat him, shot him, and threw him into the river. They were acquitted of his murder by an all-white jury. Till's murder and his murderers' acquittals sparked national outrage and helped catalyze the Civil Rights Movement of the 1960s. Till's memory reemerged during the George Floyd (he/him) protests of 2020. For one, Floyd was one more Black man murdered. For another, in the midst of a rise in hate crimes, Till's memorial was vandalized repeatedly. It has been secured behind protective measures—more than what was done for Till himself.

The Infinite Loop was written by Pierrick Colinet (he/him) and illustrated by Elsa Charretier (she/her). The two have a history of working together on projects, including several *Star Wars* titles. *La boucle infinie* was originally published in France in August of 2015 (Glénat), with its English title translated in the comic as *The Infinite Loop*. The English-version collection appeared in November 2015 (IDW). It earned the Virginia Library Association Graphic Novel Diversity Award for its LGBTQ+ advocacy and its civil rights history lessons.

The book falls into roughly two halves. The first half largely deals with the romance, and the second half deals with the time travel paradoxes (which all lead back to the romance). Our protagonist, Teddy (she/her), works as a temporal agent at the Brigade, an organization that tries very hard to keep the timeline intact. On the other side, the Forgers disrupt history as we know it. Just who are the good ones here? Teddy and her colleagues travel through time in order to clean up the "anomalies" left behind by the temporal missions and by the "Forgers."

On a routine mission to New York City in 1970—the time and place of the first Gay Pride Parade—Teddy encounters the anomaly of a woman with purple hair. To date, the Forgers had only left behind inanimate anomalies. Why are they becoming animate? Of course, Teddy's job requires that she "suppress" any and all anomalies. Suppressing something basically means disintegrating it. Her job makes no exceptions for women with purple hair who are "hot" (Teddy's word). And, so, she breaks protocol and runs off with her. Teddy calls her Ano (she/her), short for Anomaly. She never has any other name throughout the book. Telling, wouldn't you say?

Initially, the two retreat to Teddy's company-owned apartment, not the best idea. Luckily, Teddy has her own little Fortress of Solitude. She has constructed a bucolic farm outside of space and time—her own personal "time warp." They escape the apartment, and she takes Ano there. They no sooner land on terra infirma, when the sex begins. Teddy was too nervous to make a move the night before, but now, Ano takes the initiative. The two lovers spend five months outside of time. They have sex; they watch movies; they read; they talk. All any lovers could ask for, really.

But things are happening back inside the flow of time. The Brigade and Teddy's old boss, Tina (she/her), are not going to take this lying down. They eventually find their way into Teddy's time warp. And then all hell breaks loose.

In the second half, Ano is suppressed, and Teddy goes off the rails. She rages and destroys timelines and causality. Her future self speaks to her through her mother. The graphic depicts anomalies in a timeline via small yellow rectangles. They float around a page; they cover a character. They become more and more pervasive as the flow of time breaks down. In the warehouse that rather conveniently holds copies of every suppressed anomaly, Teddy meets the androgynous, genderqueer Andromeda (pronouns unknown). She also finds the copy of Ano. Except, Ano is not material, not tangible. Would she be okay with a life with a version of Ano she cannot touch? Ano is not having it.

So, they have three options: they all die when the Brigade shows up; they run away, never able to touch again; or Teddy breaks the time-stream and reboots it. Andromeda tells Teddy: "You're gonna woman up, you're gonna pride up and you're gonna break this goddamn loop you keep talking about" (147).

Teddy has spent her life trying to keep order, but now the Infinite Loop has to be broken. The Loop is the order of things, the system that keeps order in place; it is the way that the powers-that-be have maintained power. And, in many respects, Emmett Till is a central—if not overtly stated—figure in *The Infinite Loop*. Teddy mentions Eric Lembembe (he/him), an LGBTI activist found murdered in Cameroon in 2013. She mentions Jean Jaurès (he/him), a French Socialist and antimilitarist who was assassinated in 1914. She mentions Rev. James Reeb (he/him) a Unitarian Universalist minister and civil rights activist, who was murdered in 1965 by white nationalists during the Selma to Montgomery marches. She mentions Qiu Jin (she/her), a Chinese revolutionary and feminist, who was publicly beheaded in 1907 for her purported role in an assassination attempt. Ano also rather problematically mentions Aung San Suu Kyi (she/her), the icon of democracy and peace turned symbol of ethnic and religious persecution.

What do each of these individuals mean? Each one confronts Teddy. They tell her that she *could* have changed the past. They say that she *allowed* them to be murdered over and over again, all in the name of order. But that order is patriarchal and racist and heteronormative. And that order must be broken. The loop must be broken. As they tell her, as Andromeda tells her, she must stand and fight.

Teddy returns to that moment in 1970 when she and Ano first met. Along the way in the wormhole, Teddy is encouraged by Susan B. Anthony (she/her) and Malcolm X (he/him). This time, she finds Ano among the protestors outside Stonewall. A sign next to Ano reads: "Stonewall means fight back" (157). Teddy breaks all of time. Teddy reboots the system—the very definition of radical activism and systemic change. But it's not that simple, is it? It happens again. A headline reads: "They Are Not Like Us." The patterns start over. "It's happening again" (160). Patterns of discrimination, of exclusion, and of hatred have crept back in. Ano stands up. Ano proclaims that it doesn't matter. They will stand and fight every time. Their movement has gotten larger, and "even those who aren't victims of the infinite loop are joining our cause, every day" (163).

Ano proclaims that "History proved us right. The world and humanity always moved forward. No matter how many wrenches were thrown at it" (162). A nice thought, but I would just trouble that statement a bit. (a) I do not believe that history and humanity have always moved forward. We've moved by lurches and stumbles. We've taken huge steps backward. (b) It all depends on whose history we're talking about, right? Progress has not worked the same for everyone. To paraphrase

William Gibson (he/him), the future has not been distributed equally. Progress for some is not necessarily progress for all. And (c) Ano's statement sort of undermines the premise of the graphic novel. How does time function? Is it linear? Is that a Western, scientific model that we have imposed?

And what does any of this have to do with queerness?

In *In a Queer Time and Place*, Jack Halberstam (he/him or she/her) writes about "queer time and space." Halberstam argues that "queer time" emerged as a consequence of the AIDS crisis, through which so many queer folx, and particularly gay men, saw the very idea of the future diminish. What future did they have in the face of this disease? So, on the one hand, queer time is a collapsing of time. On the other hand, queer time also represents alternate possibilities outside of the heterotemporality. As Halberstam writes, "Queer subcultures produce alternative temporalities by allowing their participants to believe that their futures can be imagined according to logics that lie outside of those paradigmatic markers of life experience—namely, birth, marriage, reproduction, and death" (2).

In *The Infinite Loop*, time is also kind of queer. It doesn't exactly flow in an ineluctable line. After all, time agents go back and make changes. It doesn't really flow in a cyclical pattern, though those cultures that hold a cyclical notion of time also tend to play a long game in planning. Ano argues for a long game. For another, Teddy and Ano develop their relationship *outside* of time altogether. Time passes inside their paradise, and they experience one day after another, and yet, time does not pass relative to the world they stepped out of. It is a queer space outside of time altogether.

In *The Infinite Loop*, time is both linear and cyclical. Time is stoppable; time is re-bootable; time is malleable. In *The Infinite*

Loop, Teddy and Ano use time to queer the world, to undo the history and presence of racism,[§] sexism, and homophobia.

So, it's time to "pride up" and break the loop.

§ Even so, it must be said that the ways in which the French artists, Colinet and Charretier, appropriate US history is fraught with complications. To what extent is their use of US history—and, in particular, Black US history—an aspect of superiority? They might have looked to racism and sexism within their own history, for example, but instead find racism and sexism in another country's history. In what ways is their use of US history a manifestation of US cultural imperialism?

Shade 13 — *Kaptara* (2015)

The Glomps Want to Make Kaptara Great Again

WHAT ARE THE odds? On June 16, 2015, Donald Trump (he/him) descended the staircase to announce his candidacy for President of the US. Little did we know what would follow. It was also in June of 2015 that the Supreme Court of the US ruled that refusing to grant same-sex marriage licenses was a violation of the 14th Amendment, the so-called Equal Protection Clause (which seems under threat post-*Dobbs*). Things went south after that. Even as Trump claimed to have done more for "the gays" than any president ever, he, in fact, did quite a lot to undermine LGBTQ+ rights in the US. He signed a law that undercut anti-discriminatory protections; he argued that civil law does not cover federal employees from sexual orientation discrimination; he attacked rights for trans individuals, in the military and as civilians. And now, the three Supreme Court Justices appointed by Trump provide legal cover for Trump's vision of the US.

What does all that have to do with *Kaptara*? Perhaps nothing more than a coincidence. Perhaps oracular-level prescience. Nevertheless, on April 22, 2015, Chip Zdarsky (he/him) and Kagan McLeod (he/him) released the very first issue of *Kaptara*. It ran for five issues, and was subsequently released as a graphic novel, *Kaptara Vol. 1: Fear Not, Tiny Alien*, in December of 2015.

The campy comic begins with five individuals on an exploration ship, headed for who knows where. The group appears to be racially and gender diverse. The primary character is a bio-engineer who is a queer Black man, Keith (he/him). Keith and the pilot Lance (he/him) don't get along. Lance is a typical jock, super-jacked and always conspicuously working out. It annoys Keith, a skinny gay dude who would rather play video games. Nevertheless, the physician on board, Dr. Laurette (she/her), a tall Black woman, *sees* Keith. She understands that he had been picked on as a queer youth and that he was not going to allow it any more. She suggests that he not always rise to the obvious queer baiting.

As they sail along, they encounter an anomaly. They see what appears to be a tunnel in a field of asteroids and decide to make their way through the tunnel. You can scream "Don't do it" all you want; they're still going through that tunnel. It doesn't go quite as planned. The tunnel draws them in at a very high rate of speed. As they make their way through, the ship takes a lot of damage. The pilot Lance orders the crew into escape pods. He soon follows, and their pods crash land on the planet below. Then things really go south.

The pods have crashed on Kaptara, a world filled with bizarre people and even more outlandish and garish monsters. After a near-fatal run-in with Fusciabeast, Keith finds himself in the royal chambers of Jinli (she/her), Queen of Endom, the Fourth Kingdom of Kaptara. Her son, Darfor (he/him), is a scantily clad man and a champion dart blower. He just loves blowing darts. Keith also undertakes battle training, and he and his trainer Pongord (he/him) flirt. A lot.

The Kaptarans discover that the human ships have come through a rift usually used by villains. If the humans came through, then it is quite likely that the evil Skullthor (pronouns unknown) has found Earth and is destroying it. Keith, however, is fine with that. He had been treated poorly as a gay man; his family had turned its back on him. He's fine with whatever fate the Earth faces. He—at least initially—is content in Endom.

As a group goes off to find a way to Earth to kill Skullthor, the entire party from Endom is taken captive by a group of Glomps. They are rude; they are crude; they are sexist; they are racist. They were exiled from Endom for their behavior. However, they doubled down and claimed reverse discrimination. Further, they blame their bad reputation on the media: "Freedom from those who would censor out glomptruths! Freedom from the %$#&s and $#%@s and of course the %$#@s who control the media!" (62). You see, the Glomps are a group of all straight men who draw erotic pictures of "ladies" for one another. As Darfor tells them, "Your repression is adorable." And here's the thing: they are hideous little guys who look an awful lot like Donald Trump (though some of them look just like Steve Bannon). They look like a cartoon Trump, like the giant floating naked baby Trump, and they act like him, too.

So, what's with the horde of toddler Trumps? As I noted, 2015 was a pretty good year in the US for LGBTQ+ rights and regulations. The actual Donald Trump had just declared his candidacy, and no one knew if it was for real or if he could get elected. So why are Zdarsky and McLeod painting such a portrait of the future-and-onetime Hair Fuhrer? Well, I don't actually think that they were prescient about Trump; however, the seeds of Trumpism were already present. Despite the fact that rights for LGBTQ+ individuals had improved in the Obama years, undercurrents were already in motion. A Newton-like truism says that for every social and political gain, an equal and opposite backlash will appear.

In 2015, White Supremacy was already a thing. After all, we had just elected the first Black president. In 2015, incels were already a thing. They were already planning the Beta uprising. Politicians were already complaining about the "liberal media." After all, the Media Research Center was founded in the US in 1987. They produced and offered their "I Don't Believe the Liberal Media" bumperstickers in 2010.

On top of all that, Zdarksy and MacLeod both worked in journalism for years. Zdarksy worked at the *National Post* for 14 years. MacLeod worked for the *National Post* as well. They were doubtless well aware of these trends.

Oh, to be sure, the comic book is absurd, campy fun (see Shade 40 for more on camp). Still, the situation is unbelievable. The "pollen" that rewires the brain to allow them all to speak a common language is improbable (and a bit of a pet peeve for me). The monsters and villains are, well, cartoonish. The "vehicles" that the Kaptarans "drive" and the beasts that they "fly" are of Seussian proportions.

Furthermore, the lead character Keith is something of a stereotype. This situation happens all too often when only *one* character is gay. Keith (in this case) becomes the "representative" of the queer community. He stands in for all gay men. And, of course, that's impossible. No one gay man can represent the entire range of experience of all gay men. And so the authors rely on stereotypes. He's sassy and quick of wit but scared to death of conflict and fighting. He introduces himself to the Queen of Endom as Keith, Prince of the Dance Floor. He's always ready with a pop cultural reference.

And, yet. Isn't the absurdity in part the point?

Keith's dilemma is all-too-real and all-too-absurd. On Earth, he was rejected by all those who mattered to him. Keith was hoping for a clean slate, a tabula rasa, a fresh beginning on Kaptara. Maybe he can be accepted here. Maybe he will find community here. Maybe a new beginning is possible. Alas, all of Keith's dreams are dashed.

The monsters are here, too, whether they are archfiends like Skullthor and Villektra (pronouns unknown), or snarling beasts like the Fusciabeast, or the hated-filled, bigoted Glomps.

Maybe it's time to stand and fight....

Shade 14 — *Paper Girls* (2015-2019)

Eyes Wide Open

HOW OFTEN HAVE you wanted to meet your older self? Maybe when you're having a bad day, some advice from a future you might be reassuring. Maybe if you get a less-than-desirable medical diagnosis, knowledge from your future self might help with the anxiety. Maybe you're a nerdy teenager, and you'd like to hear that it won't always be quite so difficult. Maybe you'd like to know that we do not destroy the Earth and that you have a future ahead of you. Maybe you're struggling with your sexuality and you'd like to hear that it gets better, that you won't always be uncertain, that you won't always be a pariah, that you won't always be unloved.

Brian K. Vaughn's (he/him) *Paper Girls* explores some of these possibilities, and more. *Paper Girls* is a *long* comic—thirty issues, collected into one volume totaling 773 pages. The first issue appeared in October 2015, and the final issue appeared in July 2019. And one really needs to read all of it to get any answers. Over the course of those 30 issues, the comic was nominated for four Hugo Awards (never won). It was nominated for two Eisner Awards and won one (2016) for Best New Comic. The television series adaptation premiered on 29 July 2022 (Amazon Prime) but was cancelled after only one season.

Set in 1988 in a small, fictional town outside of Cleveland, Ohio, *Paper Girls* features four twelve-year-old girls who deliver papers. In 1988, that was kind of a big thing. Only boys had paper routes. But Mac Coyle (she/her) broke the mold, and others followed. Soon KJ (she/her) and Tiffany (she/her) also delivered papers. They were a bit of a support group, especially on the morning after Halloween, when all the low-lifes are still lurking around. The "new girl" is Erin Tsieng (she/her). On November 1, 1988, the four of them meet in the middle of the road, and everything starts to go a little bit strange.

In an interview, Vaughn and Cliff Chiang (he/him) explain that they were trying to get inside the heads of 12-year-olds, at a point just as they are about to enter the real world. At this point in their lives, they are still idealistic and have not been ground down by the vicissitudes of life. Moreover, they are more willing to see the forces battling over the fate of all time as two competing philosophies rather than as good guys and bad guys (Tucker Stone, "Interview"). Nevertheless, these four see a future, see others working for that future, and they are determined to have a hand in shaping what it will look like.

Before they know it, they are front and center in a millennia-long fight for the survival of Earth. After Dr. Qanta Braunstein (she/her) invents time travel (for semi-fictional AppleX), anomalies begin to appear. Much as we saw in *The Infinite Loop* (Shade 12), one faction is committed to cleaning up the anomalies and making certain that the temporal flow of events is not altered. These Old-Timers are committed to the "first draft of history." Their primary tool is to scoop up people who have witnessed anomalies and to wipe their short-term memory. Afterward, they have no recollection of anything out of the ordinary.

On the other side of the battle are the Teenagers, who are equally as committed to changing history in order to assure a "fairer, more just world was possible for everyone" (648). The Teenagers travel through time trying to undo the corrections of the Old-Timers. They gather pieces of technology that might be useful to them in the future. But because the Teenagers travel through time a *lot*, they have developed a new kind of cancer. They wear implants to help cope with the cancer, but, ironically, they appear old and scarred.

As readers, we're never quite sure whom to trust, and we're never quite sure whom to root for.

Still, the complications don't end there. As the four paper girls flee near certain death, they make a time jump to the year 11,706 BCE. There they meet a young woman (about their age), Wari (she/her), who has a son, Jahpo (he/him). They are surprised to learn that Jahpo has three biological fathers, and those fathers will stop at nothing to get Jahpo back. When Dr. Braunstein makes her initial time jump, she also (conveniently) lands in 11,706. With her help, they all get out. However, Braunstein takes Jahpo and raises him as her own son. He has no idea of his past. And our young pre-historic man becomes the leader of the Old-Timers, known as Grand Father.

It takes 773 pages and 4+ years to resolve the conflict. (More on that in a sec.)

At first blush, it sounds as though *Paper Girls* is a straight-up (puns are always intended, right?) time-travel romp. Lots of factions, lots of time frames, lots of confusion. Which version of Erin is this? Which timeline are we in now? Will I puff out of existence if my younger self gets eliminated? Can I influence the creation of myself? What happens to the fabric of time if we start mucking about with it? True, that's all here.

Nevertheless, I would argue that *Paper Girls* is a queer (and not straightforward) comic in a number of ways. First, as noted above, the comic undermines and challenges the tradition of newspapers being delivered by boys. Vaughn structures the comic around a couple of keys texts, including the *American Newspaper Delivery Guild Handbook*, 1932. The *Handbook* offers tidbits about the ideal attitude and behavior of a newspaper boy. And it is definitely gendered. The idea of a young girl out there, riding her bike around in the dark, responsibly delivering papers, collecting money from (sometimes) bellig-

erent customers was all unthinkable—until, of course, someone did it. Mac shattered a stereotype in this fictional Ohio.
And, yet, it was not all smooth sailing. The local boys insult-
ed her and intimidated her (or tried to). She always held her
own. The paper girls make the town and their neighbors *see*
them differently and *see* possibilities differently. Vaughn has
said, "Subverting the expected was something we wanted to
do" (Tucker Stone, "Interview").

Second, the comic ends not with a giant battle scene nor
with a conflagration, but with an agreement to hold the peace.
Isn't it a staple of comics to have lots of big battles? Lots of
explosions? Lots of BIFF and POW? The staples of giant
beasts and gigantic robots are all here, if, perhaps ironically.
The conventions of giant weapons being brandished about are
all here, if a bit ineffectively. No, even though the two sides
seem thoroughly entrenched, even though the two sides seem
hell-bent (literally and figuratively) on defeating one another,
they simply decide to call a halt. It's not even so much negotiation or making concessions. When Jahpo learns the truth
about his own life, his own identity, his own ironic existence,
he says, "Enough." Anti-climactic? *Exactly.*

Third, the comic takes on some of the political issues of the
1980s. Vaughn and Chang have said that they did not want
the comic to be political, that they wanted to avoid those larger political issues since the comic is from the perspective of
12-year-old girls in 1988 (Tucker Stone, "Interview"). Even
so, those issues are present. Early on Erin has a dream, and
in that dream she is ice skating with Ronald Reagan—syn-
onymous with the conservative turn of the 1980s. However,
Reagan is also associated with the AIDS crisis, particularly
for his failure to acknowledge the crisis. Despite the desire
to remain apolitical, these background characters and events
cannot help but cast light on history, and in particular on the
history of the queer community. Vaughn and Chiang may

have wanted the comic to be apolitical, but one simply cannot invoke Reagan in the '80s and *not* conjure up politics.

Finally, we learn that at least some of the Teenagers are queer. Jude says that he was much older when he came out. But one of the narrative and emotional centers of the entire comic is young Tiffany coming to terms with her sexuality. She has a vision when she touches one of the 4D beings. She sees several things—all of which come to pass. She believes that they *are* the future. And this is key, right? Is she locked into this future? Can she do anything at all to change it? Does she *want* to change it? In one of her visions, she kisses Mac. She later confesses to Mac that she thinks she is—or will become—a "lesbo." Despite the horrors of the 1980s, despite the AIDS epidemic, despite her friend/crush's homophobia, Tiffany can no longer deny what she feels and for whom. The derogative terms may shock someone in 2022, but in the 1980s, Tiffany would not have had much else at hand to understand and to talk about her identity.

We watch Mac's journey, too, but hers is a different path. Vaughn describes "that full-page reveal of Mac where she uses a homophobic slur against another kid. It's this moment that feels like a traditional superhero splash page, and we really wanted to undercut it as a reminder of the casual homophobia of the past" (Tucker Stone, "Interview"). Initially, Mac makes homophobic comments. Mac calls Tiffany "disgusting" and a "pervert." And, yet, in a flashback scene, we see the young Mackenzie Coyle at the local library, checking out a book. The librarian expects her to check out something violent and gory. Instead, Mac shyly hands the librarian the *Secrets* volume of *Sweet Valley High* (Francine Pascal [she/her], 1983). The book either suggests a sweeter side of Mac, or an interest in school social machinations. In addition, the book selection suggests that Mac has a secret. Despite her front, she initiates the kiss with Tiffany.

Vaughn and Chiang have been clear that their primary interest in telling this story is to look at childhood, adolescence, and coming of age. The center of the story is the bond among four girls, and their unwillingness to let one another go. And, yet, in telling that story, Vaughn and Chiang have pushed at the boundaries of the comic form, even as they employ many of the standard tropes and forms. In the end, they have pushed at the readers' expectations of just what a comic can and should do.

Shade 15—*Joyride* (2016-2018)
A Universal Language

A FEW YEARS ago, in 1835 to be precise, Henry Wadsworth Longfellow (he/him) wrote that "music is the universal language of mankind." That quote took on a life of its own and became a truism, often with no sense of where the quote—or idea—originated. Some years later, in 1890, George Bernard Shaw (he/him) referenced Longfellow's quote, but with a variation on the theme: "Though music be a universal language, it is spoken with all sorts of accents." To be honest, I have always been skeptical of this claim. For one, I like some categories or types of music a lot; I don't like other kinds of music at all. A friend can be absolutely moved to near rapture by a song that leaves me cold. I'm certain the reverse is true, as well. For another, I have doubts that a contemporary urban teenager in the US would immediately see the beauty in, say, Qawwali music from Pakistan, or that a contemporary factory worker in Guadalajara might enjoy Tuvan throat singing. My own skepticism notwithstanding, perhaps Longfellow and Shaw are correct.

Indeed, a group of Harvard scientists decided to put the universality of music to the test. The scientists examined 315 societies and found that all 315 have music as an element. They collected 118 songs from 86 cultures covering 30 geographic regions. What they discovered was that all societies have music for "infant care, healing, dance, and love" as well as "mourning, warfare, processions, and ritual" (Gottlieb). One of the researchers noted that seeing the cross-cultural prevalence of music points toward "the social, cognitive, and cultural evolutionary foundations of complex traditions found throughout societies from music to law, narrative to witchcraft" (Gottlieb). Further, the similarities in form and function might point toward cognitive similarities.

So, we here on Earth might share a love of music due to "cognitive similarities," but is the love of music really *universal?*

From 2016 until 2018 (just about the exact same time that the Harvard researchers were conducting their study), writers Jackson Lanzing (he/him) and Collin Kelly (he/him) published *Joyride* for BOOM! Studios. The limited series ran for 12 issues and was then reprinted in 3 collections (*Ignition*, 2016; *Teenage Spaceland*, 2018; and *Maximum Velocity*, 2018). Although undated, the events of *Joyride* seem to take place in a future Earth. In the *mise en scène*, humans have already developed space travel, gone out there and met something really, really scary, retreated to Earth and built a fortified wall around the *entire Earth*. So, yeah, that's well into the future.

Uma Akkolyte (she/her) is a child of the '60s, or so it would seem. After all, she listens to Miles Davis's (he/him) *Kind of Blue* on repeat. Her parents were part of the Akkolytes, a group-family based on shared interests, especially art, culture, and music. As one of the Akkolytes, young Uma was exposed to a wide rage of cultural experiences. Just as importantly, the Akkolytes were committed to personal freedom. They told her that she could do whatever she wanted to do—even go to space. The problem: the Triumvirate has cut off access to space, cut off sight of the stars, and controlled the narrative about space. That's OK. She has a plan to break free.

Her best friend (not quite sure how *that* happened) is Dewydd Abderizai (he/him), the son of some true believers. Everyone in his family has bought into the controlling narrative. Dewydd himself followed the whole patriotic pathway, took military training, and became a Young Ally. But this pathway never quite sat well with Dewydd. In fact, he just loves Uma's free spirit, and he has hitched his wagon to the Uma juggernaut. Off they go to the moon in order to steal a spaceship.

The third member of our teenage triumvirate is Princess Catrin Cosanova (she/her). She is the daughter and heir-apparent of the Cosanovas, the family that envisioned and built the SafeSky shield that covers Earth. One day she will be the leader of the not-so-free world. Even so, she has to pay her dues. She is a Private assigned to a back corridor on the station on Luna. When Uma and Dewydd flash through to meet their alien contact, she jumps into action and gets beamed up into the middle of it. Off she goes with our other wandering teens.

Teenage hijinks ensue on a galactic level. They get in and out of sticky situations; they upset a lot of local authorities; they meet many aliens. Along the way, they are exposed to some alien ways of seeing the world. They also learn that humans are not well regarded in the galaxy. For example, the Regulatrix (she/her) has some choice words about humans: "The human race is…a wart, a cancer, a small world of small hearts, content to writhe in filth" (87, vol. 3). You see, the quarantine works both ways. The humans want to keep the scary, evil aliens out, and the aliens want to keep the uncivilized humans *in*. And they are happy to destroy the entire planet, if necessary.

One of their acquaintances is Kolstak the Wander (he/him), a 10,000-year-old member of an ancient race. Kolstak, though, has been sitting on a grudge for a very long time. And these teens have given Kolstak an opportunity to retaliate and wipe out the Ultravoid, a race of beings older than the stars. In order to stop Kolstak, Uma sacrifices her own life. Let's look at the parallels here.

Uma hates the Triumvirate that rules Earth for a lot of reasons. For one, the Akkolytes are all about freedom, and the Triumvirate has a fascist stranglehold on the Earth. For another, she holds them responsible for her parents' deaths. The Cosanovas had seen the Akkolyte community as "aberrant" and "abnormal." So, with their giant laser mounted on the moon, they wiped out the Akkolytes. But, understandably, she also blamed her parents for getting killed. She saw it as selfish. And now here she is herself. She has made a group of friends—a new chosen family. And now she is going to sacrifice herself in order to save them all. In that moment, she understands her parents in a way she never could have before.

The other irony, of course, is that she sacrifices herself just as she and Catrin have cemented their relationship. The queer girl has to die so that they all may live. Rest assured, though, that that is not the end of Uma. Because of Uma's sacrifice, the Ultravoid lives on, Catrin becomes a freedom fighter, and Dewydd becomes a disciple of the Wander.

These shenanigans, though, have stirred up some trouble. The reincarnated Uma wants to go back home and blow the lid off of SafeSky. She wants the entire Earth to see the lies behind the Triumvirate. The problem is that the galactic peacekeepers are not happy with her. And when Uma blows open the SafeSky and breaks Earth's quarantine, the galactic authorities get involved. They want to "cauterize" the festering wound that is Earth.

How on Earth does Uma save the day? Well, the Akkolytes do. In a way. Part of their daily practice is to collect cultural artifacts. They have a large collection of music. Uma beams a soundtrack to the Regulators (the playlist is available at the end of the comic). Based on what they hear, they can only conclude that humans have just demonstrated "regulation-level sentience" (89, vol. 3). They must now be protected. Apparently, these aliens prove the point about music and "cognitive similarities."

Joyride beggars the imagination in a number of ways. Okay, fine; lots of SF and lots of comics do that. A certain suspension of disbelief is required. Some texts work hard at plausibility while others do not. That is not their concern. So, what is *Joyride*'s concern?

(1) The importance of found family and community. *Joyride* offers three human families. The Abderizai family consists of two parents (mother and father) and two sons (Dewydd and Jorn). Jorn (he/him) is the most "successful," in that he has risen to a high rank in the military. And yet, his loyalty to family is limited. When Dewydd heads off-world, Jorn is tasked with returning his brother. He hauls his parents out in the middle of the night to inform them that their son is "aberrant." After Dewydd rescues Jorn and Jorn has a change of heart, the parents reject them both. Like devoted Fox News viewers, they spout ideology and misinformation. For them, ideology trumps family.

The Cosanova family is no better. For four generations, they have held Earth in an iron grip. When Catrin's father Heller is killed, Uma blames herself. Catrin takes a different view. Her father built a giant space laser on the moon, aimed at Earth, in order to control Earthlings. As Catrin notes, that laser was pointed at *him*, too. He was unable to take in new information, unable to compromise on his beliefs. For Heller, it was SafeSky shield or war. He, too, chose ideology over family.

The Akkolytes, however, are held up as a positive model. The Akkolytes value children. They value culture. They value experience. They value difference. They value community. They are the people who can encounter the radical Otherness of space aliens and not react with weapons. Moreover, they are the people who can encounter *any* kind of Otherness with acceptance. For them, "aberrant" and "abnormal" make no sense. And, they are a non-normative family. Instead of a traditional nuclear family (as above), they are a queer family.

(2) The importance of friendship. In the beginning, it is quite clear that Dewydd fancies Uma. He lusts after her, re-

ally. He's ready to throw everything away for her. She does not, however, reciprocate those feelings. When he says "I love you," she says that he is her "friend" (12, vol. 2). The word "friend" shatters Dewydd. However, over the course of the series, friends become central. Much like with family, having friends is an important part of community.

(3) Individual liberty is tantamount. *Joyride* offers a dichotomy: fascism or freedom. In the name of "protection" and "safety," the Triumvirate has total control over Earth. They control the news, the narrative, and the culture. The inhabitants of Earth have *no* idea what is happening outside the SafeSky shield; they only know what the authorities tell them. Furthermore, they must act in accordance with Triumvirate rules. The inhabitants must toe the party line. The Akkolytes, on the other hand, value freedom of choice. In a flashback scene, a very young Uma asks her parents if she'll be able to do anything she wants when she gets older. "Absolutely," they tell her.

However, *Joyride* also demonstrates the irony in that. Uma chooses to sacrifice herself. She chooses to return to Earth to end the fascist regime. She chooses to take on the Regulators. However, in order to save Earth, she must agree to stay on the planet. Even though space travel has long been her dream, she must give it up. In the end, she does make a choice, but a heavily limited choice.

(4) Top-down power (such as patriarchy) corrupts. The Cosanovas have had a male leader for generations. Their sense of privilege and power only seem to have ossified. As Uma's family watches a TV broadcast of Heller Cosanova, her mother notes: "Like Chancellor Heller Cosanova, the guy that [sic] ordered aberrant oophorectomies, is gonna hand his carefully cultivated patriarchy over to a woman" (51, vol. 3). No, the patriarchal model of the Triumvirate does not work. Or, it

works only by making some members Others, aberrant, and abnormal.

Instead, what emerges is a female-headed collectivity. Uma and Catrin, now married, lead a group of autonomous agents who work to better the world. Uma reconnects with the Akkolytes and travels the world making connections. These two queer woman work toward a new way to govern. And the third member of our triad, Dewydd, now freed of romantic interests, finds his own way in the world.

(5) Music is a universal language. Lanzing and Kelly take Longfellow's dictum a bit further. Music is not just the universal language of *humans*, but is the universal language of every *being* in the *universe*. The aliens immediately recognize the artistic and aesthetic worth of the music by The Rolling Stones, The Beatles, NWA, Radiohead, and Beyoncé. While I would submit that that is a *really* narrow slice of human music, nevertheless, these pieces convince the aliens that we, as humans, do have valuable insights and abilities. We are able to see and think beyond ourselves.

Maybe, just maybe, we have what it takes to be acolytes to a universal community.

Shade 16 — *Merry Men* (July 2018)
The Community of Men

IN 1972, THE anthropologist Sherry Ortner (she/her) published "Is Female to Male As Nature Is to Culture?" In the essay, Ortner attempts to explain the near-universal secondary status of women. For Ortner, the underlying cause was the near-universal evaluation we humans have about nature, and our near-universal alignment of women with nature. We have tended to code nature as bad and culture as good. Nature is something we have to overcome (weather, the elements, animals), and culture is an improvement upon nature (cooking raw vegetables, carving a rock). Because we view women as being closer to nature (not that they actually *are* closer to nature; we just think so), we view them as closer to animality and further from culture. However, she notes that women participate in the culture system on a daily basis. As women give birth, raise children, and cook sustenance, they are participating in the very system that says they are secondary. So, Ortner asks, *why* would women want to participate in the same system that denigrates them?

I was struck by a very similar question asked in *Merry Men* — to which I will return.

Robert Rodi (he/him), the writer of *Merry Men*, has been called "the gay Molière" (Rodi, "Home"). He has written a series of books set in the gay demimonde of Chicago. Illustrator Jackie Lewis (she/her) has worked on *The Lion of Rora* and *Play Ball*. In this comic, they reanimate Robin of Sherwood

Forest and his band of Merry Men. The limited series ran for 10 issues, which have been collected into a single volume.

In the final pages of *Merry Men*, Rodi offers a brief "Queer History of England," with biographies and analyses of the historical figures Richard the Lionheart (he/him), Alcuin of York (he/him), William Rufus (he/him), Edward II (he/him), John Rykener (he/him), and Joan of Arc (she/her). In doing so, Rodi gives credence to his own telling of Robin Hood. Men and women who lived outside the social order, and men and women who were considered deviant and marginalized have existed throughout English history. Further, the pages of the introductory and concluding material have the look of handmade paper, again lending authenticity.

In this version of the Robin Hood story, Robert Godwinson (he/him) had been the "boon companion" of King Richard (he/him). Robert was both a soldier for Richard and his bed companion. At the beginning of the comic, Richard is on his Crusade to take back the Holy Lands. When the army begins to find dismembered soldiers, Richard puts the task of solving the mystery onto Robert, who discovers that the culprit is Sir Guy (he/him), who is angry that Richard will not let him torture and kill infidel prisoners. He had hoped to stir Richard and the others to bloodlust. By the time the mystery is solved, Richard's eye has wandered, and he sends Robert back to England. Robert is given a pension and is meant to live out a comfortable life. Of course, that's not quite what unfolds. The Sheriff of Nottingham (he/him) is rousing the villages, punishing all those who are "unnatural" or "merry men." Here, Rodi plays with the multiple meanings of the expression "merry men." Historically, a "merry man" was any follower of a knight or an outlaw. In this case, the "merry men" are both followers of the outlaw Robert and men who have sex with other men. When Robert and his band of "merry men" are driven into the forest, they find comfort in one another's arms.

Many of them have wives and children back home, but their true natures and their hearts belong to the other merry men.

Initially, Robert (now Robin) and his men seem content to stay in the woods. They live simply, and they love strongly. A young woman shows up at their camp and changes everything. Scarlet (she/her) is a trans woman, and she has been driven from town, as well. The only person who ever accepted Scarlet for her true self was Daniel of Doncaster (he/him)—a good friend of Robin. When Robin receives a bag with Daniel's severed hand, he knows he must finally take action against the Sheriff and against the purge of merry men.

Meanwhile, Prince John (he/him), King Richard's brother, wants the throne. One way to do so would be to undermine his brother. He employs Sir Guy, who wants his own revenge against the King. In order to undermine all favor for King Richard, Guy and the Sheriff wage a campaign against the merry men that is meant to turn public opinion against Richard. Guy also wants revenge against Robin, and he savages the local villagers to draw him out. His plan works, and Robin and his band are caught in Guy's web.

So, Rodi makes the case that gay men have existed throughout time, specifically throughout English history. Here, Rodi is careful not to say that "homosexuality" as we understand it today was what the merry men practiced. Instead, people engaged in same-sex *behaviors*, but which were not seen as constituting an identity. King Richard is suspected of being one such individual. However, in having Robin and his band identify *as* "merry men," Rodi does run the risk of retroactively imposing an identity on them. The characters frequently refer to themselves as "merry men" individually and collectively.

Gender scholars have also long noted that men frequently married for inheritance purposes, but found their satisfactions outside marriage (see also Shade 42). That was true, in part, because they viewed their wives as pure and wholesome, and they saw their mistresses or courtesans as profane and corporal. They would procreate with their wives, but they would love and have sex with others. In *Merry Men*, Little John (he/him) and Kenneth (he/him) and Arthur (he/him) all have wives and children. They want their family names and properties to carry on. But in their hearts, and in their true natures, their desires are for other men.

On the last page of Chapter 7, we meet Joan (she/her), Kenneth's wife, who is now betrothed to the Sheriff of Nottingham. She has come along with the Sheriff to gloat over her husband's impending demise. Before that happens, Joan fills Kenneth in on what happened to her after he left for Sherwood Forest. Although he believed he was leaving his wife behind in good standing, everything fell apart for her. Neighbors shunned her; her servants robbed her; her house was destroyed. She became destitute and resorted to petty crime to feed herself. It was then that the Sheriff found her and decided to use her as a pawn in his revenge strategy. But Joan describes for Kenneth the difficulties of being a woman in dangerous times. Kenneth, Robin, and the Merry Men simply did not understand the reality of being a woman.

Their worldview is further shaken, however, by Scarlet. For one, Scarlet is appalled that they would take a vow and make a commitment to their wives and then leave them behind. For her, that lack of integrity is unforgivable (106). For another, she is appalled that the merry men would participate in the very system that denies their existence. They marry and sire children to perpetuate a social order that does not allow for their existence. "What advantage lies in perpetuating a system that is *alien* to your natures?" (106). Ortner answered this question for women by saying that, as humans, they too valued culture over nature. But as women, their only available means to participate in culture was in ways that demeaned them. Even so, they *were* participating in a valued system. Does the rationale hold for the merry men? Their society does not value them for who they are, and so they participate in the society in whatever way they can.

Finally, Scarlet is furious that the merry men were able to build one identity (husband and father) and then abandon it when it no longer suited them. They are then able to build another life and another identity as a merry man (there's that slippage again). "For some of us yet struggle, who have no such freedom" (106). From Scarlet's perspective as a trans woman, the merry men have a freedom of identity and of existence that she will never have. Only Daniel accepted her fully, and he was murdered for it.

On the one hand, *Merry Men* is a positive take on the historically suppressed category of men who have sex with other men. Rodi illustrates and illuminates their existence and to some extent the lengths to which they would have to go to live and love. As the "Queer History of England" notes, we do not know just how many such men existed, or how often they were persecuted and prosecuted. Ironically, though, *Merry Men* is something of an indictment of the strategy the merry men employed. They have found ways to live "in the chinks in the world machine" (Tiptree 154) but have left the machine unchallenged (see Shade 5).

Interestingly, Scarlet and Joan operate as the conscience of the graphic novel. They point out the inconsistencies in the practices of the merry men; they point out the blind spots. They encourage the merry men to think beyond themselves. Given that the comic is set in historical times with historical characters, Rodi chooses not to simply overturn historical reality. However, creating a fictional world with "merry men" and telling a historical recounting of "merry men" are two different projects.

Rodi and Lewis have given the merry men a new life.

Shade 17 — *Kim & Kim* (2016)
Let's Take This on the Road Again

I REMEMBER VIVIDLY the first time I watched them hold hands, gun their 1966 Ford Thunderbird, and head out over the cliff's edge. That event followed 2 hours of tension, delight, and fear. They were finally trapped; they had run out of options. They wouldn't do it, would they? They couldn't. I'm talking about *Thelma and Louise* (1991), of course. The two women who refuse to accept abuse, who refuse to be victims, and who refuse to be hauled back into the patriarchal system in which they have no voice and no place. No, flying over the cliff is a better alternative than what awaited them. Over the edge they flew.

The buddy film has a long and storied history. Initially, buddy films featured pairs who undertook an adventure, frequently in the form of a road trip. The two individuals generally had different personalities, causing a clash and producing tension—and humor. The duos of Stan Laurel (he/him) and Oliver Hardy (he/him) and Bud Abbott (he/him) and Lou Costello (he/him) were popular in the 1930s and '40s. Duos Dean Martin (he/him) and Jerry Lewis (he/him) and Walter Matthau (he/him) and Jack Lemmon (he/him) ascended in the 1960s. The teams were most frequently pairs of (white) men, and those teams operated in the absence of women. The relationships at the center of the films were man-centric.

Comics have an analogous history. The escapades of Batman and Robin resemble a buddy film—two men who undertake a lot of adventures together. True, Robin is more of a sidekick and Batman the star. In recent years, Robin has come out as gay, but not back then. In 1941, Green Arrow was introduced and was later teamed up with Green Lantern. True to form, they were two very different men (superheroes) doing manly things. Power Man first appeared in the 1970s. He was soon paired with Iron Fist (and all of his issues of cultural appropriation), and the pair fought alongside one another as an interracial buddy team. The shift to an interracial buddy film also took place in the buddy film genre. Writer Magdalene Visaggio (she/her) said, "In a lot of ways, I use Abby and Ilana from *Broad City* as a model, but that 'sober one/crazy one' dynamic is kind of built into the buddy dynamic" (Collins, "Buddy Story").

All of which raises a couple of questions.

What would a queer buddy film—or in our case here—a queer buddy comic offer? How might it imitate the form? How might it alter the tradition? Writer Visaggio has some ideas about this. In an interview, Visaggio notes that she explicitly wanted a comic that was rooted in female friendship (Whitbrook, "Trans Comic Heroes"). "I landed on doing a book about two women because I wanted to do a woman-centric book, and I wanted to do a buddy story" (Collins, "Buddy Story"). Further, as someone going through transition herself, she wanted one of her characters to be a trans woman. So, for Visaggio's *Kim & Kim* (Black Mask Studios), the two Kims are best friends, even if they have to work through the hard stuff. Additionally, they are both queer—Kim Q (she/her) is trans and Kim D (she/her) is bisexual (Whitbrook, "Trans Comic Heroes").

The comic series centers, of course, on the two Kims. Kimiko Quatro, or Kim Q, is the daughter of a very powerful man, Furious Quatro (he/him), who is the head of The Catalans, the Omniverse's most successful and powerful bounty hunters. Kim Q is a trans woman with neon pink hair and a guitar as her weapon of choice. Kimber Dantzler, or Kim D, is a former necromancer. She just wasn't very good at it. Kim D's weapon of choice is a Howitzer. The two friends are trying to be independent contractors, but making a living as a freelance bounty hunter does not run smoothly. Every job they pick up seems to fall apart. They are running out of money and getting really desperate—just not desperate enough to work for Furious Quatro.

As luck would have it, they stumble into a lucrative job. Tom Quilt (he/him) is the most hunted man in the Omniverse. He's a polyform—i.e., he can shift into any form he chooses—in part because he is the result of an experiment with gene enhancers. The Kims locate and apprehend Quilt, but the problem is that Kim Q has stolen the idea from her dad's men. They are stealing the bounty out from under her dad. But when the Kims catch him, he turns out to look a bit like a young Harry Potter (he/him), and he has nice sob story. True to form, they can't turn him in and, instead, they help him get back to Dimension 12.

Along the way, we learn that Kim Q *really* wants to open a "punk bakery." "We'd bake like transgressive muffins and cakes that had 'queeriarchy' written on them in fondant and we'd live on love" (17). We also learn that their relationship is strong. Kim D describes Kim Q as her "business partner, platonic significant other, and personal whole world" (75). When they crash-land on Never-Look-Back, the Kims sit inside their smoldering kombi (combination van/spaceship), and, as they wonder just exactly when they first met, they reach out and touch pinkie fingers. A kind, loving, subtle gesture. The interpretations are many. A simple moment of human contact in the face of mortality? A reassurance that they will survive the current crisis? An overture to affection? A bit of sexual tension? All possible in this Omniverse.

Unlike, say, Shade 4, in which *The Pride* announces the gender, sexual identity, and pronouns of every superhero, Visaggio takes an approach more like SF writer Octavia E. Butler (she/her). She was well known for her approach to race. Butler would not announce a character's race or sexuality unless the narrative called for it. For example, in *Dawn*, the reader has no clues as to Lilith Iyapo's racial identity. In a brief flashback, the narrative indicates that Lilith's husband had been of Nigerian descent. Taken by itself, that might not mean anything at all about Lilith. Much later, one of the alien Oankali notes that it was surprised that Lilith did not choose one of "the dark ones" as a mate, since the mate would look more like her. In both cases, it is not the narrator announcing Lilith's racial and ethnic background. Instead, that information arises organically from the events of the narrative. Visaggio takes a similar approach. The reader learns that Kim Q is a trans woman, but only through clues.

So, one might ask, what good does it do to have a trans woman who is not explicitly trans? Well, it does a *lot* of good. First of all, Visaggio notes that she never wanted to make Kim's transness explicit. However, she acknowledges that she is, fundamentally, writing for a cis audience, and for that reason she *had* to make it explicit. And "why should it? Why should that fact get mentioned when everyone but her stupid dad has moved the f--- on with their lives and just accepts her as the woman she clearly is?" (Whitbrook, "Trans Comic Heroes"). Kim Q is a trans woman who just *is*. Her transness is a part of her; it's not the whole of her.

Furthermore, Visaggio also notes the impact that the *kinds* of trans representation had on her. She notes that learning about trans women and trans identity via news stories and after-school specials meant that she saw only a miserable existence for herself (Whitford). The presence of negative representations on TV and in books had a negative effect, and the lack of positive representations did, as well. Visaggio says she had just begun the transition process herself when she began writing *Kim & Kim*. And "Kim Q provided me this vehicle to imagine myself, I dunno, a couple of years down the line" (Collins, "Buddy Story"). Maybe, just maybe, Kim Q can fill that representational void.

And finally, as I argued in the Introduction, the representation of a whole range of narratives about QUILTBAG individuals is vital. (Here, I use the acronym QUILTBAG instead of the more familiar LGBTQI primarily to acknowledge the character Tom Quilt. His name cannot be a mere accident.) While it's true that *Kim & Kim* has only two main characters, the comic still offers a number of kinds of queer people. As was the case with Kim Q's transness, Kim D's bisexualness is similarly muted. But in an interview, Visaggio states clearly, "Both Kims are queer—Kim D is bisexual. Just wanted to get that out there!" (Collins, "Buddy Story").

So, the two queer Kims take their show on the road. The two different personalities clash with and complement one another. Their incompetence is part of their charm, and their hearts are (almost) always in the right place—all part of a new model for a queer buddy adventure.

Shade 18 — *Love Circuits* (2017)

Speculating Sex

THE LATE, GREAT Tanith Lee (she/her) left a very rich body of work behind. She published works in high fantasy, in horror, and in science fiction. Her science fiction novels include *Don't Bite the Sun* (1976) and its sequel, *Drinking Sapphire Wine* (1977). *Electric Forest* (1979) was a stand-alone novel though it raised a few of the themes of her next SF novels: *The Silver Metal Lover* (1981) and its sequel, *Metallic Love* (2005). These last two novels featured romantic relationships—love *and* sex—between humans and robots.

Love Circuits begins to examine some of the same questions that Lee raised in her novels.

Taneka Stotts (she/her) "eats, sleeps, and breathes" comics (Horne, 15 March) and is a force to be reckoned with in the industry. Some of her early writing in comics was for *Steven Universe* and *My Little Pony*. Since that time, she has been the writer on *Casual Hex* and *Déjà Brew* (which was nominated for an Eisner Award). Stotts is also "fiercely dedicated to publishing the work of talented marginalized voices, specifically women of color and the LGBTQIA community" (Horne, 15 March). To that end she has also done some important editing, including two volumes in the Beyond series, including *Beyond: The Queer Sci-Fi and Fantasy Comic Anthology* (2016). That anthology won a number of awards, including an Eisner Award for Best Anthology and a Lambda Literary Award for Best Anthology. It was followed by *Beyond II: The Queer Post-Apocalyptic and Urban Fantasy Comic Anthology* (2017).

She has also edited two volumes in the Elements series, including *Elements: Fire—A Comic Anthology by Creators of Color* (2016) and *Elements: Earth* (2019). Perhaps just as importantly, Stotts co-created the publishing company that produced and published these anthologies, Beyond Publishing.

By 2022, though, Stotts had begun working in TV, including in the Cartoon Network series *Steven Universe Future* (2019) and *Craig of the Creek* (2019), Discovery Network's *My Little Pony: Pony Life* (2020-21) series, the animated Netflix series *Magic: The Gathering* (2021), and on Dreamworks's *Pinecone and Pony* (2022). For a number of projects, including *Love Circuits* (2017), Stotts has teamed up with comic artist and illustrator Genué Revuelta (she/her).

This particular Shade differs from the others in this collection because it addresses a very brief, unfinished webcomic. *Love Circuits* premiered online on 17 February 2017. Stotts and Revuelta posted semi-regular updates. They published a total of 23 pages, the last page appearing on 22 September 2017. Just 23 pages.

What happened? Did Stotts run out of ideas? Run out of money? Had a falling out? Got involved with other projects? All possible, I suppose, though each of those ideas is equally speculative. Even so, we do know that Stotts was extremely busy during that period. Stotts has teased a return to the webcomic via her Twitter account, but those updates have not yet materialized.

So, why write about a partial comic? Why write about 23 pages? Let me count the ways….

One, as I have noted above, Stotts is and (I suspect) will continue to be a major voice in animation and comics. Her *Casual Hex* (2019) is a multi-racial, multi-ethnic queer supernatural comic. Her two *Elements* anthologies and her two *Beyond* anthologies raised the bar on queer and multi-ethnic representations in comics. The anthologies are slick, striking, vibrant, and well-crafted.

Two, Stotts and *Love Circuits* work to give voice and representation to marginalized voices. As I have already noted, Stotts foregrounds marginalized voices. That philosophy continues in *Love Circuits*.

Three, the webcomic begins with an interesting premise, one not explored much in these pages—namely, is having sex with a robot inherently queer? (cf. Shade 44).

The *Love Circuits* fragment picks up with a character from an earlier webcomic: *Glass Castles* (2016), also by Stotts and Revuelta. *Castles* follows three brothers, Lalo, Chuy (pronouns unknown for the brothers), and Javier (he/him), who try to keep their family together. Javier also shows up in *Love Circuits*, as the ex-boyfriend of Yvonne King (she/her), proprietor of King Repair, situated in Nuevo Miami.

At the beginning of *Love Circuits*, Yvonne has celebrated a birthday. Her apartment is a bit of a mess, and she's lying in bed. A phone call from Mom (she/her) gets her up and moving. Mom suggests that Javier would help her clean up—a notion that Yvonne rejects. They've moved on!

Just as Mom's harangue kicks into high gear, a very large gift arrives. Once the package opens, Yvonne meets her full-sized "heartbreaker" robot named Lucos (pronouns uncertain). Yvonne discovers that the gift is from her friend Frankie (they/them), a queer, nonbinary hacker. According to Frankie, a somewhat drunk Yvonne had asked them for a heartbreaker at the party—Frankie was happy to oblige.

Lucos initiates a contract—which reads like a variation of Asimov's Three Laws. And, with the consummation of the contract, Lucos belongs to Yvonne. Although Yvonne appreciates Lucos's *nalgas* (his butt), she decides he needs to wear clothing. It is at this inopportune moment that Javier enters the apartment, carry two boxes.

Although Javier never actually sees Lucos, he gets the idea that Yvonne has someone there with her, and he apologizes and leaves. It would appear that Javier has not moved on after all.

Two central mysteries remain: Lucos occasionally spaces out. Lucos and Frankie determine that it is probably due to a missing file. But what is the missing file? And why is it missing? The other question is, will Yvonne and Lucos become lovers?

The graphics are amazing.

The world-building is amazing.

The diversity of representation is excellent. Given that the characters often speak Spanish (with no translations given) in Nuevo Miami, the assumption might be that they are Latine. As Stotts notes in interviews, she is interested in telling the stories of marginalized individuals and communities. She is interested in those characters being the protagonists of their own stories, not sidekicks and not secondary characters. Unlike in *Kim & Kim* (Shade 17), in which Magdalene Visaggio laments that her primary audience is a cis audience, Stotts makes a different assumption. Stotts writes for her people, and if someone from outside the group wants to come along, then that's great!

In addition, Yvonne has a prosthetic left leg. She never mentions it, but she does not hide it, either. The prosthetic is not a naturalized leg but a styled and clearly metallic leg. (Whether or not the leg is connected to her business or profession is unknown. Perhaps the backstory would have eventually been provided.) In this case, Stotts chooses to have her protagonist wear a prosthetic, but she does not make much of an issue with it. Yvonne's leg is what it is; it is a part of her body, but it does not define who she is or what she can do.

Finally, at least some of the characters are queer. As I noted above, Frankie is queer and nonbinary. Javier seems to still be interested in Yvonne. But the tensions are there between Yvonne and Lucos. I guess, then, that one of the central questions is: what is human-robot sex? Lucos's morphology resembles that of a human who was assigned male gender at birth, and his gender, at least as far as we can see, is traditionally masculine-ish.

The romantic/sexual relationship with Lucos is, of course, speculative.

In Lee's novels *The Silver Metal Lover* and *Metallic Love*, the relationship between the two lovers, Jane (she/her) the young woman and Silver (he/him) the robot lover follows the heteronormative benchmarks: girl meets robot; girl falls in love with robot; girl throws away all her privilege, and they live in poverty; robot uses his skillset to eke out a living; girl and robot live happily ever after. In that narrative, anyway, the relationship doesn't seem particularly queer. Oh, it pushes against cultural norms, and it costs Jane her fortune, but it does not queer romance or sex.

Just three years after Lee published *Silver Metal Lover*, theorist Donna Haraway (she/her) published her "A Cyborg Manifesto" (1985), in which Haraway discusses the breakdown of former boundaries. She saw in the new world order a breakdown of the human/machine distinction. More and more, machinery is finding its way inside of us (heart transplants, stents, eye lenses, and so on) even as we shape machines (they respond to humans, they behave more like humans). The relationship is a feedback loop; the distinction becomes fuzzy. Although Haraway does not say this, extrapolation would suggest that the taboo of human robot relations would begin to erode as well.

Along similar lines, physicist and philosopher Tanja Kubes thinks that sexual relations with robots could be liberating and queer. Kubes writes, "The construction of sex robots offers a great potential for reducing stereotypes and promoting diversity. For people to sexually interact with robots, traditional dualisms have to be dissolved. Thus, the strict separation of man and machine needs to give way to a view accepting the latter at least to some degree as an equal" (n.p.). And yet, as we see in *Silver Metal Lover* and in *Love Circuits*, Kubes notes that "[c]urrent trends in sex-robotics, however, do not explore these rich possibilities. Instead, hetero-normative ideas of male hegemony are mirrored in the design of both hardware and software. While the robots' anatomy exaggerates pornographic fantasies of hyper-femininity" ("New Materialist").

Oh, the possibilities—in robot design, in storytelling, in *Love Circuits.*

Maybe, just maybe, Stotts will resume the comic and explore these possibilities....

Shade 19 — *Contact High* (2017)
Love Is the Drug

IT'S EASY ENOUGH these days to want to read every narrative as an allegory about COVID. We have been through the outbreak, the lockdown, the vaccine, and the re-opening (several times). The pandemic has shaped and reshaped our jobs, our schools, our families, and our personal habits. So, in this moment, every disease narrative, every mention of a contagion, every instance of quarantine, every limitation of personal space and movement seems as though it must be about the COVID pandemic—even when the narrative was published in 2017.

Contact High (2017) is a very short, one-shot comic—just a 26-page pdf. Josh Eckert (he/him) and James Wright (he/him) have committed all proceeds to The Southern Poverty Law Center and to Lambda Legal. In 2018, *Contact High* was nominated for the Eisner Award for the Best Digital Comic.

So, obviously, then, *Contact High* cannot be about COVID. Nevertheless, the tendency to read an older text through the lens of current events really does add credence to reader response modes of reading and interpretation. But as the late great Argentinian writer Jorge Luis Borges (he/him) demonstrated to us in "Pierre Menard, Author of *Don Quixote*" (1939), no text can be read the same at different moments in time. A reader in 2017 would have read *Contact High* one way; a reader in 2024, or whenever your "now" is, cannot help but read it differently. Who knows what new layers of meaning and interpretation will accrue at future dates?

Other allegories apply, as well.

The poet Sappho (she/her) writes of this kind of desire. In Fragment 39, Sappho writes of desire for a married woman. For Sappho, the man who gets to sit next to the married woman, the object of her passion, is more than a god. For Sappho, if she meets the woman on the street, "I can't // speak—my tongue is broken; // a thin flame runs under // my skin." Passion burns. Passion is felt on the skin. The desire to touch the woman's skin pains her. Even the very thought of touching her brings her close to the "little death" (Sappho 39).

In *Contact High*, Eckert and Wright also write of the desire to touch one another, to feel the other's skin. For Eckert and Wright, that desire is like a craving, an addiction, a drug. The 2017 reader doubtless read this text in light of conversion therapy debates. Using faulty research and ideological aims, some conservative groups claimed that they could "convert" queer people. They have used lobotomies, chemical treatments, aversion therapies, and prayer as ways to redirect a person's sexual desire. No scientific evidence supports the claim that a person's sexuality can be converted nor the techniques they have used to do so. Even so, they believe that they can redirect or retrain a person's desire. The desire to regulate love is all too real. The desire to stop (at least certain kinds of) love is all too real.

In *Contact High*, in some unnamed future, the government has banned all touching. Every single person is required to be covered by a special suit at all times. A lover cannot caress the other's skin. A mother cannot breastfeed her child. Worse, Dr. Pound (he/him) and the Veneer Institution want to eliminate any and all *desire* to touch. For Pound, that would be true freedom.

Not so for Ziggurat (he/him). Not so for Apex (he/him). Not so for all the "addicts" committed to Veneer who are undergoing conversion treatment. In the opening scene, Ziggurat is hauled into Veneer, a criminal, a socially undesirable "addict." He is clad only in pants. The guards treat him with disrespect. They are quite sure that Dr. Pound will, well, pound some sense into him. *Contact High* is a digitally created comic, and the backgrounds and figures are clearly digital. In this particular case, that fact works in the creators' favor. The large landscapes seem impersonal and alienating. The buildings seem menacing.

At an AA-like meeting, Ziggurat relates the story of how he got to where he is. Ziggurat once toed the line. He once followed the policy, but he always wondered whether the policy was justified. He wondered if we could actually touch one another. He wondered if whatever justification used by the government still applied. When he first met Apex, his world exploded. Apex showed him that compliance was unnecessary. Apex showed him that touching each other was "the most natural thing in the world" (6)."How I do love that man" (15), he says.

Another addict committed to Veneer, Summit (she/her) (I'm sensing a theme here with the names), tells him that she spoke to Apex, and that Apex spoke to her about Ziggurat. She tells Ziggurat that Apex is located on Level Four.

Ziggurat is a large, powerful man. Ziggurat is a highly motivated individual, and he has a bit of knowledge about the guards' weapons. He finds his way to Level Four. There, Apex is strapped to a table; there, Dr. Pound attempts to cleanse Apex of all desire for contact.

Ziggurat lovingly disconnects the electrodes. Ziggurat and Apex embrace, skin to skin. And it is electric. The page explodes with rainbow colors. A contact high.

So, do we read *Contact High* as an AIDS narrative, about the dangers of bodily contact? About the dangers of same-sex contact? Do we read it as a narrative about conversion therapy and the ways in which some people have tried to erase same-sex desire? Do we read it as a plague narrative, as a tale about how the powers that be have forced us into bubbles and regulated "social distancing?" Do we read it as a cautionary tale about the effects of the Supreme Court ruling in *Dobbs v. Jackson Women's Health* (2022)? In that ruling, the court says that the states have the power to regulate social issues, not the federal government. In his concurring opinion, Clarence Thomas invites new cases that would challenge other landmark rulings, such as *Obergefell v. Hodges* (2015), which established a federal guarantee for same-sex marriage.

In the vein of Borges, I would suggest that *Contact High* contains all of these readings—and more. The way any given reader reads the comic depends upon that reader's background and experience. I would also suggest that new crises will prompt new ways to read *Contact High*. The palimpsest of layers upon layers of meaning is one of the great joys of reading and makes texts relevant far beyond whatever original intent they may have had.

Shade 20 — *FTL, Y'All!: Tales from the Age of the $200 Warp Drive* (2018)

Step Right Up!

WHEN I WAS a young reader, one of my primary introductions to science fiction was through anthologies. I clearly recall a large red hardback copy of the *Omnibus of Science Fiction* (1952) edited by Groff Conklin (he/him). It still sits on a shelf in my office, the spine a bit the worse for wear, containing forty-three short stories by names familiar and strange. Indeed, the SF anthology has a rich history, and Conklin was the go-to editor in the 1940s and 1950s. By the 1960s, the number of anthologies had exploded. In fact, I have compiled a list of 302 anthologies published in the 1960s alone.

Anthologies seem to be a rarer breed in the world of SF comics. A number of well-known comic series began their life as anthologies. For example, *Detective Comics* operated as an anthology until the 1960s, and *Action Comics* was in anthology format until 1959. Other anthology titles such as *Tales of the Unexpected* appeared in 1956 and remained an anthology format. More recently, in 2012 Marvel introduced *A+X* as a monthly anthology, though it ran just two years.

However, I'm more interested here in one-shot anthologies, in which an editor has an idea for a theme and collects a number of short comics under that theme. In 2014, Shannon O'Leary (she/her) and Joan Reilly (she/her) edited *Big Feminist BUT*, which contains some SF elements. In that same year, Rob Kirby (he/him) edited *QU33R*, a collection of queer-themed comics from 33 different creators. Although it was pitched as forward looking, it contains little speculative material. Just two years later, *Oath: An Anthology of New Queer Heroes* was edited by Audrey Redpath (she/her). It offers 21 short comics about heroes, some of them of the super variety. The following year (2017) saw the publication of *Pinoy Monster Boyfriend Anthology*, a Filipino collection of stories edited by Motzie Dapul (she/her). It features six stories about LGBTQ+ individuals and their monster boyfriends. In 2017, however, the SF comic anthology went full gloss. Joamette Gil (she/her) edited *Power & Magic: The Queer Witch Comics Anthology* (P&M Press), and the anthology was presented on high-quality, high-gloss paper in full, dynamic color. *Power & Magic* was honor-listed for the Otherwise Award in 2018. Following its success and reception, Gil edited a second volume, which was published in 2020.

For this Shade, however, I want to take a closer look at another anthology, *FTL, Y'All* (2018). The collection is edited by C. Spike Trotman (she/ her) and Amanda Lafrenais (she/ her), and published by Iron Circus Comics. That publishing company is owned and operated by Trotman and is a publishing company specifically designed to sell projects that Trotman has funded through Kickstarter. Trotman has effectively turned crowdsourcing into a viable business model.

Trotman's first interaction with Kickstarter was in 2009 for a project called *Poorcraft*. In those days, the platform was different and, perhaps more importantly, it was disreputable, for a bit of aroma attached to any project that was funded by readers and buyers. How serious could it be when it hadn't gotten past the gatekeepers? That attitude has shifted since 2009. According to Trotman, the key to her crowdsourcing model has been the pay structure. When a project collects more than the original goal, she pays a higher per-page rate to the contributors. No more getting paid in copies and exposure. Real paychecks! So, for example, the original goal for *Poor-*

craft was $6,000. The Kickstarter campaign raised $13,000. That additional money went to the contributors (MacDonald, "Interview"). The Iron Circus model has become the gold standard for comics publishers using crowdsourcing. In a meta move, Trotman published an ebook on how to run an effective Kickstarter campaign (*Let's Kickstart a Comic*).

Trotman queered the comics publishing industry.

By mid-2022 Trotman had run 31 Kickstarter campaigns and collected $2.5 million. I dare say that that's a bigger budget than any other small, independent comic publication. The model has worked for Trotman and for comic artists. However, when Kickstarter announced it was shifting to blockchain, Trotman, like many others, left the stability and safety of Kickstarter. She started her own crowdfunding mechanism. While the initial launch was rocky—they weren't prepared for the hit the servers would take; since then, the mechanics have all been worked out (MacDonald, "Interview").

And with the changes at Kickstarter, a number of other sites are now vying for Trotman's customers. The crowdfunding environment is bound to get bigger and to become less centralized.

But what of this particular anthology?

Like all great extrapolative SF, the stories in *FTL, Y'All* are all built on a simple premise: some presence suddenly makes the schematics for an FTL (Faster Than Light) drive available to everyone. Even better, the drive can be built quite simply and cheaply—for no more than $200. What would a future world in which space travel and exploration are democratized look like? How would it change social structures? How would it change relationships? How would it change space exploration? How would it change colonization? How would it change Earth?

Trotman and Lafrenais have selected an excellent range and variety of artists and stories. What was true of the Conklin

anthology in 1952 is also true of *FTL, Y'All* in 2018. The selections will not fit every reader's tastes. What they do do, however, is showcase a wide range of talents—some well known,
some unknown—and offer a starting place.

The delightful Blue Dellaquanti (they/them) opens the
collection with a short called "Soft Physics." With humans
spread out all over the place, the fundamental entertainment
economy has changed. People subscribe to packets of files
distributed by hand. Two very popular content providers are
Phoney and Mandy, who send back videos of them exploring
new worlds. Dellaquanti employs multiple modes of storytelling (images, drawings, texts, etc.) in order to relate the story.
But, in a familiar pattern, online posters quickly doubt and
debunk their posts. In other words, the more things change,
the more they stay the same. FTL travel has changed neither
our post-truth world nor the thoughtlessness of anonymous
online posting.

In "Senior Project," Maia Kobabe (e/em/eir) writes of a senior class that undertakes a 36-week project. All but one of
the class elects to build an FTL engine. Willow Ramsey (pronouns unknown) elects to gather data on adzuki beans. Willow
is looking for a more efficient way to feed the world population
amidst the effects of climate change. A couple of weeks in, Kai
(pronouns unknown) joins Willow's lab, and the two form a
strong bond. Both of them are working on something that will
improve the lives of everyday citizens. Over the next 30 weeks,
they collaborate, brainstorm, and problem solve. They may or
may not have a romantic relationship, but they certainly form
a personal bond based in mutual values and actions. Willow is
wracked with fear that Kai might not return.

In the "Introduction" to *QU33R*, Rob Kirby (he/him)
suggests that a collection acts as a snapshot, as a glimpse at
both the field of comics and the lives of queers today (i.e.,
in 2014, when it was published). I would suggest that *FTL,*

Y'All performs something similar. Yes, *FTL* might be more forward looking, inasmuch as it is extrapolating about the social, cultural, and personal effects of faster-than-light travel. Even so, *FTL* offers 21 glimpses into issues that queer artists are thinking about, are dealing with, on a daily basis. Furthermore, the anthology is edited by a queer BIPOC artist. While not every story is by a queer artist, and not every story features queer characters, the anthology queers the worldview. The underlying premise asks its artists and readers to imagine a future society that is structured differently. It suggests that the world would be altered by FTL technology. Whether such alterations would be positive of negative remains to be seen....

Shade 21 — *Moth and Whisper* (2018-2019)
Paying It Forward

IN 2021, STREAMING network Netflix had something of a breakout hit with the French thriller *Lupin*. The series was created by George Kay (he/him) and François Uzan (he/him), and stars the French actor Omar Sy (he/him). The protagonist is Assane Diop (he/him), a man who is the son of an immigrant to France from Senegal. When his father is framed for robbery, the now-adult Diop sets out to avenge his father's false conviction and subsequent (alleged) suicide. Diop is inspired by a book that his father had given him: *Arsène Lupin, Gentleman Burglar*. The very real book that inspires Assane Diop, and the books upon which the series is based, is by Maurice Leblanc (he/him). In fact, Leblanc was a contemporary of and rival to Sir Arthur Conan Doyle (he/him) and his own Sherlock Holmes (he/him) character.

Assane Diop is a gentleman. He is a man of integrity. He is quite skilled as a thief. He is primarily motivated by a desire for revenge. He is also quite skilled with technology, which frequently aids him in these burglaries. In the end, his ultimate goal is to bring down the Pellegrini family that framed his father.

In *Moth and Whisper* (2018-2019), writer Ted Anderson (he/him) and artist Jen Hickman (they/them) have produced a similar kind of character. Given the timing of their appearances, it is not that Anderson and Hickman borrowed from or were inspired by *Lupin*. After all, the five-part limited series *Moth and Whisper* appeared three years earlier. (Inasmuch as

Anderson is a librarian, he just *might* have known of Leblanc's books.) Nevertheless, their protagonist shares a number of important traits with *Lupin's* Assane Diop.

The eponymous Moth and Whisper never actually appear in the comic. The Moth (she/her) was a legendary impersonator and a master of disguise. She pulled off job after job with no one the wiser. No one had ever seen her true face. All they ever saw was her iconic calling card, the image of a moth. Similarly, Whisper (he/him) was a complete cypher. No one knew who he was. He targeted primarily corrupt governments and nefarious corporations. But now they are both gone. Disappeared. And no one knows where they have gone or why they left.

But six months after their disappearance, their infamous calling card reappears. Why are they suddenly back?

In fact, they are not back at all. Their child, Niki (they/them), has decided to carry on the family business, primarily in the name of finding out what happened to their parents. Niki learned from the best. Niki inherited the best resources and learned a few skills. Can they find their mom and dad? Can they bring down the wealthy family that (they believe) is responsible for the disappearance of their parents? (The *Lupin* similarities build.)

The comic takes place in a future, super-corrupt city: think Gotham or Metropolis. The police are in the pocket of the crimelord Ambrose Wolfe (he/him). Wolfe is bad news, two-dimensional cartoon villain bad. Niki's parents had taught them that Wolfe was truly evil, and they had always maintained that, if anything ever happened to them, it would be because of Wolfe. So, guess who Niki targets first?

Ah, but one doesn't just walk up to the most powerful crimelord in the city. Niki takes a roundabout pathway, through another corrupt crime family, the Waverlys. Derry Waverly (he/him) is nearly as evil as Wolfe, but not quite. However, Niki wonders who wants Wolfe out of the way *almost* as much as Niki does? Yes, Derry Waverly. Niki marshals all their infiltration skills and waltzes into a posh party being held at the Waverly house. Risky, but Niki gets in, no problem. At the party, Niki happens to run into Waverly's son, Walter (he/him). Fortuitous. Except that Walter busts Niki on the disguise.

After a few twists and turns, it turns out that they have a common enemy and could use one another. Waverly the younger wants to show Waverly the elder that he is ready to handle responsibility, and Niki wants to take out the family that took out their parents. A match made in corruption. Despite the righteous suspicions on both sides, they agree to work together and bring down Wolfe.

When Niki and Walter begin their mission, Walter asks: "Are you a *him* or a *her*, Niki?" "Them. I'm genderqueer" (6). For one, Niki says their parents were fully supportive when Niki came out as nonbinary. Better parenting skills already. For another, Niki's nonconformity seems to make them a better spy. Niki, not locked into rigid gender norms, behaviors, and movements, moves back and forth among identities and disguises with ease.

Even so, when Niki and Walter infiltrate a Wolfe facility, things don't go quite as planned. They are captured. Wolfe says he had nothing to do with the Moth and the Whisper's disappearance. Instead, Wolfe wants Niki to work for him. Wolfe pulls up incontrovertible video evidence that Whisper did work for Wolfe, but we are in a post-truth era, after all, and sometimes a partial truth is as good as a lie.

When Niki and Walter escape (you knew that, right?), they make another discovery: Moth and Whisper had a silent partner. Moira (pronouns unknown), aka the Mole, has an office inside the municipal building. And, Moira is a tech whiz. With Moira's help, Walter and Niki effectively steal business data from Wolfe and hand it over to Derry Waverly.

That's it. Sort of. Niki has brought down Wolfe, though they still do not know for certain whether Wolfe played any part in their parents' disappearance. They also do not know the status of their parents: alive, dead, injured, retired? It's all a mystery.

What does Niki's enby *identity* matter? What does it contribute to the comic? Well, first off, that assumes that it *needs* to have a purpose. It does not. The question "what does Niki's identity contribute to the story or plot?" perpetuates that heteronormative assumption. We would not ask "what does Lois Lane's identity as a cishet woman contribute to the Superman series?" It has only been when a character deviates from the norm that we ask such a question. Otherwise, we assume the normative. Asking what Niki's enby identity contributes to the plot is rooted in the notion that a character would be enby *only* if it served some plot point.

What does Niki's enby identity *matter*? Well, verisimilitude. Queer and enby folx exist in the world. That's a given. If we are representing a world, then that world must also include queer and enby folx, whether or not their identity is germane to the story. Well, one might say, *Moth and Whisper* is a comic and *not* an accurate representation of the world we live in. Fair enough. One could build a world in which none of the inhabitants are queer. However, that choice has all kinds of consequences. For one, it says something about the writer. Furthermore, it has an effect on any potential readers.

What does Niki's enby identity *contribute*? Perhaps most importantly, representation. We have seen through this collection (and I would suggest it holds outside this collection, as well) that lesbian and gay identities abound in comics, but enby ones not so much. In other words, the binaries of woman and man persist, and the binaries of straight and queer do, as well. In this narrative, Niki challenges that binary. We know that nature does not like binaries very much, and I see no reason that binaries should be the norm in comics, either.

In addition, Niki's identity helps build character. We learn that Moth and Whisper (or, we are told so by Niki) fully supported Niki's enby identity and pronouns. That tells the reader something about Moth and Whisper's character, about their commitment to justice and fairness, about their humanity. By contrast, when Wolfe commits utterly dehumanizing atrocities and Waverly follows in his footsteps, we see the kinds of people they are. People make choices, and their choices reveal a lot about them as human beings. Moth and Whisper are humane and loving human beings and parents who want to bring down corrupt individuals and corporations and want to leave a better world for their child, Niki.

As we learn about Assane Diop's father's character, we learn a lot about Assane's character, as well. What will he do once he avenges his father's suicide? Similarly, we will see if Niki reappears after this limited series, and we will see what their commitments to justice are.

Shade 22 — *The Wilds* (2018)

You People Need to Get in Line

ONE OF THE enduring science fiction films—against all odds and despite its initial reception—has been *Blade Runner* (1982). Based on the Philip K. Dick (he/him) novel *Do Androids Dream of Electric Sheep?* (1968), the film enacts one of Dick's common concerns: what does it mean to be human? For Dick, consumer society, technology, and televised war were de-humanizing us all. For him, the metaphor of the robot was the de-humanized human. Robots were copies; robots lacked emotions; robots lacked empathy. They were not human. Although the film, I would argue, flips the book on its head, it illustrates the same dilemma. In what ways are the replicants Pris (she/her), Zhora (she/her), Leon (he/him), and Roy (he/him) different from any of the humans on Earth?¶ Do they not want the same things? Do they not contemplate their own mortality? Are they not motivated by connections and friendships? In the penultimate scene atop the Bradbury Hotel, the question becomes: is the Blade Runner Rick Deckard (he/him) more or less human than the replicant Roy? Does Roy gain humanity in his final act of selflessness and salvation? The white bird flying up into the heavens suggests that he does.

So who is human, and what makes them a human? *The Wilds* offers some suggestions.

¶ In the film, the two female androids are referred to only by their first names, while their two male counterparts have both first and last names, thereby re-enacting a long-standing gendered bias about familiarity and authority.

The Wilds was a limited run series of five issues, from 28 February 2018 through 3 October 2018. Writer Vita Ayala (they/them) has worked previously on titles such as *Black Panther* (2019-2022), *Black AF* (2021), *Nubia and the Amazons* (2021-2022), *Bitch Planet* (2017), and *Marvel's Voices: Pride* (2022). In an interview, Ayala has said that: "Marvel had a bunch of Black and Brown characters and DC had well-developed female characters and queer characters—I'm all about those. One of things that just doesn't make sense to me is when people make up entire universes and it doesn't include Brown people and queer people; it just doesn't make sense to me. Like, we're real, we're right here, and we're at any big event in history. We're right there" (Stone, "Vita"). Ayala clearly has some things to say about this topic.

The Wilds takes place in some familiar-looking future, where a contagion breaks out. The progression sounds familiar: flu-like symptoms followed by fever and chills. It settles into the mucus membranes. And then the madness begins, followed by mutations. The infected body becomes quite fertile. Any seed or spore that lands on an infected body sprouts. Colloquially, these people are called "abominations" or "flowers." They act an awful lot like zombies. They roam around in small groups. They attack the uninfected. They no longer need to eat as they are able to photosynthesize their energy. In the world of *The Wilds*, they are no longer considered human.

The numbers were staggering. Some 38% of all people died in what became known as the Reckoning. Some 40% became abominations. That left just 22% of all people as "humans." And that's the central question in *The Wilds*: who counts as human? What makes someone human? What makes someone un-human? What are our responsibilities in this situation?

Through a series of flashbacks, we learn of the history leading up to the comic's present moment. We learn about the lawlessness, and we learn that people like Mr. Smith (he/him) founded "compounds"—walled-in safe havens that protect humans from flowers. But the problem was resources. Being walled up inside the compound left the survivors vulnerable. So, Smith set up a system of "runners," people who would leave the compound to search for goods and resources. They would bring back food, medical supplies, hardware, books, and whatever else they could find. The work of the runners was dangerous, so Smith offered incentives. Few runners lived to see those incentives. Although we see only a small sample from *one* compound, the runners do seem to be composed of people of color and queer folx. In other words, once again the most marginal people find themselves having to take the risk.

Enter our current heroes: Daisy Walker (she/her) and Heather Whitebull (she/her). They are both runners; they are both women of color; they are lovers. Heather has kind of had it with Smith and the compound system. As a nomad, she prefers to be outside the walls and in nature. As a runner, she is tired of the exploitation. In her mind, Smith *uses* runners. He knows the job is dangerous; he knows that some people are desperate; he nickels and dimes runners to keep them in debt.

Daisy, though, is not quite ready to make the move outside the walls. For one, she appreciates the comfort and stability of the compound. It's just too dangerous out there in the wilds. For another, she sees it as the only way she can help other people. She imagines what would happen to those in the compound if she stopped being a runner. She imagines what would happen to the little 12-year-old girl she found medicine for. That little girl would have died, and so would have countless others. How could she turn her back on all that?

Well, Smith makes it easy.

In the vicinity of the compound is a medical research lab. Seems pretty high tech in the wake of the Reckoning and the loss of 78% of all humans, but OK. Let's roll with it. The medical facility makes medicines, but they also conduct research to develop a "cure" for the contagion. The botanist Dr. Odutola (pronouns unknown) has been working on means of communicating with the flowers via pheromones. Odutola and others have also found a basic way to inhibit the flowers via those same pheromones. Dr. Richard Knott (he/him), however, is also working on fertility. His research is effectively a positive eugenics project. He wants to take those who seem to be immune from contagion and have them breed. To that end, he kidnaps both flowers and humans in order to experiment on them. He sees Heather as a perfect candidate. Worse, Smith effectively sells Heather to Knott for the project.

Both Smith and Knott—two white men—employ similar arguments: they say that they are looking out for the greater good (of the compound and of all of humanity, respectively); they say that this project is larger than any one person and, therefore, any one person's rights. And they say, quite pointedly, that "you people" need to be grateful for what they already have. In their minds, Smith and Knott will be the saviors of all mankind (and I use that word advisedly). We recognize the logic and language of these demagogues.

And, so, the central question: who counts as human? Who is worth saving? Who is expendable in the name of progress? I think we all know the answers.

Daisy tells Knott: "Men like you act like hurting people is *objectivity*, as if it is *brave* to *use* people as a means to an end. But it *isn't*. It's just selfishness and fear pretending to be *logic*" (vol. 5, 24). Daisy also challenges Knott on who counts as human. "You and your thugs, clearly, but *who else*? Certainly not *me* and *definitely* not the people you kidnapped and treated as *disposable*" (vol. 5, 24). For most readers, I suspect, the words ring true, but they have no effect on Knott. He has wrapped himself in an out-of-context phrase from the Hippocratic Oath to justify his actions. Odutola, a black woman and a physician, tells Knott: his work is useless if it destroys as many as it saves. The cost is too high (vol. 5, 23).

The Wilds does represent the arguments and struggles in the midst of a pandemic. Now, we are all too familiar with the terms. In the midst of a global pandemic, what is our responsibility? Where do our individual rights fall next to the needs of the community? For some, getting a vaccine was too much responsibility. For some, wearing a mask was too much to ask. Imagine what would happen if all social and political order breaks down....

But the pandemic also laid bare (as if it were not already as plain as day) the structural racism in our society. Who got the vaccines and when? Whom was the vaccine tested on? To which communities were the tests distributed? For which communities did the CDC recommend ending lock down? In its calculations, the CDC (knowing full well that there were *people* behind the decisions of the CDC) seemed to decide that immuno-compromised people were worth *less*. This logic seemed to suggest that low-income and communities of color were lower priorities.

The Wilds illustrates this very same logic.

What it does *not* demonstrate is the ontological status of the flowers. Both the people in the compound and the people in Medical seem to agree that the flowers are un-human. Well, why? On what basis? What are the criteria? What fundamental thing(s) have they lost? What are they (not) able to do? Why did those immune to the contagion turn so quickly and so fully against the flowers?

Maybe all these questions are answerable, but the comic does not take them up. And I think it should have. Look at the parallels here. Audre Lorde (she/her) said it loudly, did she not? In the world of *The Wilds*, the runners, the queer folx, the BIPOC, are all marginalized and dehumanized. But here, anyway, they seem to be willing to do the same to the flowers.

"The master's tools will never dismantle the master's house" (110).

Or, maybe that was the point all along....

Shade 23 — *Crowded* (2018)

Well, There Is Now....

IN 1954, FREDRIC Brown (he/him) published a *very* short story titled "Answer." In the story, a scientist has created a supercomputer. When the computer is powered on, the scientist asks the computer one simple question. The question is common enough: "Is there a god?" (16). Very quickly, the computer answers: "Yes, *now* there is a god" (16). Of course, the *coup de grâce* is that the computer zaps (in shades of Zeus almighty) a bolt of lightning that fuses the switch closed. Extrapolation has long been one of the functions of science fiction. A story of extrapolation, sometimes called an "if this goes on. . ." story, takes a current technological or social development and imagines it into the future. Where will it lead? What is a possible outcome? Though written in the 1950s, Brown's story takes up the development of supercomputers. Where will they lead? What form might they take? Brown's answer skips quite a few steps and goes right to the apocalyptic (in all the religious senses of the word).

Even today, extrapolation stories remain a staple. SF imagines where computers might lead us. What changes might cloning technologies bring? What changes might global weirding bring to the environment and society? Christopher Sebela (he/him), Ro Stein (any pronoun you like), Tríona Farrell (she/her) have created an extrapolative comic series in *Crowded*. The comic began in 2018. The limited series has three story arcs, each consisting of 6 issues. The first 12 issues were published as single issues between 2018 and 2020 and then collected into Volumes 1 (*Soft Apocalypse*) and 2 (*Glitter Dystopia*). The final five issues were published all at once in Volume 3 (*Cutting-Edge Desolation*) in 2022. *Crowded* has been nominated for an Eisner Award in 2019 (Best New Series) and a GLAAD Award in 2020 (Outstanding Comic Book). *Crowded* extrapolates what a social media-obsessed future might look like. It imagines just where crowdsourcing might lead. I mean, we're not far off, are we?

Crowded begins with Charlie Ellison (she/her), a woman who pieces together a living in the gig economy. For example, she drives for two ride-share companies, Muver and Drift; rents out her car via Weelsy; rents out a dress via Kloset; walks dogs via Dogstrol; babysits kids via Citysitter; lends out money via Moneyfriender; rents herself out to an old man via Palrent (merely as a companion); and tutors calculus for a high school student (this one comes back later). The future Sebela imagines is not all that appealing. On top of all that, Charlie is addicted to social media. She cannot not post her life online (this also comes back to bite her).

Even so, Sebela takes this concept someplace even darker, crowdsourcing a murder. The newest app is called Reapr, through which anyone can crowdsource a hit job on anyone else. As we eventually learn, the original Reapr contract was on the US Secretary of State and several Cabinet members. In the end, 5,000 people donated to that campaign. Of course, the government responded, but, as is frequently the case, the servers quickly all went underground and out of reach. But the precedent had been set. "People finally had the charge to strike back against the jerks in power" (Vol. 1, 52). As with most things online, the precedent gave way to other kinds of hits. Soon, someone set up a Reapr campaign on a director who had "ruined" the *Star Wars* franchise. People set up a Reapr campaign for someone who posted a tweet, or took too long in the Subway line. Most Reapr campaigns never get any backers, and no one gets killed. If a campaign is backed, then the contract lasts for thirty days. If the target survives, double jeopardy attaches, and the target is free to go. Reapr is a bit like "The Most Dangerous Game" (1924) on a smart phone.

In light of that development, another industry emerges: Dfenders. These are paid bodyguards who try to keep the target alive for 30 days. Enter our Dfender, Vita Slatter (she/her). Vita is a queer woman who is down on her luck. She is a former secret service agent. Her ex-girlfriend is a cop, and her Dfender jobs tend not to go well. Clients like the warm and fuzzy approach—they're paying a lot for the service, right? Vita is not warm and fuzzy. However, her survival rate is really good. She's not lost a client yet. Her new client, Charlie, will put that to the test.

The first arc (Vol. 1) centers on the campaign to kill Charlie, particularly the "killstreamer" Trotter (he/him) who fulfills Reapr contracts while live streaming. Trotter has millions of followers and has made a career out of executing people for the reward. It also introduces Circe (she/her) another apparent assassin tracking Charlie. In the second arc (Vol. 2), set in Los Vegas, Vita tries to reconnect with an underground cult, thinking that going underground (literally and figuratively) might help them stay alive. As luck would have it, the cult also needs the reward money. Circe has followed them, as well. The third arc (Vol. 3) is all about redemption and resolution. We all learn who originated the contract on Charlie. We learn who started the initial Reapr campaign. We learn why the bounty on Charlie (a relative nobody) swelled to three million dollars. Our primary characters (Charlie, Vita, Jo, Circe, and Doug the Dog) all live happily ever after.

How queer is *Crowded*? Well, sort of. To begin with, all the primary characters are queer. As we have seen here, some comics will add a secondary queer character, or offer a primary character who is queer though that character's queerness is not an element of the story. To reiterate, none of those things is necessarily bad. I maintain that a whole range of configurations of queer characters is the ideal goal. *Crowded*, however, has multiple queer characters, and their queerness is a present factor in their lives and in the narrative. Charlie, Vita, and Circe are all attracted, at various times, to one another. Charlie and Vita have sex (a lot of it) while on the run. Vita and Circe make out. Vita and Jo reunite. And Charlie and Circe end up together as a couple. No word on Doug the Dog.

The series is also filled with queer breadcrumbs. For example, the narrative casually mentions "President Monáe," referring to the queer singer/songwriter/author/actor Janelle Monáe. While on the run, our crew travels through Oklahoma City, which has been taken over by queer folk. They casually refer to it as "Oklahomo" (Vol. 3, 89), where everyone is welcome—except TERFs and Nazis. That sounds fair. In this sense, then, *Crowded* offers tidbits for the queer reader.

The comic, though, does not treat queer folx as a monolith. Circe is a stone-cold killer. Circe is happy to fulfill the murderous desires of her wealthy clients, from whom she has benefitted financially. Vita, on the other hand, dislikes violence and killing. Oh, Vita is very good at it and does kill a number of people. But Vita prefers negotiation; she prefers outmaneuvering a target; she prefers the least damaging option to handle a situation. Charlie is, in many ways, a lover and not a fighter. In the final confrontation with Nexus Specialty Corp., she's driven to violence, though Vita talks her down. It's not who she is, and she would have regretted killing them.

Finally, *Crowded* asks readers to take a different look at apps and the gig economy. Charlie's daily routine, which barely allows her to live, is absurd. It's no way to make a living, and yet it is completely normalized in the series. Sebela pushes the envelope a bit, asking, "What if this goes on?" How many jobs does it take to make a living? What level of poverty pushes someone to thievery (which can lead to a Reapr contract)? What kinds of services will be offered in the gig economy? Where is the limit on what we will farm out? Perhaps the idea of a murder app seems far-fetched. Is it, really? Based on what I have observed since 2016, I get the sense that a significant portion of the population (I was tempted to say US population, but I think it really extends beyond the US) would be fine with a murder app.

Crowded provides a vision of what that might look like.

Shade 24 — *Archival Quality* (2018)

Tear Down the Past

IN SEPTEMBER OF 2020, pop star Demi Lovato (they/them or she/her) opened up about their own life-long struggles with depression and addiction. On that World Suicide Prevention Day, Lovato talked about their struggles, their doubts. And they talked about the importance of seeking help, of working on oneself. They wrote and released a song titled "OK Not to Be OK" for the occasion. They released another single when they fell off the sobriety wagon. As in the case of Lovato, we hear about it (at least, some of the time) when celebrities struggle with depression. Not so much when it affects the local librarian.

In the "Afterword" to her 2018 graphic novel, *Archival Quality*, Ivy Noelle Weir (she/her) writes about her own struggles with depression. According to her, she struggled her entire life with "chronic illness, depression, and anxiety" (266). That depression affected her personal and her work life. She eventually got an internship in a "medical history museum," where she digitized "antique medical photographs, illustrations, and documents" (266). She tried to write about medical history from an academic perspective. Then she wrote a story called "The Archivist" that she submitted to the Clarion Writers Workshop (though she also has a MLIS from Clarion University!). After that story was rejected, she put it away. But when she found the artwork of Steenz (Christina Stewart) (they/them), Weir decided to write her story as a graphic novel. *Et voilà.*

The graphic novel centers on Celeste "Cel" Walden (she/her), who has just lost her job at the library because of her depression. As she carries her effects home, her boyfriend, Kyle (he/him), calls her a loser. He looks for every opportunity to put her down and even to institutionalize her. Nevertheless, she finds a job as an archivist—though it's all a bit mysterious. The museum is local, but she had never heard of the place before. It is a public museum, but no one ever visits. Still, she is eager to work with the Director, Abayomi Abiola (he/him) and the librarian, Holly Park (she/her). One of the perks of the job is an apartment located within the building. The arrangement is ideal for Cel, not so much for Kyle.

One night in her apartment, she sees a woman in her dreams who asks for her help. Shortly thereafter, she sees a picture of the same woman in one of the images that she is digitizing. That simply cannot be a coincidence. And then strange things begin to happen in her apartment and in the museum—strange noises, objects being knocked over, papers flying around the room, initials carved into a doorframe. Eventually, we discover that the woman in her dreams was Celine Wanamaker (she/her). She had been an (unwilling) patient in the asylum that later became the museum. The doctors there had experimented on her. The real revelation is that the museum directors have been selling off body parts for their personal profit. Celine asks Celeste to get them ALL out.

How, then, is *Archival Quality*, a graphic novel about depression and about unethical experimentation a queer comic? As always, that depends.

For one, the graphic novel takes up the topic of depression. Despite the efforts of Demi Lovato (and Michelle Obama [she/her], and Justin Bieber [he/him], and others), the stigma still remains. The comic is asking the reader to think about depression—its effects in our lives and our responses to those suffering depression—in a different way. All too often, patients who seek help for depression are marginalized and ignored. They are (over)medicated and warehoused. They are dismissed as hypochondriacs or as hysterical (and I am using that word advisedly given the history of medical treatment in this book). Celine appeals to Celeste; Celeste cannot but empathize with Celine. They have both been treated badly by the medical establishment.

In a related issue, the graphic novel takes up the question of medical records and medical remains. Who handles them? Who controls them? Who is responsible for them? What is the responsibility? *Archival Quality* asks its readers to rethink those questions, as well. We may not have had anything to do with the bodies or the records, but that past haunts all of us (cf. Shade 27). We see this question in the news all-too frequently. Consider, for example, the "treatment" of Indigenous children in the US and Canada. Who is responsible for the records? Who is responsible for the remains? How should they be handled? What is the best way to "liberate" them? The only way that Cel is able to get "unstuck" and move on with her own life is by helping to correct the injustice done to Celine and the other patients of the asylum. Doing the right thing costs them all their jobs, but they do the right thing.

Finally, the graphic novel does feature two queer characters, Holly and Gina (she/her). Holly is one of the three main characters. She's front and center, and she gets plenty of screen time. Holly is not relegated to a marginal existence in the novel. Holly has a girlfriend, Gina (whom we see much less of). What's the relevance of that relationship to the narrative? Well, next to none, if I'm honest. Late in the graphic novel, Gina comes in handy because she is able to procure a key to the board room. Cel's visit to the rather macabre board room is key to unraveling the mystery. Is Gina's ability to get the key tied to her queerness? Nope. The plot point would have worked just as well if Holly had had a boyfriend and the boyfriend had gotten the key from his dad. In this sense, the queer relationship just *is*.

Nevertheless, Holly's ability to connect with Cel may be aided by her queerness. Holly's ability to address Cel's depression may be facilitated by Holly's lived experience as a woman of color and as a lesbian. As Audre Lorde (she/her) famously notes in "Will the Master's Tools Dismantle the Master's House," people who are on the margins, people who do not fall into our society's definitions of femininity, can find common cause. They share the experience of being marginalized. They collectively benefit from reimagining and rebuilding social structures. They collectively benefit from a radically reconstructed society.

And, arguably, that is what they all (Cel, Holly, and Abayomi) do. Each of them is a marginalized figure. Each of them takes a risk. Each of them puts their livelihood on the line. Collectively, they pull down the structure—literally and figuratively. They close down the building, and they close down the whole market in body parts.

In the "Afterword," Weir writes, "To go through therapy is to at once give up and regain agency—you have to put the deconstruction of what you believe in the hands of a near-stranger, and then you must rebuild yourself" (268).

Weir, like Lovato and others, wants to de-stigmatize depression. And Weir, like Lorde and others, wants to radically reimagine what we all can do to build a better society.

Shade 25 — *Open Earth* (2018)[**]

Environmental Warriors in Space

THE STATE OF California has long been at the vanguard of environmental legislation. As David Vogel argues, the intersection of four elements have led to the state's environmental policies. These elements include the unique beauty of the California landscape, the threat to that landscape due to economic and population growth, affluent individuals who have been committed to preservation, and the role that businesses have played in environmental protection (Vogel, "Why the Golden" 2-3). In the 2021-22 legislative session, the California legislation initiated hundreds of bills dealing with environmental issues. These bills have included ways to address climate change, to address wildfires (causes and effects), and to address environmental (in)justice (Kent, "California Environmental"). With the third largest land area of any US state, and with the

[**] *Open Earth* (2018) is published by the same company that published *A Quick and Easy Guide to They/Them Pronouns* (2018). The *Guide* (see Shade 1) makes the argument that everyone should have conversations about pronouns and every workplace should proactively make changes in the work culture and work practices in order to make it into a welcoming and safe space. The *Guide* points out that we should normalize the use of pronouns, that we should not single out gender-nonconforming individuals for using pronouns. And, indeed, in the beginning of the *Guide*, the page that lists all the execs and staff at Oni/Limerance Press includes the pronouns for every name. However, in *Open Earth*, published in the same year, the company seems to have reverted to old practices. The pronouns are gone. They seem NOT to have taken the lesson to heart.

largest population of any US state, the environmental trends in California have often trickled out to the other states.

The graphic novel *Open Earth* picks up the idea that (a) environmental issues will persist and, in fact, worsen, and that (b) California will continue to lead the way—this time, right into space....

In a not-too-distant future, California has seceded from the US. I mean, why not? As we have seen, it has been able to push an aggressive environmental agenda. Consequently, it has become the "undisputed global economic king of enviro-tech" (26). One of the newly independent California's initiatives was to send plants into space in order to preserve them—*Silent Running* (1972), anyone? The voyage was meant to last a year; however, the scientists who joined the plants in space had already decided that they were never going back. *Open Earth* picks up 20 years later.

Writer Sarah Mirk (she/her) and artist Eva Cabrera (she/her) present us with Rigo (she/her), the daughter of Ximena and Papi, two scientists of Latine descent. In space, they try to maintain many of their familial and cultural practices. Papi says it's important to preserve their culture. Rigo tells him that cultural differences were a big reason why they fucked up Earth. Maybe they're better off without them. Even so, all the "first-generation" stationers speak a combination of English and Spanish. The dialog in the graphic novel reflects this cultural shift.

Rigo just finds her parents out-dated and, well, incomprehensible. They have been in a 25-year, monogamous relationship, which Rigo says, "Sounds fucking crazy to me" (28). Dad especially pushes Rigo to date one person and to settle down. Instead, Rigo is in a polyamorous relationship with Carver and Franklin. *Open Earth*, then, is the tale of national divides, of familial divides, of generational divides, and of personal divides.

Even so, Papi's attitudes are really at the center of the narrative inasmuch as his views represent the current status quo. For example, Rigo wants to move in with Carver and "to partner." She does not want "to marry"; she does not want "to date"; she does not want "to be exclusive." Instead, her relationship with Carver would be the primary relationship, but both would remain free to have other sexual, social, and relational partners. Papi finds the new norms incomprehensible. Papi thinks she should date one person, should have a long-term loving relationship. Rigo says, "You're literally from a different planet than me" (24).

In addition, the ethics of the flight from Earth are questionable. The scientists were supposed to return but did not. Were they "heroes" for saving the plant samples and human samples? Or were they "fucking sneaky" for leaving everyone else behind? Earth was in dire straits. Much of Southern California was under water. Nueva San Francisco has long since stopped responding to communications. Have they merely lost power? Are they all gone? So, does the end (preserved humans and plants) justify the means? A secondary, underlying tension in the graphic novel is the technology on board. Will it hold up? Can they maintain the equipment that they have? Will they replicate the mistakes of the past?

In what ways does *Open Earth* queer comics? Well, several.

For one, Mirk and Cabrera queer the comic form through the drawings, the illustrations, and the representations of the characters. Of course, the jokes about female characters in comics with huge breasts and very little clothing abound. Deservedly so. Those kinds of representations would almost seem to be foundational and definitional of SF/fantasy comics. For *Open Earth*, the artists made conscious choices to break those stereotypes. Our lead is Latine. Not the first in comics, but still rare enough. For another, Rigo is a curvy, feminine character.

Mirk notes that she wanted a "short, curvy, girl who's confident in her body" (112) and states that Rigo grew up in the absence of pop culture and consumerism. Rigo (and several of the secondary characters) has not been forged in the crucible of hegemonic beauty. By extension, her sexual partners have not, either. Similarly, the character Atwood is drawn as femme, though Atwood would not even recognize the masc/femme distinction that we might make. Mirk and Cabrera imagine a future in which "people express gender in a more dynamic way. Cabrera says that she drew Atwood with "curviness," "intelligence," and "patience" (116).

For another, the first generation characters are all polyamorous (at least the ones we meet). Rigo, Carver, and Franklin are regular sexual partners. When Franklin walks in on Rigo and Carver in the act, his response is "I'm just here to get a wrench." At lunch one day, Atwood, the head of the First Generation Leadership Council, approaches. Rigo encourages her lover Franklin to stay with Atwood. Franklin and Atwood do go off to have sex. Before they finish, Rigo bursts into the room, sits down on the bed, and talks about her desire to move in with Carver. In other words, she is unfazed by her sometimes lover having sex with another person.

It's true that all of the sex scenes we see (Rigo and Carver, Rigo and Hex, Franklin and Atwood, and Rigo's mother and father) are all heterosexual. The comic does hint at same-sex relations between Carver and Franklin. When Franklin interrupts Rigo and Carver, Carver says, "We should get dressed" (46). Franklin quickly steps in and gives Carver a kiss and says, "Not on my account, *guapo*…. Besides, I've seen it all before" (47). Franklin gives the still undressed Carver another kiss just before he leaves (and we see a small red heart appear above Franklin and Carver (47).

Granted, Rigo is the primary character, and her primary and secondary sexual relationships are with men. If the authors wanted to show a generation with more fluid gender—and sexuality—they might have shown Rigo with partners of different sexes. While Rigo is the primary character, the creators also show people who are not Rigo having sex. Here, too, the secondary sexual relationships are heteronormative, if multiple. As another example, when Rigo's mother and father are shown having sex, they are engaged in bondage, with her mother whipping her father. So, not an example of non-heterosexual sex, but it is a representation of non-normative sexual practices.

California has been at the leading edge of environmental issues. Further, California has also long been a racially, ethnically, and culturally diverse state. In *Open Earth*, the culture that emerges on the station is a combination of Anglo and Chicano. Many of the characters have Spanish-derived or Spanish-sounding names. Many characters speak a mixture of English and Spanish. Further, in California Sur, one struggle has always been among immigrants, half-generation, first generation, and second generation family members. In *Open Earth*, the first generation are aliens. They were not born on Earth. They have no direct connection to Earth. As such, they forge new customs, new practices, and new mores.

Shade 26 — *SfSx* (2020)
Dystopia, with Kink

I DISTINCTLY REMEMBER reading *The Handmaid's Tale* (1985) for the first time. On the one hand, as a student of literature, I thought it was just beautifully constructed and written. I still do. On the other hand, I found the politics to be scary as hell. I still do. Some critics saw the premise as too far-fetched. They could not image a far-right, religious-based government taking over. They could not imagine a theocracy on our shores. After all, that kind of thing only happens in Middle East countries, right? They could not imagine women stripped so completely of every single political and social gain they had made in the past 65 years. They were incorrect. We know now that it wasn't far-fetched, at all. We move closer to that reality every single day....

In 2019, writer, teacher, and activist Tina Horn (she/her) published the first issue of *SfSx* (Safe Sex). Horn has reported on sexual subcultures and sexual politics via *Rolling Stone*, *Playboy*, and *Jezebel*. More recently, Horn has hosted a podcast on sexual kinks, called *Why Are People into That?* The comic series *SfSx* had originally been slated to be released by Vertigo, but that imprint shut down before *SfSx* could launch. Horn—eventually—found a home at Image, and the rest is history. The first seven issues were published in 2019-2020, and then issued as a single volume in July 2020. A second volume was released in November 2021.

Much like *The Handmaid's Tale*, *SfSx* takes place in a near but undefined future US. By some undisclosed means (though recent events in US history offer some clues), an ultra-conservative group has taken power. The Party consists of an alliance between two factions, "Religious Right fascists" and "carceral feminists" (Page 5). In constructing this government, Horn draws on two movements of the 1980s. The first faction is based on the rise of the New Right, coinciding with the election of Ronald Reagan, the rise of the Moral Majority, the rise of Newt Gingrich, and the Contract with America (just as Atwood was also drawing on these events). For the second faction, Horn draws on the "sex wars" of feminism that also took place in the 1980s. In these battles, certain feminists saw regression in the sexual politics of other feminists. They argued that pornography was a tool of patriarchy, and they argued that anyone who was into SM had to have been brainwashed. These anti-porn and anti-sex feminists wanted to ban certain types of erotic material and to police sexual politics. Horn extrapolates those two movements into a political party that would incarcerate those they disagree with.

In *SfSx*, these two factions have joined forces to take power, and The Party aims to create a truly pure and truly liberated society. *SfSx* sets out to demonstrate just how ludicrous that idea is.

In the comic, Margaret Jones (she/her) is the proprietor of The Dirty Mind, a club in San Francisco that is "a brothel, a dungeon, a porno theater, a strip club" (10). Is it also the refuge of many a sex worker and sexual rebel. Jones and her girlfriend Sylvia (she/her) consider The Dirty Mind to be a family. They are loyal to their workers; they create a safe and creative environment for their workers; and they create a safe (-ish—more on that in a bit) experience for their clientele.

Most of the volume is focalized through Avory (she/her), a sex worker who has found a man who respects her for everything she is. George (he/him) was initially a client, but the two eventually marry. When the Party raids The Dirty Mind, they take Jones prisoner. In the melée, Avory and George escape. Sylvia cannot forgive this betrayal of family. Even worse, the Party has taken over The Dirty Mind and converted it into their headquarters, now called The Pleasure Center. Oh, irony is not quite dead….

The Party tracks everything. A Fitbit-like wrist tracker called a Halo (more irony) records everything everyone does. It monitors when they have sex, how long they have sex, and with whom they have sex. And if they have sex, then they have to file paperwork with the Party to assure the sex police that the sex was of an appropriate kind with an appropriate partner (who can only be a spouse). No more spontaneity. No more "base" and "animalistic" thoughts (16). No more deviance. Here's the other thing: George also works for the Party. In his day job, he keeps track of everyone's "purity score."

When George discovers the sexual "reprogramming" and torture happening on the thirteenth floor of the Pleasure Center, he's arrested. When the Party finds sex toys in Avory and George's shared apartment, Avory becomes a fugitive. The remainder of the volume consists of Avory mobilizing her old comrades. They develop a plan to break Jones and George out of The Pleasure Center and to expose the Party for what it really is: a bunch of old white hypocrites who torture people. As Morgan M. Page (she/her) states in the Introduction, Horn makes it clear that the resistance will be led by "hookers, queers, trans people, and women of colour in full leather" (6).

Just so you know, the ending of volume 1 of *SfSx* is just about as conclusive and just about as hopeful as the ending of *The Handmaid's Tale*.

SfSx is a queer SF comic in just about every way that I have defined queer SF. In other words, it's queer AF.

For one, the comic asks the reader to think about things differently. *SfSx* queers the reader's perspective. Consider the subject matter—sex workers. Certainly, sex workers have appeared in SF before. But in what capacity? Typically, they have been background figures in world building. Or perhaps they have been a short-term distraction for the hero. He has a bit of down time and needs to blow off some steam. Or perhaps the sex worker is collateral damage. She was just in the wrong place at the wrong time. Or, finally, as *SfSx* likes to call it, maybe she got "Pretty Womaned." In other words, the successful hero rescues the hooker-with-a-heart-of-gold and gives her the happily-ever-after life.

Not here. Sex workers are front and center. They are represented in all their variety and glory. And they make no apologies for their profession or their preferences. Not scientists. Not explorers. Not superheros. Sex workers fighting back the rising tide of puritanical fascism, redefining the subject matter of SF comics.

For another, *SfSx* queers the SF comic. Rarely do we see the intersection of technology, politics, and sexual politics in this way. We have seen many instances in SF when technology has been used to create and reinforce a political goal. Rarely has that goal been a particular view of sexuality and the control of sexual lives. We have seen narratives in which technology invades our personal lives. It tracks our movements. It tracks our shopping. It tracks our buying preferences. Consider the very early story "Captive Audience" (1953) by Anne Warren Griffith (she/her) in which a housewife fends off the aggressive ads in the grocery store and in her kitchen. Or, consider (the many) Philip K. Dick (he/him) stories of advertising invading our private space.

But here, the control is specifically of sexual lives. As I noted above, the anti-sex feminists were focused on questions of sexuality. They saw most aspects of sexuality as functions of patriarchy. They saw heterosexual sex as rape. Andrea Dworkin (she/her), Catharine McKinnon (she/her), Helen Longino (she/her), Gail Dines (she/her), and others argued for the limitation and control of sex and sexually explicit representations. Political conservatives have made similar arguments. Politicians such as Jerry Falwell (he/him), Chuck Grassley (he/him), Mike Pence (he/him), and others have argued against sex outside of marriage, sex that is not heterosexual sex, and sexually explicit representations. In the finest SF fashion, *SfSx* extrapolates where such arguments might lead us. The answer is fascism.

For another still, *SfSx* graphically illustrates the sexual lives and practices of sexual "deviants." While much of the comic centers on the rescue mission, it nevertheless works in a great deal of sex. In an early scene, The Dirty Mind is closed to clients so that the sex workers can have the evening to themselves. They are able to engage in their own pleasures and their own fantasies. In the scene, we see same-sex partners, group sex, strap-ons, suspensions, and other scenarios. The narrator, Avory, talks of the pleasure of having an orgasm in public view. They have discussions of the pleasures of pain. We see flashback scenes when George is a client and Avory inflicts pain compared to torture scenes when George is held prisoner. One is an act of trust and compassion; the other is an act of power and hatred.

SfSx is at once a repudiation of conservative sexual politics and a validation of non-normative sexual practices. According to *SfSx*, sexual repression is not freedom. True freedom would be the ability and opportunity to explore and express one's sexuality. And when the politicians come to take that away, may the sex workers and sexual non-conformists lead the revolution!

Shade 27 — *Mooncakes* (2019)

Love Is Love

AN OLD ADAGE has it that, when times get tough—politically, socially, economically—writers and fans turn away from science fiction and toward fantasy. The argument holds that science fiction can be a bit too on the nose, a bit too relevant to provide the desired escape from tough times. Fantasy, on the other hand, is understood to be more escapist, more detached from reality. And that furthermore, in fantasy writers can make up entirely new sets of rules, as long as they are consistent. I do not mean to suggest that fantasy cannot address contemporary issues. Far from it. However, a science fiction story about a scientist racing to defeat a contagion about to destroy human civilization and a fantasy story about a wizard trying to undo a spell or a plague do not have quite the same resonance to a contemporary reader. So, in the middle of a global pandemic, when everyone is shut down and no one knows whether or not we will ever go back to "normal," who wants to read about virology or chemistry or medicine? Why not read about werewolves and witches?

I am not convinced that the adage holds true. A look at the magazine *Locus* or the website *io9* tells us that a lot of SF and a lot of fantasy are being produced all the time. Was there an increase in the amount of fantasy published during the height of the COVID pandemic? It would be an interesting study. Nevertheless, what does it mean to publish fantasy in the age of COVID? What does it mean to delve into the world of witches and werewolves when the news is filled with biomedical information about viruses? Does fantasy have any political, social, or economic relevance? Why witches? Why now?

Suzanne Walker (she/her) is a writer based in Chicago. She writes fiction and nonfiction and speaks publicly about representation in science fiction/fantasy, especially the representation of disability. Wendy Xu (she/her) is an illustrator based in Brooklyn who also works as a YA and children's books editor. In *Mooncakes* (2019), they take us into a small town that has some demon issues.

In many ways, the Hugo-nominated *Mooncakes* has a fairly traditional narrative and graphic structure. The narrative is almost entirely chronological, with just a few brief flashbacks for context. The images are full color and generally realist. The figures and backgrounds fall somewhere between the cartoonish figures of *Gingerbread Girl* and *Strong Female Protagonist* and the fully-defined figures of *Angela: Asgard's Assassin* and *Alienated*. The scenes in which magic takes place are washed with pinks and purples, rendering an otherworldliness. Even so, the queerness here derives from the narrative, which asks the reader to see the world from a different perspective.

Teenage witch Nova Huang (she/her) lives with her two Nanas (Nechama and Qiuli) (pronouns unknown for both). Nova's parents are deceased, but they do show up from time to time in protoplasmic form. Nova's Nanas run a café and bookstore; however, the real scene is in the back of the store. Any customer asking for "rare books" gets escorted into the back. The Nanas are also witches, and they are teaching Nova as much as they can. They have a gigantic collection of books about magic.

The small town gets a visitor, a white wolf. The wolf is actually the werewolf form of Tam Lang (they/them), a teenager shapeshifter. They have been drawn back to the woods outside town in order to face a demon. Initially, the demon possesses a horse. We discover, however, that the demon is meant to take over the werewolf form of Tam. The new demon-werewolf would have nearly unlimited power, invulnerable to witches' magic.

But the other piece of the puzzle is that Nova and Tam are childhood friends. They were nearly inseparable, and Nova had a huge childhood crush on Tam. They were separated only when Tam's family moved away. As they rekindle their relationship, they help one another realize their own powers and their own potential.

Do Walker and Xu intend the comic to be literal or metaphorical? Do they mean to suggest that magic exists alongside science? Do they argue that magic and science are two sides of the same coin? That argument seems to be the clearest and strongest point in the comic. For example, in one scene, the local science nerd Tatyana (she/her) is shown reading a book titled, *Science and Magic: Are They Really So Different?* In another example, Tatyana-the-scientist suggests that she wants to study Tam-the-werewolf, explicitly stating that even skeptics can be open and learn (227). As still another example, the nana Nechama wears eyeglasses. One might expect a witch to cast a spell to repair or alter vision. Similarly, her granddaughter Nova wears hearing aids. While Nova's hearing aids are partially an example of Walker's commitment to the representation of disability in comics, the hearing aids also complicate the relationship between science and magic. Why wouldn't a witch simply cast a spell to improve her hearing? Why rely on a technological device? In fact, Nova sometimes uses her technological devices to aid her magic. In other words, they work in tandem and are not opposed to one another.

Apart from the science/magic relationship, does *Mooncakes* have anything to say about today? Certainly. For one, it addresses near-universal themes of trust and betrayal, of power and misuse, and of family dysfunction.

Trust plays an important role in *Mooncakes*. Nova trusts the Nanas enough to tell them about Tam, to tell them about the demon, and to include them in the rescue mission. In turn, the Nanas trust Nova to make good decisions. They have given her the tools, and they trust her to make good use of them. On the other hand, Tam had trusted Mrs. C (she/her) only to discover that Mrs. C had been in league with Tam's stepfather all along.

The conflict in the narrative comes down to the desire for power. A neighbor, Mrs. C has been working with Tam's stepdad. He courted and married Tam's mother specifically in order to get close to Tam. The two of them want to create the demon/werewolf so that they can have unlimited power. They would be immune to the corrective spells of the witches. Because the comic was written in 2019, we can easily read the comic as a meditation on those addicted to power, those who would use any means to consolidate their power and to render themselves immune to any corrective influences.

Mooncakes also illustrates the importance—but also the pliability—of family. For one, we see very briefly the family that Tatyana nannies for. The family appears to be a heteronormative, nuclear family, though both parents work long hours. In this case, the nanny Tatyana plays an important familial role for the children. As another example, we see Tam's family. Tam and their mother (she/her) moved away when Tam's mother divorced. She remarried, but Tam's stepfather (he/him) was only interested in Tam's shapeshifting abilities. He was motivated by the power of the demon-werewolf. As a result, Tam's relationship with their mother is severely damaged. Their bio-fam has failed them, but they have found a new, queer family with Nova and the Nanas.

Nova's family is also fractured, but differently. Nova's parents appear in her life only as ghosts. While sometimes critical, they nevertheless show up to remind Nova that they are proud of her. Nova's two Nanas are loving and supportive parents to Nova. This queer family is the ideal support for Nova, and, in the end, provides the nourishment that Nova needs to move on. This queer family is able to incorporate Tam, as well.

Love is love. Nova and Tam rekindle and express their love. But it is love that conquers the demon. Love made them vulnerable. But it also made them stronger, wiser, better equipped. They tell the demon that they have love, and the demon can, too. In the end, in the midst of a plague or not, in science fiction or fantasy, *Mooncakes* argues that love conquers all.

And, in this case, queer love conquers all.

Shade 28—*Alienated* (2020)

An Alien in the Midwest

HIGH SCHOOL SUCKED. I mean, I hated it. I wouldn't go back for 10 million dollars. Primarily, I didn't fit in, and it was painfully obvious. I was frequently the butt of jokes, laughter, and pranks. One time, they even set my pants on fire. Did anyone let me know what they were doing or bother to stop them? Or did they all just laugh? I think you know the answer. I didn't (and couldn't) hang out with the jocks. I didn't (and couldn't) hang out with the cool kids. I didn't really want, too, either. What would I have said to them? We had fundamentally different experiences. They all hung out together, went to dances, got drunk, had sex. I mostly stayed home and read science fiction.

Simon Spurrier (he/him) and Chris Wildgoose (he/him), both veteran writers of British comics, offer up their own take on teenage alienation. Spurrier later went on to write for Marvel, including the *Star Wars: Doctor Aphra* series. In 2020, Spurrier won a GLAAD Media Award for Outstanding Comic Book for his work on that series. *Alienated*, a six-issue limited series published by BOOM! Studios in 2020, has generally gotten good reviews. An omnibus edition was released in late 2020.

The story centers on three disaffected and alienated youths growing up in small-town Tangletree, Illinois (which, according to Google Maps, does not exist), which resembles many small towns, including the one I grew up in. In the first Chapter, we meet Samuel (he/him), Samantha (she/her), and Samir (he/him)—the three Sams. Samuel is an angry white kid. His father is AWOL, and his mother is a cop. They've moved around a lot, and he's currently the "new kid" in Tangletree. Unbeknownst to his mother, Samuel has a secret identity. He is a vlogger who uses the name The Hooded Hierophant. A hierophant was a priest in ancient Greece who interpreted mysteries or texts. Young Samuel decodes the state of the world. Behind his mask and digitally altered voice, Samuel rails against the state of the world and at young people's apathy. His two primary impediments (as he sees it) are that he has only 43 followers and that Waxy, a vlogger with millions of followers, offers a similar take on the world.

Samantha is a white girl who is counting down the days until she can leave town and begin with a clean slate at college. There, no one will know anything about her, her family, or her past. She comes from an upper-middle-class family. We see her house and backyard pool. She is given an SUV for her birthday but refuses to drive it on principle. More than that, she wants to escape the incident that defined her in her hometown. She had gotten drunk at a party and had sex with a jock. When she discovered that she was pregnant, the boy, Craig (he/him), bailed on her. He and his friends argued that he "deserved" a normal life, but that she was just the "slut" who gave up her baby.

Finally, Samir is a queer Pakistani-American Muslim. He is an affable guy whom everyone seems to love (well, except Leon [he/him]). However, we discover that Samir carries a lot of guilt. He feels that he has been a terrible Muslim, a terrible Pakistani, and a terrible son. He believes that was why his father left the family. He has often wished that he simply no longer existed.

Oh, but they are not the only disaffected youths in town. Young Leon is a budding white supremacist and school shooter. He hates everyone and hides weapons in his bedroom. And

Chelsea (she/her) is a fame seeker. She sings of Jesus and love even as she believes that she is better than everyone else at school.

But what ties the three Sams together is an alien named Chip (the three Sams use he/him pronouns for the alien). As the three of them walk through the woods on their way to school, they see a strange blue ball dangling from a tree branch. As if they had never seen an *Alien* movie, they decide to touch it. Two of them lift the third one up, and they touch the blue ball. They are instantly connected telepathically. They now have access to each other's minds. They have access to thoughts and memories. They have become linked to the alien. Once they are linked, their interior thoughts are represented visually via three colored fonts.

One day at school, Samir tries to make peace with Leon. If anyone can get through to Leon, it would be Samir. But Leon is having none of it; he can only lash out and insult. Samir operates on the principle that one fears what one doesn't understand. You cannot hate someone you know well, right? So, why not introduce Leon to the alien? Why not add him to the group mind? It might work, mightn't it? If Leon could see Samir's humanity, then, perhaps, he would understand. Perhaps he could see Samir as a person, not as an "illegal" and not as a "homo." But when they tussle in the woods, they discover that Chip does more than link their thoughts. He has *powers*, and those powers extend to the whole group. When Leon tries to hit them with a stick, they just make him go AWAY.

Similarly, they try to get through to Chelsea—though it's fair to ask if they're really trying to get through to her or if they really just want to take her down a notch. When they get inside Chelsea's mind, they see her disdain for others, and her view of other students as pawns. Everything she does is calculated to maximize her exposure and her being *seen*. Sounds familiar, no? However, they have little luck in breaking her. She remains committed to the idea that she "deserves" (we see that word a LOT in this comic) her time in the limelight. Instead, their interventions leave Chelsea hospitalized, in a coma.

Oh, this series is like *Hamlet*. The body count is just starting.

While Leon and Chelsea are easy targets to make fun of, the strength of the series is that it shows how the Sams are pretty much the same. All three want to be seen. All three want to be recognized for who they are. All three want their visions for the world to come true. All three want to be less alienated. Ironically, our cuddly alien just gives them the means—or accentuates the means.

Samir wants to be free of his guilt, and he wants to be seen by his father. He uses Chip—even though he knows the process causes Chip pain—to locate and confront his father. His father is all-too-human. He is appalled at Samir's pain, appalled to think he was the source of it. However, he left his family behind for a woman, alcohol, and other pleasures of the flesh. As he confronts the father-sized hole in his heart, Samir slits his wrists. Through the intervention of Samantha and Chip, though, Samir pulls through. In the space of his new-found peace of mind, Samir decides to (a) apologize to Chip, and (b) come clean about their role in Leon's disappearance and Chelsea's coma. In other words, the person-to-person connection turns out to be Samir's salvation.

Samantha wants to confront her baby-daddy. She has lived with the consequences of their evening, while he simply walked away from it. So, as Craig plays old-school board games and flirts with other women, Samantha enters his mind and confronts him. She explains the hell she has been through; she explains the torment that he has escaped. She explains that she had no choice for a "normal life." And although she is filled with rage and a desire for revenge, she finds that it is enough that he knows. She has confronted him with her pain and her need to be seen by him. Further, she sees the toll it takes on Chip. Although she rejects the accusation that she treats Chip like a baby because she is trying to replace her own child, she is the only one who consistently sees Chip as a sentient subject.

And then there is Samuel, perhaps the most damaged character, perhaps the least likable. He is single-minded in his desire to change the world, an admirable desire. He is a high school student with a keen awareness of social, cultural, political, and environmental injustices, and he wants to right them. But he also wants to be seen and heard. And it's hard to say which of those two needs is greater for Samuel. He is blinded by his drive; he is blinded by his own hypocrisy. He cannot see his own shortcomings. He cannot see that he commits the same acts as do those he despises. He is ruthless in his endgame.

As a queer comic, what does *Alienated* have to say? First off, it offers a single gay character. And while Samir's being queer is not central, it does play a role in his alienation from his family and in his desire to bridge the gap of understanding with Leon. He fails. The homophobe Leon is not going to be persuaded. (Though, narratively, it might have been interesting to see Leon brought into the group mind and see how it changed all of them.) Furthermore, Samir ends up dead. Yes, Spurrier and Wildgoose bury their one gay character. True, they also kill off Samuel (and his mom). Even so, Samir is sacrificed for the redemption of Samantha and Chip.

Beyond that, though, *Alienated* represents the alienation of difference during the teenaged years. High school years can be really tough to get through. Further, *Alienated* represents every alienated kid's wish to have some means to bridge that alienation. Wouldn't all of the weird kids (queer kids, nerds, brainiacs, autistic kids) have loved to connect to an alien, to get into the mind of someone else (because we sure weren't able to understand them without one)?

Wouldn't we all have liked to be a little less alienated?

Shade 29 — *Lost on Planet Earth* (2020)
Finding Oneself

A TWEET RECENTLY appeared in my social media feeds. The tweet was about Henry David Thoreau (he/him) and his famous hideaway at Walden Pond. For many, his book *Walden; or, A Life in the Woods* (1854) was a guidepost, a roadmap. For many, *Walden* represented a goal to live a simple life of solitary contemplation. As Thoreau spent his two-plus years in the woods, he made observations about nature and about himself. The book contains sentiments about personal independence and self-reliance. The tweet attributed to Zoe Whittall, however, points out that Walden Pond was located on his mother's property, and she would bring him sandwiches and take away his laundry! (@zoewhittall). Although I have not tried to verify his dependence upon his mother and her as-ever invisible domestic labor, the meme sheds light on the improbability of just wandering off for a couple of years to find oneself. Even so, the protagonist of *Lost on Planet Earth* gives it a shot.

Lost on Planet Earth is a ComiXology original. ComiXology is an Amazon company that was originally a delivery platform to sell comics. Netflix once just licensed and sold content and later began to produce its own original content; ComiXology followed a similar trajectory. It was initially a platform for following comics, and then a platform for buying comics. Beginning in 2018, ComiXology began to produce content. The lead writer of *Lost on Planet Earth*, Magdalene Visaggio (she/her), describes herself as a trans woman with autism (Horne, 15 July). Visaggio has also worked on *Kim &*

Kim (Shade 17) and *Open Earth* (Shade 25), and she has been nominated for two Eisner Awards and three GLAAD Media Awards. Claudia Aguirre (she/her), who describes herself as a queer comic creator, has also worked on *Kim & Kim,* is *Lost*'s illustrator.

In the Introduction to *Lost on Planet Earth*, Visaggio writes of the social and political circumstances during which she was writing this comic, in particular the killing of George Floyd and the removal of Confederate statues in Richmond, Virginia. Visaggio claims that the story *began* as a semi-humorous critique of *Star Trek* and the role of Star Fleet. The story was too stodgy and too polemical and became instead a story about Basil (she/her) finding herself—her best, truest self—despite the costs.

In 2381, the Star Union is the thing that unites large portions of the population. It's also the thing that colonizes and assimilates other cultures. Against this backdrop, the Miranda family has a long history of serving in the Interplanetary Fleet. The benefits of doing so are enormous. For one, Fleet members have a sense that they are fulfilling a larger duty. For another, they are financially and materially cared for. Our young hero, Basilisa (Basil) Miranda expects to follow in her parents' footsteps and enter the Fleet. Since she was five years old, every action and every decision has been taken to achieve that goal.

One of those decisions involves her long-time friend Charlotte (she/her), another Fleet hopeful. One day when they are studying on the bed, they get a bit flirtatious, and they nearly kiss. Basil freaks out because the military does not allow same-sex relations. To be one of "those people" would mean giving up the dream. The next day, she strong-arms Charlotte into making a decision: have me as a friend or not at all. They agree to remain friends but not lovers. Nevertheless, they plan to enter the Academy together, get assigned on a ship together, and fly across space together. They plan to be together in whatever ways are available to them.

How many queer folk have had to make that decision? How many families, businesses, professions, or careers have compelled that choice? At the time, Basil seems content with the choice. She has her priorities in line, you know? Charlotte finds it harder.

The day of the big Academy exam, however, Basil flips out and runs out of the testing site. The exam, and one particular question on the exam, forces her to confront something within herself. She suddenly faces the question of what makes her happy. She realizes that it is *not* the military, after all. When she leaves the military behind, she asks Charlotte to come with her. Another ultimatum. This time, Charlotte cannot follow Basil. And so, they are kept apart again, but this time emotionally and physically.

As Basil ponders the question of what makes her happy and who she is, she dabbles in revolutionary politics. She falls in with a crowd of agitators, of individuals who are not under the sway of the Star Union. The revolutionaries consist of Academy dropouts and aliens who have been colonized and assimilated. As she works with and protests with them, Basil discovers that she is not a political revolutionary, either.

Even so, Charlotte loves Basil, and she helps Basil escape, even though that means sending her into parts unknown. The price that Charlotte pays is huge. In order for Basil to walk away free, Charlotte shackles herself to an abusive man, Dan Cantara (he/him). Meanwhile, Basil lives a life of quiet contemplation in a small cabin in the woods. She continues to listen to the meditations she heard when she was preparing for the Academy. But, here and now, they take on a new significance for her.

Like Basil, the revolutionary Velda (she/her) also loses her revolutionary fervor. She tracks down Charlotte and informs her that Basil is living on Margarten. Charlotte packs up everything and chases after Basil. To no avail. They never meet again. Charlotte and Velda, however, make a full life together on Margarten.

Basil *was* lost on Earth. It took getting away from Earth—from the economics of it, from the politics of it, from the abusiveness of it—to find herself. She sought fulfillment in the military, but that did not work. She sought fulfillment in revolutionary politics, but that did not work. She sought fulfillment in a relationship, but that did not work. Basil needed to find herself. She needed to find her identity and her purpose outside those usual social and political avenues.

Is the answer practical? In a word, "No." And that's almost always the question, isn't it? How do I find a space outside social norms? How do I find a space outside the social and political structures? To invoke Audre Lorde (she/her), how do I get out of the master's house? Thoreau pretended to get away from it all, but he didn't really, did he? He still relied on the gendered labor of his mother to make his self-discovery possible. At this moment in time, no one gets to hop on a ship and fly to a remote colony, and even if we could, we would probably repeat the same old colonization of alien spaces.

Alright, we're all lost here on Earth. Where is that space in which we can each find ourselves? Who has the time and the means to head off on a retreat? Finding such a space is a lovely thing to be desired, but not, for most, within the realm of the possible.

Shade 30—*Primer* (2020)

Run, Jane, Run

I HAVE A vague recollection of the tattered, board-bound books we were given in first grade. These primers were designed to teach first graders to read according to the (generally discredited) whole word method. The books feature the children Dick (he/him) and Jane (she/her), their dog Spot (he/him), and their parents. *Fun with Dick and Jane* was a staple in the US education system for decades. Entire generations learned to read with the antics of Dick and Jane. They learned to "sit" and to "run." They also learned that mommy is "pretty" and cooks in the "kitchen." In other words, they learned the normativity of a white, middle-class, cishet, heterosexual family. In some ways, *Primer* turns those norms on their heads. Sort of.

In the graphic novel *Primer,* Jennifer Muró (writer), Thomas Krajewski (writer), and Gretel Lusky (illustrator) offer the 12-year-old Ashley (she/her) who lives in a congregate foster home (she turns 13 about midway through). She has been in and out of family homes. It's never worked out. As a result, she's a bit…pessimistic about the whole system. When her social worker arranges a meeting with a new potential foster family, she walks in with an attitude. But, *quelle surprise*, she hits it off with her potential foster dad, Kitch (he/him). He's a bit of a rebel; he has committed his own share of delinquent acts. Looks like a match. Kitch and Yuka Nolan (she/her) take her home, and Ashley settles into her new bedroom.

Now, to be clear, *Primer* really glosses over a lot of the hardships of moving from home to home. It really makes the bonding process seem easy. In reality, kids who have been in the system as long as Ashley has have a really difficult time adjusting, trusting, and bonding. Nevertheless, verisimilitude may not be *Primer's* primary goal.

So, in one way, the newly expanded Nolan family reproduces a traditional, nuclear family—with a few differences. For one, Kitch and Yuka are an interracial couple. For another, they cannot have children on their own. Third, they reverse traditional roles. Yuka is the scientist who earns a ton of money. She works for a large lab that conducts government research. On the other hand, Kitch is a community college professor who looks a bit crunchy-granola and who lounges around, plays video games, and paints. Despite these differences, they are a cishet couple who take in a foster kid.

In the narrative world of *Fun with Dick and Jane*, everything is hunky dory. They have the picture-perfect family in the picture-perfect home. In the narrative world of *Primer*, however, the picture is a bit less perfect. This daughter sneaks out at night and tags the walls of underpasses. This father is not the family patriarch. This mother steals a briefcase from her top-secret job and hides it in her bedroom. Finally, the military baddies come hunting and take mother and father hostage. So much for perfection.

The word "primer" also signifies an easy-to-digest introduction to a subject. Someone might pick up a primer on gemstones, or a primer on html web design, or, as a final example, a primer on sourdough starter (a pandemic favorite). That person won't be an expert on the topic by the end, but they will have a basic, working knowledge.

In this case, *Primer* is an introduction to a new hero in the DC universe. As such, we learn the origin story of the superhero Primer. We learn that the military had been working on paints that imbue people with superpowers. One paint produces invisibility, one allows teleportation, and one allows the wearer to fly. Ashley constructs a handy-dandy chart of all 33 paints and powers. We also learn of Ashley's troubled past, specifically with her father. We know that he will continue to be a complication in Ashley's life.

Still, as with any primer, many questions remain. Who will her nemeses be? Will her bond with the Nolans last? How will she fit into the DC universe? Will she cross over and interact with other DC superheroes? All of that will have to wait.[††]

A primer is the first coat of paint put down to cover whatever color may already be in place and to ensure a uniformity of coverage. It sets the conditions for what the room will look like later.

And *Primer* indeed covers over several things: At the end of the novel, Major General Temple (he/him) gives Primer her superhero suit, suggesting that the military is OK with Ashley keeping the paints. That beggars the imagination. He had been hellbent on getting them back. After all, this new form of soldier was going to be his legacy. He sent the rogue warrior Cal Strack (he/him) to get the paints back. In addition, Ashley seems to have made peace with her new foster family. The ordeals that foster kids go through are no joke, and the effects of growing up with a felon for a father and then being kicked around the foster care system leaves scars. It takes individuals years—assuming they ever do—to work through those issues of trust, and abandonment, and self-worth. It would require *a lot* of primer to cover that over.

However, *Primer* does allow a few things to push through the new paint. Her father will continue to trouble her. He will continue to try to influence her—and benefit from her. She will continue to struggle with her history. Is she really like him? Is she her father's daughter and, therefore, a hardened

†† Book two came out in February 2024, but is not considered here.

criminal? In a move of Shakespearean proportions, her father gets the final panel, the final words. He is coming after her. He is one imperfection that has not been smoothed over by the coat of primer.

Primer is, perhaps, the least queer shade here, but it depends on which version of queer we mean.

At the most superficial (and I mean that in several senses) level, the book—and the superhero—are covered in rainbow hued paints. The cover page has rainbow paints dripping down. Primer the superhero has paint speckled all over her skin. Indeed, after she lands the airplane, a young girl calls her the "Rainbow Dash" (14) (that nickname doesn't stick). The surface level hints at queerness are there.

The suggestions of sexuality are muted. Ashley is 13 years old and decidedly not sexual. Though, to be fair, plenty of kids—in the foster care system and out—are sexual by 13. However, that's a tougher sell in a comic book published by DC. Even so, her new classmate and BFF Luke (he/him) appears to be gay. Luke aspires to be a hairdresser and is picked on by a jock because of the practice wig he has in his school locker. When Luke visits Ashley's house, she pushes him into Kitch and Yuka's bedroom. When he expresses alarm, she quickly shoots down the idea of anything sexual. Is that because she's on a mission, because she's 13, because she's queer, too? Maybe time will tell….

But if a young female superhero covered in multi-colored paints and called "Rainbow Dash" isn't queer, then I don't know what they're even doing….

Shade 31 — *Crema* (2020)

Café con leche

WHAT'S YOUR TAKE on ghosts? Do you believe that ghosts are material? Do you believe that they walk (or float) around and occupy houses? Or, alternately, do you believe that they are metaphors for something else less tangible? The idea of the spirit or soul of a human or animal living on past death goes way back. *Way* back. Indeed, the belief seems natural, almost inevitable. In general, we do not want to think that our lifetime is *it*. We would like to believe that we continue on, in some form or another, after we die. The scientific consensus seems to be that ghosts do not exist. That consensus does not seem to have invalidated our imaginative investments in an afterlife. In October of 2021, YouGov polled 1,000 US citizens about their beliefs in the supernatural. While very few expressed a belief that werewolves and vampires are real, more than 40% of respondents said that they believe that both ghosts and demons are real (Ballard). Further, 20% said that they have personally encountered a ghost.

Some might well argue that ghost stories do not constitute science fiction. Maybe. It depends. As I have argued vehemently in the past, much of non-Anglo science fiction actually pushes beyond the boundaries of Western science. One of the wonderful elements of magical realist texts (e.g., Gabriel García Márquez's (he/him) *One Hundred Years of Solitude* or Isabel Allende's (she/her) *The House of the Spirits*) is that they offer a world beyond the ordinary, beyond Western empirical modes of understanding. A world in which blood flows uphill and children are born with green skin—and then the characters act as if that is absolutely ordinary. The message is that the world is far more complicated—and far more lovely—than we have imagined.

But ghosts have other meanings, as well. What about something other than the physical presence of a soul or spirit? What about a haunting in the metaphorical sense? Sometimes ideas or events or people just stick with us. Haunt us. They are in our minds. They take up our thoughts. They seem real and alive to us. They just do not let us go.

Writer Johnnie Christmas (he/him) and artist Dante Luiz (he/him) have created a graphic novel about a love that just will not die. Set in New York City and in Bela Alvorada, Brazil (a small, fictional town), the novel intertwines two love stories. Christmas has earned a dozen awards, including the Dayne Ogilvie Prize for LGBTQS+ Emerging Writers; similarly, Luiz has been nominated for many awards and was named the Otherwise Fellow for 2022. Their graphic novel, *Crema*, is replete with ghosts that haunt people and places.

In *Crema*, Esme (she/her) is a barista who does not sleep. Instead, she consumes massive amounts of coffee. And when she does, she sees things. Ghosts, in particular. So, are the ghosts really there, or are they consequences of the caffeine coursing through her body? When she *really* drinks a lot of coffee, the people around her can see the ghosts, too. Like a contact-high or a shared hallucination. Esme has one "ghoul friend" in particular, the ghost of a deceased TV actor, Gerry (she/her). She's a best bud, and Gerry offers sage advice.

At the same time, Esme feels a bit like a ghost herself. She feels as though people just do not see her—and they do not appreciate her. They take advantage of her sweetness, and they take advantage of her inability to sleep. Something along the lines of, "I know you weren't sleeping, anyway, so can you cover my shift?" Keeping a low profile has its advantages, though. For one, no one notices her talking to ghosts.

The café has its own ghost. In the basement of the café, along with all the supplies and crates of coffee, lives a ghost. The narrative initially leads us to believe that the ghost is Abelardo. In a narrative flashback, we learn of the romantic and financial triangle in Yara's family history. Yara's mother, Joana had loved Abelardo, but the wealthy Tomás wanted her coffee plantation and her heart. When Abelardo goes to New York for business, Tomás follows. So, who is the ghost in the basement?

The café is in Brooklyn, NY, and capitalism is cutthroat. The beloved coffee shop where Esme works has just been sold to a company called Octane. Esme fully intends to skip the "mandatory" change-of-ownership celebration, but her stars are not aligned or they were aligned but just not as she had anticipated. This disaster leads to romance. She goes to the party and meets Yara (she/her), the granddaughter of the owners of a Brazilian coffee plantation. Esme and Yara are mutually smitten.

But when the coffee shop burns down, Esme is out of a job, and Yara and her family have lost their investment. The ghost in the basement asks Esme to deliver his love letters to Joana (she/her), whom he left behind on a coffee plantation in Brazil. Neither Esme nor we the readers know whether the ghost is Abelardo or Tomás.

With no job, Esme agrees to accompany Yara back to Brazil, to see the haunted coffee orchard. As Esme and Yara wander around Bela Alvorada, they grow closer together; one sign of that is that they begin to dress similarly. As the notes following the comic note, the illustrator modeled their appearance after a telenovela set in the colonial past. As they wander around the small town, Esme sees many ghosts who occupy the same space as they do. The layers of history, the patterns of the past, and the pressures of family never quite leave us.

However, the coffee orchard has a romantic (if sad) origin story. Two lovers, Abelardo (he/him) and Joana, lived in rural Brazil. Abelardo had to travel but vowed that he would return. To show her that she was always in his thoughts, he would buy gifts for Joana and send them to her. Once, he plucked three coffee beans from a tree that was rumored to be everlasting. Abelardo sent his fitting gift to his sweetheart. However, while Abelardo was away, the very wealthy and spoiled Tomás (he/him) decided that the one thing he still wanted was Joana. He could not convince her to betray Abelardo. Despite all his money and power, she remained faithful. Tomás left Brazil to find Abelardo and destroy him. He was so confident in his own abilities, that he signed over his estate to Joana. When Abelardo and Tomás were killed, Joana inherited the land. The coffee beans were buried with her, and from her body grew the entire coffee orchard.

Just as Tomás attempted to come between Abelardo and Joana, the conniving Gustavo Henrique (he/him) tries to come between Esme and Yara. He also whispers sweet nothings into their ears and sets them against each other. After the tensions mount and they break up, Esme brings the letters to the old mansion. There, she finds the ghost of Joana in her bed. But Esme discovers that the ghost who had sent her on a mission was not the ghost of Abelardo. It was the ghost of Tomás, and the trick was part of his 100-year-old plan to get Joana.

The two love stories have many parallels. Both sets of lovers withstand trials and tribulations. Both sets of lovers endure the machinations of those who worked against them. Both sets of lovers see love itself as their legacy. When it appears that Yara had sold off the land, Abelardo and Joana tell her that land is not a legacy. Land is not meaningful. Their true legacy is their love and the family they created. Esme and Yara have learned their lessons well. They rebuild the orchard together, and they build a new coffee shop, this time called Joana's. Through their own labor of love, they honor Abelardo and Joana.

Crema utilizes the tropes of an historical ghost story to foreground a contemporary story of queer romance. At its core, *Crema* argues that "love is love." The love between the historical figures of Abelardo and Joana was steady and true, and it outlived them and their corporeal existence. Despite any and all obstacles, their love built a lasting legacy. The queer love of Esme and Yara is much younger, and time will tell. But they, too, have a love that has withstood the tests thrown at it, and they put down the roots of their own legacy.

Shade 32 — *Don't Go without Me* (2020)

This Radiant Vessel

WHAT'S YOUR DREAM process? Do you wake up with a dream living in your head? Can you remember every detail? Do they seem real to you? Does it feel like you actually lived through it? Do you ever hold someone in your dream accountable for what they did in your dream?

Or do you wake up and find yourself unable to recall your dream? It's there. You know it happened. You know it was about…*something*. And then it's gone. Even those fleeting scraps fall away like sand through your fingers. And maybe you feel as though you have *lost* something? That that dream had been a part of you, but now it's gone. That that dream was meaningful to you, but now you can no longer even remember it. What does that loss feel like?

Rosemary Valero-O'Connell (she/her) has had an extraordinarily prolific and successful career, especially for someone as young as she is. As evidence, in 2018, she was nominated for two Eisner Awards, both for "What Is Left": Best Coloring, and Best Single Issue/One Shot. In 2019, she won the Ignatz for *Laura Dean Keeps Breaking Up with Me*: Outstanding Graphic Novel. In 2020, she won two Eisners for *Laura Dean*: Best Penciller/Inker and Best Publication for Teens. In 2020, she also won the Ignatz for Outstanding Artist. She has worked for First Second, DC Comics, BOOM! Studios, and more. An amazing beginning for an artist who was born in 1994.

Valero-O'Connell's collection of stories, *Don't Go without Me*, published by Short Box (UK), offers three thematically related pieces. In this triptych, she takes her readers on a trip through several oneiric landscapes, marked by disillusionment, loss, and decaying memories. Not quite language poetry, not quite symbolist imagery, Valero-O'Connell eschews many of the conventions of contemporary commercial comics. Lavishly drawn though simply colored, the three pieces enact an otherworldly dream-state that always feels a little bit out of reach.

In the titular piece, "Don't Go without Me," two women discuss the rumors of a rift in the time-space continuum. The rift is, of course, on Cherry Street, the place where you feel for the "catch and crack the shell." Our nameless narrator covers her eyes and takes the plunge. She crosses over and is greeted by a menagerie of gryffen-like beings. Her girlfriend, Almendra (she/her), is not there. The more she tries to find Almendra, the less she remembers her. She tells the gryffens all about Almendra's dark hair and hazel eyes: "She is the love of my life" (16).

The gryffens send her along to the Butcher (she/her). However, this hybrid peddler of useless stuff cannot help her find Almendra, either. The Butcher sends her along to The Seventh House bar, where she encounters a cacophony of sounds and shapes, a kaleidoscope of transposed bodies, long-beaked bartenders and a talking serpent crawling out from skeletal eye sockets, talking wolves and heads of flame. But Almendra continues to fade. No one can help her.

And, then, like waking from that dream that slips away, Almendra's name is gone, too.

Outside, she finds another woman who is also looking for someone. The final frame of the story shows the two women, our narrator and a woman with long dark, curly hair. Perhaps it is Almendra, after all? Unlike Shade 31 (*Crema*), the love does not last. Instead, it fades like a dream.

The second story, "What Is Left," takes a different approach. It begins with a computer screen that informs us of the details of the Memory Core Project. This technology captures the flow of memories from a donor and uses that energy to fuel a spaceship. "It's all very safe" (78).

Kelo signs up. She tells her mother: "I know, can you imagine? It's almost embarrassing how romantic the whole thing is. Every first kiss, every scraped knee…. Everyone I've ever loved, pulling us through the stars!" (78). But what happens when the technology fails? What happens when the ship implodes in space? After the ship implodes, Kelo and the biomechanic Isla (she/her) have survived. The two communicate alongside the flow of memories from Kelo's past. In the flow of memories, we see Kelo's first kiss with a dark-haired woman.

They are like Schrödinger's astronauts—both dead and alive until the rescue ship arrives. Isla thinks: "You're all that exists in here. Every bit of it is you. In here, I can still see the sky. I can almost feel the sun" (79).

When the radio voice from Mother 6 breaks through, we get no answer. Everything is slipping away, like the tear that runs down Isla's face in the final panel. Once again, it fades away and disperses like the cosmic debris of an imploded spacecraft.

In the third story, "Con temor, con ternura" [With fear, with tenderness], Valero-O'Connell shifts locations. Earth? Maybe not. It is set along a coast, and just off the shore is a colossus, a giant figure sleeping in the waters. The prophecies say that one day the colossus will awaken. But then what? People speculate wildly, verbiage flies, and sects are formed. It's a mash-up of the doomsday cults in *Contact* (1997) and the sleeping giant in *Moana* (2016).

But one night, the residents celebrate. Perhaps it is the eve of the awakening. Perhaps it is an excuse to party. During the celebration, women kiss one another. The oldest woman in the world dances with her wife. And off the coast, the giant sleeping female figure sleeps on. The prophecy seems to have been wrong. Uncertain of what would happen (that night, the next night, some night ten years from now), they decided to live and to love. They think: "You are here, aboard this breathtaking doomed spaceship. This radiant vessel carrying everyone you've ever loved in its belly" (105).

The story ends with a countdown: "Three. Two. One" (110).

Fin.

Fade to gray.

Valero-O'Connell's artwork is dazzling. It invites the reader to pour over every panel, to wonder at every reference and every connection. The storytelling similarly draws the reader in, inviting them to linger over the story, to wonder about the ambiguities of each tale to—perhaps more than anything—settle into the ambiguity and find a home.

Valero-O'Connell offers three tales of relationships, mostly between women. These worlds are the worlds of women. She writes and draws these tales with much love and beauty. And, yet, the three stories contain a pessimism. Each ends with uncertainty. They land on a place of uncertainty. I will admit that maybe that says more about me. After all, that ambiguity and that uncertainty could be read as positive.

And maybe that's the queerest part of the whole book.

Shade 33 — *Séance Tea Party* (2020)
The Golden Age of Twelve

THE OLD ADAGE is that the Golden Age of science fiction is 12. The idea is that, as adults, our taste in science fiction (and, presumably, many other things, as well) is informed—if not wholly formed—by whatever it was that we read when we were 12. We're impressionable at that age. We're making a psychological and emotional shift from being a child to being a young adult. We're shifting from being reliant on others to being an independent agent in the world. Indeed, *Séance Tea Party* opens with a C. S. Lewis (he/him) quote that tells the reader it's time to "put away childish things."

Every time I've heard that quote from Lewis, I've taken it to mean that we *need* to grow up. In order to be a functioning adult (whatever that means), we need to leave behind the behaviors, tastes, and activities of our childhoods. And, yet, the full quote from Lewis suggests the opposite. Lewis writes that he once read fairy tales in secret for fear of being thought childish. Now that he is (was) an adult, he reads fairy tales openly. No. According to Lewis, the thing to put away is the fear of being childish. The thing to put away is the desire to be grown up.

In *Séance Tea Party* (2020), Malaysian writer and illustrator Reimena Yee (she/her) has captured perfectly that conflict between staying a child and becoming an adult. Yee tells the story of a 12-year-old girl who is a bit of an outsider, Lora Xi (she/her). She is not an outsider so much in terms of racial or ethnic identity, but in terms of her maturity level and interests.

Lora may be 12, but she still engages in imaginative play with her stuffed animals. She may be 12, but she still has imaginary friends. As she rides her bike to school with her stuffed animals in the front basket, she pretends that they are aboard a pirate ship that is stuck in the ice. She arrives at school and puts her stuffies in her locker. And that moment is a tipping point for her friend Bobby (he/him). He ghosts her. In his view, she's just too immature. When Bobby does not contact Lora on her thirteenth birthday, she's crushed. Even Bobby has turned his back on her.

Because she plays "like a child," because she believes in the supernatural, because she eschews the technological interests of her peers (TV, movies, the internet, social media), she feels like an outsider. And rather than try to socialize and feel like a weirdo, she self-isolates; rather than risk the reminder that she is child-like, she rejects growing up. That is, until the household ghost appears. On her birthday, she assembles her coterie of stuffies and familiars and has a séance tea party. It's a big hit because that's when Alexa (she/her) reveals herself. In her time of loneliness and isolation, Lora finds her BFF. They become inseparable.

Just having Alexa as a friend boosts Lora's confidence. Unlike Esme (Shade 31), who sees ghosts that no one else can see, other people can also see Lora's ghost. So, while trick or treating, Lora knocks on the door of Sunni (she/her), a slightly older girl who had been her mentor in school. Sunni invites Lora and Alexa to join her at her party. After much hemming and hawing, they agree. Despite her lack of social skills, despite her fear of the socially current, and despite having a ghost following her around, she has a great time at the party. It is the beginning of her social life. It is her first step in "growing up." It is also the beginning of the end of her relationship with Alexa.

Alexa, too, is in the midst of a crisis. She died very young and has befriended all the children who have lived in the house where she died. But she recalls nothing of her death, nothing of her life. She has seen a number of children come into her (after)life, outgrow her, and move on. She now sees the writing on the wall—Lora will do the same. To exacerbate things, Alexa has been fascinated by all the changes in the world—she loves Lora's tablet and the internet. Maybe she, too, needs to "grow up."

Diana Rodriguez (she/her) brings these two storylines together. Diana is the author of children's books, most of which feature some element of magic or the supernatural. As (narrative) luck would have it, Diana was best friends with Alexa when she was alive. Diana is able to fill in all the details of Alexa's life and death. As Lora spends time with her new friends, Alexa spends time with her old friend. She sees that Diana has lived a full life and has aged (physically, emotionally). Alexa realizes that she cannot stay as she is. She gives up the ghost.

But Alexa and Diana teach Lora that she is *not* alone, and that plenty of people exist in the world who keep their inner child alive. Beginning with Diana, Lora will find and make friends who live just a little outside the box.

In what ways, then, is *Séance Tea Party* queer? Oh, so many.

Number one, it queers the way we look at the world and at growing up. Asking the reader to think about growing up is not a particularly new, or particularly queer, idea; however, the graphic novel does ask us to think about the motivation and desire to leave childish things behind. Can one be an adult and still be childish? Why, yes.

Number two, it queers the graphic novel form in four ways. Oh, it's fairly straightforward in its (roughly) chronological story. It's fairly conventional for a coming of age narrative—though with a slight twist regarding adulting. No, Yee breaks a number of the formal conventions. (a) the drawings themselves are not super sophisticated. Compare these drawings with those of the Marvel or DC comics, and the difference is stark. Nevertheless, they are perfectly suited to this comic. The drawing style suits the story of a 12-year-old girl resisting growing up. They are drawings of the world from Lora's perspective.

(b) Yee breaks the page. Almost all of the drawings cover two pages. The panels of a comic are traditionally contained on a page. Six or eight panels on one page, with a flow from upper-left to bottom-right. Occasionally comics will feature a two-page spread. But those pages are remarkable for their scarcity. In *Séance*, they are the norm. They allow for a free flow of ideas and images. They allow for pages to work as gestalts.

(c) Yee breaks the panel. Yes, sometimes Yee contains the action inside traditional panels. However, those panels will appear separately, or in small clumps in the midst of a full two-page image. They are the exception, not the norm. It's as if the rigidity and linearity of comic panels cannot contain the imagination of a 12-year-old girl. Even on a page that DOES have six semi-traditional panels, those panels are imposed over a full background image.

(d) Yee breaks the separation of foreground and background. Behind the panels, beside the panels, the images flow freely. Landscapes, wind-blown leaves, a group of familiars— they are a representation of the wild and full imagination of a child. It's busy; it's hectic; it's chaotic; it's queer.

Number three, *Séance Tea Party* takes place largely in the world of girls and women. True, Lora's gay friend Bobby pops in and out a bit, but the narrative centers on Lora, Alexa, and Diana, and to a lesser extent, Lora's new friends, Sunni, Emily, Aya, and Hiya. No Bechdel Test necessary here.

Number four, *Séance Tea Party* demonstrates the love among these women. The graphic novel does not really suggest that they are lovers. Even so, they love each other. Sunni and her friends are close, and Lora and Alexa love one another. On several occasions, they look as if they might kiss.

Consider Adrienne Rich's essay, "Compulsory Heterosexuality and Lesbian Existence" (1984). Rich notes the ways in which woman-to-woman relationships get devalued in a patriarchal society. Frequently, girls are best friends. But once the boyfriends start, once they get married, once they have children, they find they no longer have time for the other women in their lives. In this graphic novel, Yee demonstrates the centrality and importance of women's relationships.

Lora ages chronologically, and Lora grows up. But Lora will retain the Golden Age of 12.

Shade 34—*Apsara Engine* (2020)
This

THIS. THIS IS it. This is what I have been looking for. This is what I have been writing about. This collection queers comics in all the ways that I have been talking about. This is *Apsara Engine*.

Apsara Engine by Bishakh Som (she/her) is a remarkable book. It is a massive book, large in size and length. It is published by Feminist Press (NYC) and not by one of the many comics publishers already represented here. I wonder about that. What does it mean? Did Som not want to publish with a comics press? Does Som have some bias against comics? Does she even see her work *as* comics? Som comes out of a background of architecture, so maybe she doesn't. Or would comics publishers not touch it? Was it just too different that comics publisher wouldn't know what to do with it? What would they even call it? How would they market it? It certainly does not fit into a superhero or an action mold. On the one hand, none of those things matters. On the other hand, they matter a great deal. Who is selling and marketing the book? To what audience? Will comic book readers even see it? I, for example, could not get a copy from my local comic book dealer—he didn't have it; he couldn't get it; it didn't show up in his distributor's database. I found it because I was researching, and I ended up ordering the book directly from Feminist Press. That's not something a casual reader would do. In short, who publishes it *does* matter.

The book itself is a massive collection of eight illustrated stories. Som's other books include *The Prefab Bathroom: An Architectural History* (2014) and *Spellbound: A Graphic Memoir* (2020). Som also contributed a piece to *We're Still Here: An All-Trans Comic Anthology* (2018). In the current volume, each of the eight stories is distinct from the others. And yet, unsurprisingly, they all share some qualities. "'A lot of these stories I wrote before I "hatched," before I came out as trans, so a lot of the characters reflect what I was going through,' says Som, who opened up about her identity roughly halfway through writing the collection" (Shadel, "Surreal Femme").

The first story, "Come Back to Me," tells the story of a woman, walking along the beach, who is pulled underwater by an aquatic creature. "Throat" centers on an encounter in a café. A woman accompanied by a half dog/half girl creature runs into an acquaintance. But the creature, Kiki (she/her), tries to make a declaration when the woman steps away for a glass of wine. In "Meena and Aparna," two old friends celebrate a birthday, but nothing goes quite as planned, for anyone involved. The title story, "Apsara Engine," is no story at all, but a very short piece near the center of the book that serves to connect the tissues. It foregrounds Som's beautiful architectural drawing and offers tidbits about characters mentioned throughout the book. The very long "Pleasure Palace" tells a story within a story. A woman has taken a small vacation at a nice hotel—her "pleasure palace." A young, white man interrupts her dinner and forces his way into her life, apologizing the whole way, though she puts him in his place in the end. "Love Song" is another unusual piece. A woman eats her lunch on a bench as a creature carries her away. The narrative, though, is all about her connections to people throughout her life. And finally, "I Can See It in You" tells of a time-traveling ex-lover who stalks her ex.

Some of these stories have fantastical or otherworldly elements. Some do not. Some have futuristic elements while others do not. Most of them feature unusual, out of the ordinary characters. Most of them feature surprise endings. In many cases, they do not end well. Nearly every one of them features Som's lovely architecture. Some of them rupture the link between the narrative and the images. For example, in "Come Back to Me," the narrator talks about her relationship with her husband and how they met, how he came to settle down, how they came to buy a beach house. All the while, the images are of a half-naked woman on the beach, a woman pulled down under the water and a woman submerged under the water in her own bathroom and her husband freaking out. What do they have to do with one another? Why speak of the mundanities of relationships while drawing the fantastical encounter with an aquatic being? The connections are there. Just as she is talking about James being "dragged to the bar" by his friends, the creature drags her into the water. She says (of their dating), "I didn't know what I was doing," even as she plunges deeper into the water (15). Even so, that rupture, that dislocation is important to Som's storytelling. It demonstrates a kind of narrative/graphic storytelling mode. The images are not mere adjuncts to the narrative. The images do not merely fill in details of the background as the action unfolds. No, the words and images each do something particular. They each add something to the narrative.

Other examples take a more traditional approach in the relationship between words and images. In "Pleasure Palace," for example, the images show Edith (she/her) and the young man Craig (he/him) sitting at the dinner table, engaged in a (frustrating) conversation. Later, as they drive to her home, we see them sitting in the car, sometimes exchanging information, other times in tense, awkward silence. But even here, Som takes her time. She fills panels and pages with wordless images. The narrative is in the image, in the faces, and in the expressions.

The sixth story in the collection is "Swandive." It is worth the price of admission. We begin with the title page. It features two nude women. We will eventually know who these women are. They are floating, perhaps in water, given the colors, but perhaps in space (though probably not *outer* space). Their figures are overlaid with a map. The palimpsest speaks volumes. When looking at the bodies, they appear to be tattooed. When focusing on the map, it appears to be unconventional. None of the lines are straight. They curve and bend, much like the bodies. They map out an unknown and futuristic space.

The narrative begins in a space I am all too familiar with—an academic conference. Onima Mukherjee (she/her) is giving a talk on trans geography. Standing in front of a map, Onima says, "I imagine trans geographies to be a means of using cartography as a generative tool rather than as a descriptive device. A way to chart possibilities, ways of being that have yet to manifest themselves" (128). Furthermore, Onima says that the "trans imagination" will conjure up new spaces and places, new arrangements of space, new uses for space. These maps will be drawn from (if not literally upon) trans bodies and their everyday lived experiences in the world. She says, "I imagine trans geographies as maps of a multiplicity of unknown destinations, each unlocking access to a further myriad of open nodes, a kaleidoscope of addresses—a churning constellation of whereabouts" (129).

After her talk, Onima retires to the bar for a drink. She's joined by Amrit (they/them), another conference attendee. They had been intimidated by all the A-list academics, but they approach Onima because they loved the work, but they especially loved seeing another Desi trans person. On that basis, they bond. They share a split-world identity; they share a need for invented family; they share an experience of gender nonconformity in Indian culture. When it is time to retire, Amrit impulsively kisses Onima, who is startled. Even so, she invites Amrit to her room.

This is not going where you think it is.

Onima places a large blank sheet of paper on the wall of her hotel room. She then draws her own blood into a container. Understandably, Amrit freaks out a little. However, Onima calmly talks to Amrit and begins to draw a map. She begins with a river, which she names the Amrit River. Onima asks Amrit to join in. They imagine a park in which young trans girls can play soccer on Sundays. They imagine an art school built on property donated by a wealthy lesbian philanthropist. They imagine public gardens with free food and public housing for gender-nonconforming kids. They imagine a disco in which they play Sister Sledge, Bauhaus, and Nusrat Fateh Ali Khan.

When they have finished, Amrit is astounded. They say, "How is any of this even possible? It's like…like something out—out of the future." Onima responds, "It's a future, I guess" (158). In other words, trans geography is performing similar work to science fiction. Both are modes and methods of envisioning future spaces, future arrangements, and future possibilities. Amrit and Onima have speculated about future spaces, arranged on the bodies and lives and experiences of queer folx. As science fiction so often does, the story takes the metaphor and makes it literal. This map has literally been drawn in the blood of a trans woman. It has literally been drawn from a trans body.

The remainder of the story imagines a series of possible futures. In some futures, Amrit and Onima meet. In some they already know one another. In some they are lovers. In the final two-page panel, images of Onima and Amrit float over jagged and layered architecture. The words ask: "Do. You. Want. To. Know?" In the final image, Amrit and Onima embrace. The word "Yes" appears (169). Who says it? Who knows?

This Yes is a Joycean Yes. In James Joyce's (he/him) Ulysses, the 18th chapter is Molly Bloom's (she/her) "soliloquy." The long and unpunctuated section represents Molly's thoughts as she lies in bed next to the now-returned Leopold Bloom. Molly thinks about possibilities and love, and she thinks, "and I thought well as well him as another and then I asked him with my eyes to ask again yes and then he asked me would I yes to say yes my mountain flower and first I put my arms around him yes and drew him down to me so he could feel my breasts all perfume yes and his heart was going like mad and yes I said yes I will Yes" (1078).

In this chapter, Joyce broke a lot of "rules." This chapter shifts from Leopold to Molly. The entire chapter consists of eight "sentences," though they are not really. The entire chapter has two punctuation marks: a period at the end of sentence four and one at the end of sentence eight. In "Swandive," Bishakh Som breaks some, if not rules, then conventions. The two Desi trans people imagine a future predicated upon queer folx. It is a consummation devoutly to be wished. It is a future to which—and in which—Onima and Amrit can say Yes.

Shade 35 — *América Chávez: Made in the USA* (2021)

América's Potential

IN 2020, KEVIN Feige (he/him) announced that Xochitl Gomez (she/her) would be joining the cast of *Doctor Strange in the Multiverse of Madness*. In that movie, she would play the character América Chávez (she/her), who had first appeared in the comic *Vengeance #1* (2011). She then joined the *Young Avengers* and appeared in *A-Force* (2015). In 2017, she got her own series, *America*. That series lasted just one year, but was nominated for a GLAAD Media Award for Outstanding Comic. She is the first LGBTQ+ character to headline a Marvel series. Then in 2018, she joined the *West Coast Avengers*.

So, in 2020, when it was announced that América would be included in *Doctor Strange*, it was a big deal. She would be the first Latine character and the first LGBTQ+ superhero in the MCU. Unsurprisingly, not everyone was thrilled. Some fans of the comic and the franchise have been concerned about the lightness of Gomez's skin color. They argue that casting Gomez whitewashes América's character. To be fair, that does happen a *lot*. The 2017 series (*America*) was written by Gaby Rivera (of Puerto Rican descent) while the 2021 series (*América Chávez: Made in the USA*) was written by Kalinda Vazquez (of Colombian and Puerto Rican descent). In the former series, America is drawn as a bit older. Her body type is a bit curvy. In the latter series, América is drawn as younger and skinnier. Her body type conforms more closely to a white aesthetic of femininity and desirability.

Others are concerned that she's queer. The governments of several countries demanded that Marvel edit out references to América's "two moms" and to her queer identity. Marvel, to its credit, refused. The end result was that the film cannot be shown in those countries. Some MCU fans in those countries directly blame Gomez for that. And the abuse has been heaped on her. It's obviously her fault—a 15-year-old actress who had nothing to do with writing, casting, or editing the film! Importantly, some of her co-stars have defended Gomez, as an actor and as a person.

The 2021, the five-issue limited series by writer Kalinda Vazquez (she/her) and artist Carlos Gómez (he/him) serves primarily as a backstory for América. The comic begins with the Santanas finding a young girl on a beach, taking her home, and adding her to their family. I understand that they did not want to involve the police or child protective services. A kid placed in the foster care system in NYC would have a rough time of it. But how does someone just add a child to their family? How do they take her to the doctor? Get her vaccinations? Enroll her in school? Willful suspension of disbelief is required.

Young América has only the haziest of memories of what had happened to her prior to landing on that beach. Much later, with the help of a truth serum, América remembers it all.

The Santanas (Ceci [she/her] and Papi [he/him]) are of Puerto Rican descent and own a bodega in Washington Heights in the Bronx. When young América Santana begins to demonstrate superpowers, she believes that she must use those powers for good. She stops robberies and bullies. Of course, that gets the cops involved. The cops rarely show up, but they bring trouble when they do. The Santanas tell América that "people like us" need to keep our heads down, not call attention to ourselves, and focus on *familia*.

In short, then, América has to make a choice, and she decides that she would rather be a superhero than a Santana. From that moment on, she is América Chávez. She takes on the last name of her two mothers: Elena Pecoso Chávez (she/her) and Amalia Pecoso Chávez (she/her). The action in the series is limited. She and Spiderman battle giant moles in LA. At the very end, the superheroes are all set to battle a giant snail. No, the focus here is on América, her origins, her loss of powers, and her interpersonal relations.

For the purposes of this Shade, I am less interested in how América Chávez fits into the Marvel universe canon. I am not that interested in how she fits into the Avengers or the West Coast Avengers. The details of that discussion are all over the web. No, I'm interested instead in what role her queerness plays in the comic and in the Marvel universe. Does it matter that América is queer? Does it matter that she had two moms? If so, how so?

First, América Chávez *is* queer. Early in this series, an intrepid young local reporter asks América about her relationship with Ramone Watts (she/her), another of the West Coast Avengers. América's response to the reporter is to declare "the interview…officially over" (8). Why? Why bring it up almost immediately in the comic, only to have América quash it just as quickly? Well, for one, she is in the midst of a knock-down, drag-out fight with some gigantic, genetically modified moles. The subject is a bit of a distraction. But no, that's not it. She's been multitasking the whole time. Perhaps their relationship (América and Ramone) is not ready for public scrutiny? Maybe they haven't decided on their status? Are they exclusive? Are they dating? Is it casual but open? Perhaps. At the very end of the series, they have a heart-to-heart about América's past—a lot of which, to be fair, she had only just recovered. They agree to take a bit of time apart. Ramone will head back to the West Coast, and América will stay in NYC to protect her neighborhood and family.

Could it be that they (the powers-that-be at Marvel) don't want to have a lesbian relationship front and center? Despite their Pride Month specials? Ramone barely comes up during the entire series. True, América is busy with rodent infestations, a family trapped in a fire, and a newly remembered sister. Nevertheless, the narrative *might* have included Ramone in all those battles, in all those situations, and in all those decisions. As it reads now, América's lesbian partner is a minor detail and in no way integral to who América is or what happens to her.

Perhaps her relationship with Ramone is not germane to the plot of the comic—except that it totally is. The crux of this limited series—*the whole point*—is for América to examine the importance of family and of relationships (her moms, the Santanas, her sister, the Bronx, her *latinidad*). And, one might presume, with Ramone. It is true that after their heart-to-heart, they share a kiss. A romantic kiss, but only on the final pages.

And then we have Elena and Amalia Chávez, both accomplished physicians, both have daughters, both are concerned with their daughters' health. In a desperate move, they bring their daughters to the "Utopian Parallel," the private island of a billionaire (Gales [he/him]), who claims to be working toward a cure for Edges (a disease). Of course, that goes about as one would expect. One of her moms sacrifices her life to help her family get away, while the other mom is shot in cold blood. What role do the Chávezes play in the series, and for Marvel?

On the one hand, representation matters. All kinds of representation matters. While it *is* important to have queer families, it *is* important to have queer families that are front and center, and it is also important to have queer families that are not the center of the story. In other words, queer SF comics should exhibit the entire range of possibilities. Nevertheless, in this particular case, I would suggest that Marvel has missed some real opportunities. To be fair, Marvel *did* resist the erasure of the queer family in the movie version. That fact suggests that having a queer family is at least as important as the money lost by closing off those national markets.

In this 2021 series, the two moms represent loving parents who care deeply for their children. They are committed to their health and well-being, and they are willing to risk a great deal to care for them. What would any parent do to save their child? In this sense, the argument is that a queer parent is just as committed as a non-queer parent. The two moms also serve as role models for América. She later recalls that her moms made sacrifices and wanted their daughters to do good in the world. Part of the reason that América splits with the Santanas is the tension between being an agent of good in the world versus being a *familia*-oriented person. In this sense, they do play an important role in América's development as a person.

So, her moms *are* models of courage and integrity; however, that commitment does not *seem* to stem from their queerness. But it *could have*. Perhaps Gales could have invited them to the Utopian Parallel because they were a queer couple and he thought that queerness had something to do with the Edges syndrome (positively or negatively). Perhaps their experience as queer women and as a queer family might have informed their response to their daughter's illness. Perhaps their response to Gales's experimentation might have been informed by their Puerto Ricanness (think of *la operación*) or by their queerness. The history of AIDS research and medical arguments about queerness might have been a factor in their participation in experimentation. Or, perhaps, their valor in the face of impending death might have been tied to their valor as queer women in the US in the field of medicine.

América Chávez adds an important character and element to the Marvel canon. Just as I think Marvel suggests that

América can add something to the franchise, I can see the enormous potential the queer Puerto Rican superhero América Chávez has for queer representation in SF comics.

For now, no sequel is scheduled. However, we can hope that the series is extended to fulfill that potential....

Shade 36 — *Cyclopedia Exotica* (2021)
Seeing Things through More Than One Lens

THIS BOOK IS so delightful, one hardly knows where to begin....

According to Aminder Dhaliwal (she/her), *Cyclopedia Exotica* started off as something of a one-off joke, and then it just grew. It became something so much bigger.

I suspect that we all know that the Cyclops has one eye (cf. Shade 9). Like many mythological creatures, the Cyclops has taken on a life of its own. The Cyclops appears as a monster in science fiction, in comics, in movies, and in video games. Cyclopes appear in *Doctor Who*, in *Star Wars*, in *Godzilla*, in *Harry Potter*, in *Jumanji*, in *Dungeons and Dragons*, and so many more. And they are, indeed, nearly always monstrous (Minions notwithstanding).

Cyclopedia Exotica imagines a world in which Cyclopes and Two-Eyes live alongside each other, if not very harmoniously. The opening pages of *Cyclopedia Exotica* provide stilted, encyclopedia-like descriptions of an *alternate* history of Cyclopes. We learn that the Cyclopes originated in Italy and on its surrounding islands, and that they herded sheep. Two-Eyes hunted Cyclopes—though perhaps they were really hunting for their sheep. The history claims that Cyclopes' supposed tendency toward violence is a complete myth. They have never been violent. Acts of violence against Cyclopes, however, spiked after a series of murders attributed to Cyclopes in 1987.

The comic breaks into this encyclopedic narrative with Etna (she/her) herself saying that no encyclopedia could ever capture the subtleties of real life. I guess a comic can do it better. In a bit of ironic meta-commentary, this Shade will not do the *Cyclopedia Exotica* justice, either.... Just read the comic first.

According to the Appendix (250), Dhaliwal began with some sketches: a joke about a Cyclops with one eye, one breast, and three vaginas. She imagined this Cyclops, Etna, as a pin-up, as a sex symbol. Etna appeared in an erotic magazine, the name of which might have rhymed with *Playboy*. Her appearance was so successful that another magazine was spun off—*Playclops*. And with that act, an entire genre of sexual exploitation began.

But notice her name: Etna. Unless you are a fan of life insurance, you probably know of Etna from one place: Mount Etna. Indeed, Dhaliwal fashions all of her characters after Greek myths. In Greek mythology, the Cyclopes made their home in Mount Etna, which is a still-active volcano. In the comic, Etna the Cyclops is the touchstone, the home place for the other Cyclopes in the narrative. And while she does not exactly explode, she *does* explode the taboo around Cyclopes and sexual objectivity. She demonstrates that Cyclopes could also be sex symbols and that she could be a role model for others to follow in her footsteps.

The other nine characters include Latea (she/her) (fashioned after Galatea, the sea nymph); Tim (he/him) and Pari (she/her), the only married couple in the comic (Pari is fashioned after the Island of Lipari, associated with Cyclopes); Pol (he/him), who is truly motivated to find love (is fashioned after Polyphemus, the man-eating Cyclops who appears in *The Odyssey*); Bron (he/him), who had attempted corrective surgery to become Two-Eyed (fashioned after the Cyclops who creates thunder); Jian (she/her) and Grae (she/her), the two sisters who create activist art (the Graeae are witches in Greek mythology, and Jian is a bird from Chinese mythology that has one eye and one wing; like the two sisters here, the Jian depend on one another); Vy (she/her) (whose name derives from Virgil, the author of *The Aeneid*, in which the characters revisit Polyphemus); and Arj (he/him) the earnest and clumsy fuck-up (named after the "bright" Cyclops Arge, brother to Brontes and Steropes) (250-263).

Ten characters: nine Cyclopes and one Two-Eyes. The Cyclopes each represent some of the difficulties of living and loving in an Otherized body. The Cyclopes live alongside Two-Eyes, but they are not equals. For example, early in the book, Latea and Pari go shopping, they find a copy of the first issue of *Playclops*, and that discovery sparks a conversation. They decide that, although some things have changed, in reality, capitalism had simply found a new niche to exploit. And while many lauded the fact that equal numbers of Two-Eyes bought *Playclops* and *Playboy* (not actually named in this book), the bias still remains. Cyclopes undergo eye surgery (like Bron) to look Two-Eyed. They see no trend in Two-Eyes having surgery to look like Cyclopes. They see Cyclopes buying into the marketing for a bra that "lifts and separates" the single Cyclops breast into two breasts. They do not see women with two breasts using surgery or bras to form a single breast.

The biases are all too real. The consequences are all too familiar. The costs are too high.

Pol cannot find love. He has used every app on the market. All he finds are fetishists and racists. Pol is not conventionally attractive, and when he and Latea begin to date, she notes that he does not fit her usual type. Her friends make similar comments. The commentary here is multivalent. It reflects attitudes about appearance, the valuation of appearance over substance, the aesthetic for Cyclopes being driven by Two-Eyes, etc. All of these issues are layered onto Pol. Latea, who has been through a lot herself, finally gets it.

Bron had attempted surgery. For a while, the surgery worked. He had two functioning eyes, and his self-esteem soared. Eventually, one of his eyes failed, and he was left wearing an eye patch and seeing out of one eye, again. Well, the social pressures that led Bron to attempt the surgery are familiar. Entire industries exist based on these anxieties, and Bron had internalized the standards that surrounded him. While we can certainly see the parallels to white standards of beauty in the media, can Bron be read as a *trans* character? No, not exactly. The fundamental argument here is different. Bron, as he eventually realizes, wanted to be something that he is not. Gender confirmation surgery, on the other hand, is becoming the person they truly are.

A number of the interactions among our characters take place at one of the art shows given by Jian and Grae. Initially, they seem superficial, like a stereotype of hipster artists. That changes, to my mind, anyway. When the sisters begin to think they no longer need each other, they go their separate ways (see the Jian birds above). One continues to make art—though no one really wants her work now that she's a solo act. The other goes to Hollywood but finds she is asked to be a token and work on stereotypical pieces. Through their shows such as "Siight" and "Eye Sore," they challenge cultural assumptions and stereotypes. The interactive "Eye Sore" explores the cultural violence against Cyclopes, and we see Bron perpetuate the cycle (223).

The couple Tim and Pari illustrate a number of other issues. Tim is a Two-Eye and Pari is a Cyclops. Pari becomes pregnant and goes on maternity leave. Cyclops biology affects the pregnancy process. A pregnant Cyclops will have two or three babies sequentially: one fetus develops while the other waits. Once the first child is born, then the next fetus begins to develop. So, Pari has her first baby, a Cyclops boy, and then her second baby, a Two-Eye girl. For one, Pari is the only Cyclops at her job, and so she feels as though everything she does reflects on all Cyclopes. For another, she had always seen herself as being a stay-at-home mom. In addition, they face all kinds of prejudice from people who do not favor mixed-race children.

Throughout *Cyclopedia Exotica*, we see the children's book, *Suzy's One Eye*. It is ubiquitous. It is a run-away best seller. Is it a classic of children's literature? Is it another instance of capitalism exploiting a market? We eventually discover that it was written by a 68-year-old white male Two-Eye, Leonard Cartemis (he/him). The literature accompanying the book says: "No one can write the story of a young Cyclops girl and her friends better than Cartemis" (83). The comic raises the question of who can write for whom.

Bron hates the book. He recalls reading it when he was younger. He recalls the scene in which Suzy gets beaten up by her so-called friends. He cannot understand the cultural hype. At the very end of *Cyclopedia Exotica*, Bron decides he needs to re-read the book. Dhaliwal then writes and includes the entirety of *Suzy's One Eye*. It is a heart-warming tale of bravery and acceptance. Suzy is never beaten up. Bron says, "Hunh. That wasn't what I remember" (244). At that moment, Etna (again) interrupts the text. She notes that "Sometimes there's a story we tell ourselves" (245). In the Appendix, Dhaliwal explains that the book's story of "be true to yourself" did not fit with Bron's own experience of the world, and so he constructed a narrative about the book to justify his own experience.

This reading does not do the comic justice. All ten tales are interwoven beautifully and skillfully. The models who follow Etna, the (sometimes questionable) marketing campaigns, the running TV show *Tough Talk*, the dating apps, the instances of prejudice, individual and institutional, and the mythological layers all add to the comic. The characters are types, but they are not stereotypes. They represent different kinds of individuals who are trying to cope, to adjust, and to make a difference. The issues faced by the Cyclopes, and the responses by Two-Eyes, all reflect current racial, ethnic, sexist, and homophobic attitudes common in 21st century society. The fiction of the Cyclopes allows the reader a bit of critical distance to understand the relationship to our own world. The style in which the comic is drawn assists in that understanding. The figures here are not detailed, not photorealistic. Instead, they are iconic cartoon figures. These stripped-down figures allow the reader to recognize them as human, even as the lack of details allows the reader to universalize them, and just perhaps, see themselves in them.

Aminder Dhaliwal's Cyclopes are a delightful addition to contemporary political discussions.

Shade 37 — *Barbalien: Red Planet* (2020)
Lessons Not Learned, Battles Not Won

AH, THE 1980S. Quite a few things from popular culture from the 1980s have stuck around. It's pretty hard to move around public spaces and not hear something from *The Wall* by Pink Floyd (1980) or Michael Jackson's (he/him) *Thriller* (1983). In movies, the *Top Gun* (1986) and the *Batman* (1989) franchises are still going strong. From TV, well, we won't mention *The Cosby Show* (1984-1992) but *The Golden Girls* (1984-1992) is still a fan favorite, especially after the death of Betty White (she/her) (2021).

Politically speaking, though, the 1980s were a bit of a horror show. The election of Ronald Reagan (he/him) was a turning point, though he was really only a symptom. The election of Newt Gingrich (he/him) and the Moral Majority's Contract with America did not bode well from the social and political progress made in the 1960s and '70s. Furthermore, the emergence of AIDS—and the Reagan Administration's response to it—was devastating.

Incidents of some mysterious new disease appeared in the first half of 1981, followed by a clinical diagnosis shortly thereafter. Because the first reported cases in the US were associated with a cluster of IV drug users and gay men, some assumptions were made about the disease. Several of the early names for the disease directly linked it to the gay community. At early stages, the terms GRID (gay-related immune deficiency) and 4H (homosexuals, hemophiliacs, heroin users, and Haitians) were proposed. When doctors discovered that the disease affected more than those named groups, the term AIDS was introduced in mid-1982.

Because of the early associations of AIDS with marginalized groups, the religious, governmental, and medical response was, to put it mildly, awful. Jerry Falwell (he/him) of the Moral Majority called AIDS "the wrath of God" (King). He believed that those infected deserved it because of their sinful lifestyle. Ronald Reagan and the Reagan White House did not take AIDS seriously. Quite (in)famously, Reagan refused to meet with activists and refused to provide funding for research. Reagan was surrounded by bigots, including Pat Buchanan (he/him) and Larry Speakes (he/him), and Reagan did not publicly acknowledge the AIDS crisis until 1985 (King, "Drama"). Although the CDC understood the mechanism and the severity of AIDS by 1983, the lack of funding hampered its research and response (Bennington-Castro).

With this historical backdrop of the AIDS crisis, writers Tate Brombal (he/him) and Jeff Lemire (he/him) take up the question of AIDS, AIDS history, and AIDS activism in their 2020 comic *Barbalien: Red Planet*. In the comic's "Afterword," Brombal writes, "Queer writers don't often get to write queer stories for queer superheroes in mainstream comics—let alone one set during the AIDS crisis, a disease buried under metaphor or weaponized by supervillains. *Red Planet*, I knew, was a chance to right those wrongs" (124).

Barbalien (he/him) is a character who is a part of the *Black Hammer* series by Lemire and artist Dean Ormston (he/him). The series, which has won four Eisner Awards, takes place in a fictional Spiral City (which resembles San Francisco). Black Hammer and six superheroes defend Spiral City against the Anti-God, though they end up trapped in rural Rockwood in the process. In the *Black Hammer* books, the Martian Chancellor Lok Lokz (pronouns unknown) sends Barbalien as an ambassador to Earth to meet humans. When he arrives, he sees mobsters attacking a police officer. He kills the mobsters, and he takes over the human form of the dying officer, Mark Markz (he/him).

Barbalien: Red Planet employs an unusual narrative strategy that begins near the end of the story and then circles back. In the opening pages, Barbalien is on Mars and is sentenced to death for disgracing the Martian race. His disgrace is to take over a human form and to "couple" with other humans. The comic then jumps backward to fill in the events that led up to Barbalien's conviction.

In human terms, *Barbalien: Red Planet* takes place in 1986 in the midst of the AIDS crisis. The gigantic, red-skinned Martian Barbalien can shift back and forth between his Martian form and his human form. As Officer Markz, he is assigned to patrol an AIDS protest. Outside City Hall, a speaker with a bullhorn and a Pride flag (the six-colored Pride flag appeared in 1978) argues that the government has ignored them for five years. He points out that the government has refused to fund the research necessary to stop the deaths of thousands of fellow queers. The speaker, Miguel Cruz (he/him), climbs the flagpole, intent upon replacing the US flag with the Pride flag. He doesn't quite make it, but the cop Mark Markz sees him falling, and Barbalien, as the cop Mark Markz, swoops in to save him.

Thus begins his relationship with Miguel Cruz.

But, the thing is, he cannot reveal himself as a Martian, and he cannot appear as the police officer Markz. So, Barbalien takes on a third persona, Luke (he/him). The handsome, Caucasian appearing Luke follows Miguel and finds himself in an underground club, Café Knight Klüb. Luke gets a sudden introduction to the underground scene, drag queens, and ball culture. Miguel tells Luke that this club is the one place that they are safe, the one place where they can be whomever they truly are.

Barbalien learns a lot about Miguel and about queer culture. He learns that Miguel lost a partner to AIDS. He learns that the community has lost thousands to the disease. He learns that the doctors and hospitals often won't treat them. He meets Dr. Day (she/her), "a black, super-powered lesbian treating a majority gay population inside of a Catholic church" (64). Miguel points out that most of the nurses at this clinic are "gay"—"We call them Dr. Day and the Sunlight Sisters" (66). As Dr. Day treats Barbalien (Luke, in this moment) for a beating, she notes "I find myself counseling a gay Martian struggling with an identity crisis at an AIDS clinic run by nuns" (65).

After the police raid the Knight Klüb, the *one* safe place they'd had, Miguel has had enough. Miguel and other activists plan a series of protests throughout the city. Miguel once again climbs a flagpole; this time, he succeeds in replacing the US flag. At that moment, though, he is shot by a police officer. Barbalien once again swoops in, though this time it's too late, and he cannot undo the gunshot wound.

Barbalien has now lost everything. He has lost Mars. He resigns his job as a police officer. He has lost his romantic and sexual partner, Miguel. He has hit bottom. He says, "I used to hate who I was [Barbalien]. So I tried to be someone I wasn't [Mark Markz]. And then I tried to be someone I *loved* [Luke]" (119). He realizes that what he *does* is more important than who he *is*. Yes, we are each the sum of our choices. However, it is not a goal but a process. As Dr. Day points out, we are constantly making new choices, constantly redefining ourselves.

Why tell the history of the gay community, of the lives lost to AIDS, of AIDS activism through a science fiction comic? For one, it places that history in front of a readership that may or may not be aware of it. Yes, the tale has been told in history text books and in Broadway plays, but not in SF comic books.

The history itself is important. The lives lost are important. The lessons of how a government treats its vulnerable citizens are important, and, based on what we saw during COVID, we have not yet learned those lessons.

Furthermore, telling the story of queer history and AIDS activism through a comic allows Brombal and Lemire to do things they might not have been able to do otherwise. For one, what is humanity, who is human, and what is a humane response? The Martians are giants compared to humans. Indeed, in the scenes on Mars, they appear to be just that. Their response to Barbalien's choices is one of disgust. They would rather Barbalien die than that he become human, or that he "couple" with a human male. Their response is, as Barbalien tells them, barbaric. Their height, their weight, their horns, and their red skin suggest to us (humans) an angry and violent race. It is who they are. In this sense, they visually represent the human bigots who hold similar viewpoints.

These angry Martians share a response with the many humans who do not see the humanness of LGBTQ+ folx. They, too, see their choices and their actions as betrayals of the species. They see, as Falwell, Buchanan, and others did, their *deaths* as *justice*. Perhaps if we can see that response as fundamentally wrong, as fundamentally alien (a loaded word, to be sure), then we can rethink our response to AIDS.

Furthermore, Barbalien fundamentally changes over time. He redefines himself through his choices. Even though he comes from the violent Martians, he no longer sees himself as one of them. And his actions demonstrate that he is not. Even though he was a police officer who made some questionable choices, he no longer sees himself as one of them, either. His choice—to quit—redefines who he is. Barbalien is now Luke, and Luke is a queer man living with the loss of his partner. Miguel did not die of AIDS, but he died in the fight to stop AIDS. He died from the same attitudes about AIDS and about queer men that killed Miguel's partner. Miguel had vowed to fight until the end. Now, Barbalien/Luke takes up the torch.

The comic ends as defiantly as it begins: "And we will never stop fighting" (123).

Shade 38 — *The Girl from the Sea* (2021)
Change Is Hard

IN MAY 2021, the children's author Eric Carle (he/him) passed away. Carle was a successful author, and he used a particular and peculiar style of cutting up pieces of paper to build animals and figures. They always had a slightly angular look to them. Nevertheless, his books were beloved. In our household, *The Very Hungry Caterpillar* was a favorite. I read it over, and over, and over. According to *Forbes*, that particular title sold more than 55 million copies worldwide (Durkee). I believe that one of the reasons that that book was so popular is because of the way it deals with metamorphosis and transformation. Children find metamorphosis appealing (and very cool) because they go through it themselves. Like that caterpillar, they eat everything in sight and change on a daily basis. The notion of change is elemental. The idea that we could be (or become) something else is appealing. Take, for example, the selkie.

The selkie is, perhaps, a less common mythological creature than some of the others in this collection — the Cyclops, for example (cf. Shade 36). In some of the northern traditions, Celtic and Norse in particular, the myth of the selkie is prevalent. It's easy to imagine why people who live close to the sea would have tales about sea creatures. The versions vary widely, but the idea is that the selkie looks and lives like a seal but can transform into a human shape and move onto land. In general, the selkie can do so periodically, say every seven years. And, as in so many myths, this transforming figure is primarily female.

Writer and illustrator Molly Knox Ostertag (she/her) takes the idea of the selkie and, well, transforms it….

The Girl from the Sea is a young adult graphic novel published by Graphix, a graphic imprint of Scholastic (which publishes *Harry Potter*). The imprint includes *The Baby-Sitter's Club* (1986-2000), *Amulet* (2008-2024), *Dog Man* (2016-present), *Cat Kid* (2020-present), and a *Black Panther* graphic novel *Into the Heartlands* (2022). The pacing is different from that of an adult graphic novel. Ostertag typically (with exceptions) uses three panels per page. That format pushes the pace forward and keeps the focus on action. It holds the young reader's attention. The graphics are also different. They are more cartoony though, in very much the same style as the other book that Ostertag illustrated, *Strong Female Protagonist* (Shade 5). The characters and landscapes don't have the hard edge and detail common in many adult comics.

In this graphic novel, fifteen-year-old Morgan Kwon (she/her) and her (fractured) family live in Lunenberg, Nova Scotia. The family moved to Wilneff Island, though her dad lives elsewhere. Wilneff is a small, coastal community with some of the best kayaking in Canada. (For real!) However, Morgan has a secret and is just biding her time; she just wants to finish high school so that she can head off to college and finally be *OUT*! That's her dearly held plan: no dating, just graduate from high school, go to college, come out. Nothing will make her deviate from that plan.

Morgan is part of a circle of friends that includes the African Canadian Lizzie (she/her), the redhead Jules (she/her), the über-wealthy Serena (she/her), and the Asian Canadian Morgan. They hang out all the time; they have endless text strings. They're teens. And they share everything. But not *everything*. Morgan wants to tell them that she's queer, but she just can't do it. She wants to make that transformation away from everyone who has known her for her whole life.

As fortune would have it, a selkie changes all that. Since her dad left, everyone in the house feels tense. Mom yells a lot; her younger brother Aiden (he/him) is angry. To escape the tension, Morgan heads out onto the rocks in the rain, but she slips off the rocks and falls into the sea. As she sinks deeper and deeper, she sees her neatly compartmentalized life disappear before her eyes. When the selkie sets her on a rock, she's not quite sure if it's real or a dream. If it's a dream, why not make it a romantic dream? She kisses the selkie. (Whoops.)

After the kiss, the selkie takes a human form. Keltie (she/her), as she's now known, doesn't understand much about the human world. It's confusing, and she's always saying the wrong thing, but she's baffled that Morgan does not welcome her with open arms. In fact, Morgan does everything she can to keep Keltie a secret. However, Morgan and Keltie decide that Keltie will be allowed one day to convince Morgan that they are meant to be together.

It turns out that Keltie also has a secret of her own.

Serena's wealthy parents have bought a new yacht. It's gigantic. They intend to give tours around the islands. Serena will hold her birthday party on the yacht, mostly so she can sell the tours to everyone in town. The problem is that the tour pathway goes right past the rookery, the cove where the seals hatch their young. And that's the thing about a selkie—it's bound to protect the seals it lives with. Consequently, Keltie will do anything to stop those tours, and she needs Morgan to get her onto that party boat.

That doesn't go over well with Morgan.

This teenager who is already dealing with an identity crisis—and the fact that her angry grieving brother has publicly outed her—let her guard down and let a woman into her heart, and she was used. It was all, as far as Morgan is concerned, a pretense. She had abandoned her grand plan, only to be played. How does one come back from that?

With the help and support of her family. Her mother (she/her) only wants her daughter to be happy and to have a better relationship with her parents than she did. She tells Morgan that she just has to let her life get messy sometimes—that's where the good parts come from. OK, *maybe* that's true, but it works as a plot point. The advice catalyzes Morgan's resolve to embrace the change in plans. Her brother apologizes, and she enlists him in her grand gesture to make up with Keltie. He gets to be a mannequin!

Morgan, the aspiring designer, makes a lovely dress for Keltie so they can go to the party. Morgan creates a dress that is a combination of Keltie's favorite dolphin T-shirt and a gauzy skirt that resembles Keltie's seal skin. Morgan makes a dress for herself that incorporates the actual seal skin. The dress is atypical for Morgan, who has a "low-key, carefully curated sense of style" (250). They look quite beautiful together on that boat. Morgan marches right up to her friends and introduces her girlfriend.

Well, they save the rookery, though not without difficulty and heartbreak.

The course of true love never did run smooth, now did it? When Serena is knocked overboard because of something that Keltie did, Keltie has only one recourse—to don her seal skin and save Serena. It's the decent thing to do. However, it also means that Keltie will have to stay in seal form for the next seven years. Morgan's new plan has just taken a hit.

But Morgan is down-to-Earth and pragmatic if nothing else. She can wait seven years. It's not that much longer than her original plan, anyway. And Keltie, bless her heart, says, "Don't you dare" (228). The messiness continues, and Morgan's plans change once again.

Selkies are, by their very nature, shapeshifters. They move between seal form and human form. Keltie, however, says that *she* does not change. Keltie is Keltie no matter what shape she is in. Morgan, on the other hand, changes depending on circumstances and company. Keltie notes that Morgan is a completely different person when she is around Keltie versus when she is around her friends. Indeed, Keltie calls Morgan the true shapeshifter.

And that's what Morgan has to figure out, isn't it? Just who is she? What will she become? And to answer that question, Morgan has to become her true self. She has to stop hiding. She has to stop waiting to transform. Her love for Keltie has helped her make that transformation. Her metamorphosis into her higher form is complete, except that humans, unlike butterflies, never quite finish their metamorphosis.

Although her illustration style is nothing like Eric Carle's, Ostertag's book about transformation struck a chord with readers. It did not quite reach Eric Carle numbers, but *The Girl from the Sea* debuted at #1 (YA charts) in June 2021.

The beautiful butterfly Morgan takes wing and flies toward her next transformation.

Shade 39 — *I Am Not Starfire* (2021)

Becoming Mom

As I noted in Shade 36 of *Queering SF*, YA SF has changed a lot. The characters tend to act more like kids and less like small adults. They tend to come from a wide range of racial and ethnic backgrounds with a wider range of gender and sexual identities. They tend to deal with more real-world issues instead of intergalactic intrigue (maybe both at the same time). They still tend to be a bit predictable in their plot points and in their outcomes. I admit that that is an age-biased response: I suspect that an adult reading *I Am Not Starfire* might say, "Oh, I knew exactly what was going to happen. I've seen this before." I also suspect that a teenager reading *I Am Not Starfire* would respond differently. They have *not* seen it all before. They do not know the likely outcome. They read with suspense and anxiety. Will it work out? Will she survive? Will they get together? Will they kiss! And for a good number of readers—adult and young adult—they just would not care. The fact that it all works out is part of the pleasure. People read one Harlequin Romance after another for a reason. The fact that they have seen the formula before is a comfort.

And if they've read comics, they're likely to know who Starfire (she/her) is.

Starfire was first introduced as a character in 1980 in *DC Comics Presents*. Some of her backstory becomes clear in the current graphic novel, though not all of it. Starfire was a princess on the planet Tamaran in the Vega system. Her father was the king and her older sister, Blackfire (she/her), was in line to take the throne. However, a disease prevented Blackfire from fully developing her powers. Because Blackfire did not have her full powers, she was denied the throne, and Starfire was made queen instead. Furious at being bypassed, Blackfire tried to kill Starfire. However, Starfire survived and found her way to Earth, where she met Robin, and they formed the Teen Titans. Since these initial events, Starfire has appeared in countless comics, TV shows, movies, and video games.

Mariko Tamaki (she/her) and Yoshi Yoshitani's (no pronouns) *I Am Not Starfire* is a YA graphic novel that picks up in the middle of Starfire's story. She has come to Earth and established herself as Kory Anders (she/her); she has had a child (father unknown but publicly much speculated about). Her daughter Mandy (she/her) is 16 going on 17. Predictably, Mandy hates being the child of a superhero. All the attention, all the scrutiny, all the insults she receives on a daily basis pretty much insure that. Plus, who the hell can live up to a mom like that? We might all *think* our moms are superheroes at some point in our lives, but it's another reality altogether to have a mom who is *actually* a superhero. Instead, Mandy sees herself as the anti-Starfire.

Mandy Anders is unlike her mom in a number of ways. For one, she does not have superpowers. Her mom has waited for them to appear, but they just never have. Mandy does not have Starfire's trademark long, flowing hair—though that may be as much a style choice as anything. And she does not have the body shape of a conventional female superhero. In fact, one of her classmates calls her, in a doubly hurtful insult, "superchub" (26). And, unlike her mother, Mandy does not wear a bikini all the time.

Instead, Mandy tends to wear black, has hair that is dyed black, and sports a few noticeable piercings. In other words, she's a pretty typical-looking contemporary teenager. She doesn't really socialize at school (see above) and has one really good friend. Lincoln (he/him) is of Vietnamese descent, super intelligent and driven, and probably queer, though that is never specified. He does not socialize much in school, either. They are besties, though they don't see eye-to-eye on everything. Mandy has decided that she will not be attending college, and she informs her guidance counselor of this fact—which, of course, eventually gets back to good ol' mom. Mandy argues that it's not what she wants; she does not have to live the life that her parent has envisioned for her. Lincoln sees it a bit differently. He says that their parents work so hard as immigrants to give them the life they imagined, that they owe it to them to at least *try*. It takes Mandy a while to agree with him, but she will.

I Am Not Starfire contains several central tensions. Will Mandy ever be like her mother and develop superpowers? Will Mandy take the SAT and go to college? And will Mandy get together with her classmate Claire (she/her)?

Claire is one of the cool kids. Claire's friends Derek (he/him) and Deb (she/her) are just too cool for Mandy. They look down on her, and Deb calls her "superchub." Claire herself is super popular. She has active social media pages with tons of followers and even more likes. Claire is the captain of the soccer team and the swim team. Mandy cannot imagine living Claire's life. What would it be like to be so popular? But the kick is that Lincoln is certain that Mandy has a crush on Claire. Mandy doth protest too much.

Predictably, their English teacher puts them together on a project about *Hamlet*. They decide to rewrite Ophelia's scenes from a woman's perspective. As they work together, they get closer and closer. They spend time together. They drink coffee together. And then it's all torn apart by a social media post. A complication had to appear, no? One afternoon when they are working on their *Hamlet* project at Mandy's house, they just happen to run into a team meeting of the Teen Titans. Claire posts a selfie with the TT on her page, and Mandy loses it.

Her whole life has been about her mother. Her whole life, people have been interested in her mother and not her. Her whole life, people have used her to get to her mother. Now it appears that Claire is no different. She's dead to Mandy. But Mandy is about to be dead anyway.

Starfire's canon storyline converges with Mandy's coming-of-age tale, and Starfire's sister Blackfire shows up. She demands a battle to the death with Mandy, the rightful heir to her throne. But Mandy has no powers, so it would be the shortest superhero battle ever scripted. Starfire offers to battle Blackfire in Mandy's place and asks that she be allowed to explain to Mandy the history between the two sisters so that Mandy can understand why the battle must take place. As Mandy learns about her mother's past and her sacrifices to be on Earth raising Mandy, Mandy gains a new respect for her mother. Well, you guessed it—Blackfire knocks Starfire down. Starfire encourages her daughter to never run from her fears. And Mandy's powers kick in in time to take out Blackfire and save her mother. Justice is done.

So, in a lot of ways, it is a typical Bildungsroman, a coming-of-age story for the digital age. Young Mandy has a few real-life experiences and becomes the person she is meant to be. She just did not realize who she was meant to be until push came to shove. A new queer superhero is born.

What does that mean? Mandy is into Claire. No one seems to mind, not even Claire's awful friends. I mean, they mind that it's Mandy, but not that she's queer. But as we saw in Shade 35 (*América Chávez*), what does her queerness have to do with anything? Mandy's resistance to superheroes stems from the fact that her mom (like many moms) embarrasses her daughter: the attention, the hair, the bikini! Further, Mandy (like many daughters) does not want to be her mother; she wants to be her own thing. Mandy does realize her own potential (as a superhero) at about the same time that she becomes her true self (as a queer person). Are these related? Chronologically, yes. Causally, not so much. Mandy has to learn to face her fear, but her fear was not about being queer. She had already worked through that. Her fear was about becoming her superhero mother. The writers seem to have made a choice. Mandy is queer, and her queerness does not seem to be related to her superpowers in any way.

At least not yet.

Shade 40 — *Killer Queens* (2022)

Post-Camp

"Camp proposes a comic vision of the world."
(Susan Sontag, 288)

IN 1964, THE essayist Susan Sontag published "Notes on 'Camp,'" in which she notes that one of the defining elements of Camp was that it was private, privy to a small, select group, and not to be talked about (the first rule of Camp club…). Of course, by now, we are way beyond that.

Among the examples of Camp provided by Sontag are Tiffany lamps, Aubrey Beardsley (he/him) drawings, women's clothes of the twenties, the Cuban pop singer La Lupe (she/her), and the old *Flash Gordon* comics ("Notes," 277-78). An essay in *Time* regarding the 2019 Met Gala (the theme of which was Camp) suggests that examples of Camp might include Virgil Abloh's (he/him) use of quotations in his designs, Jeremy Scott's (he/him) aesthetic at Moschino, and Lady Gaga (she/her) wearing a meat dress to the MTV Awards in 2010 (Lang).

For Sontag, the very point of Camp is "artifice and exaggeration" (275). However, the point of the exaggeration is to "convert[] the serious into the frivolous" (276). Indeed, she writes, "the whole point of Camp is to dethrone the serious" (288). And, yet, in 2019, Andrew Bolton (he/him), curator of the Met's Costume Institute, suggests that "Whether it's pop camp, queer camp, high camp or political camp—Trump is a very camp figure—I think it's very timely…much of high camp is a reaction to something" (qtd in Lang).

So, where does that leave us?

In 2022, David M. Booher (he/him), Claudia Balboni (she/her), and Harry Saxon (he/him) released a four-issue series called *Killer Queens* for Dark Horse Comics (the references there are many, but perhaps most clearly to the very campy Freddie Mercury). Those four issues were collected into a single volume, also in 2022.

The comic features six primary characters. Alex (she/her) is stereotypically attractive and a retired assassin-for-hire. Her business partner is Max (he/him), a muscular gay man who always has a sexual joke at the ready, the cringier the better. Their old boss, Beiti (he/him), had asked them to take on a hit job that involved taking out an entire family, children included. They refused. They're cold-hearted killers but they're not *that* cold-hearted. So they steal his space ship—which is painted in the colors of the Pride flag—and they go on the lam.

Callisto (she/her)—still another very attractive woman— has some "honest" work for them—by which she means no one is supposed to get killed. As it turns out, Alex and Callisto have some history, though we're not quite sure what it is. All they have to do is go to Antigone, one of the planet Callisto's moons, and retrieve Ambassador Xixa's (she/her) two children who have been kidnapped. Simple, right?

The moon Antigone is politically divided. Half the planet is populated by democratic humanoids, while the other half is populated by rhinocorns, who are ruled by a fascist dictator. Xixa's children have voiced opinions against the fascist dictator Nastar (he/him), and so they have been imprisoned. Oh, not just anywhere, but in Prison 79, aka The Abyss, where people go in, but no one comes back out.

Well, Beiti has sabotaged their ship, so their trip to Antigone doesn't go quite as planned. They crash-land right next to a military facility and are immediately imprisoned. They just so happen to be thrown into a cell with a mountain of a man, Haws (aka Man Meat) (he/him). He and his partner Ballick (she/her) are members of the Resistance. In the meantime, Beiti has made a deal with the dictator Nastar, who reneges on the deal. Now all five—Alex, Max, Beiti, Haws, and Ballick—face the firing squad, until Ambassador Xixa and her troops swarm in and capture them all. Sending Alex and Max to Antigone was meant to fail; their capture and execution was the pretense to move in.

Sounds like a fairly conventional space opera, no? It has space ships, nefarious bosses, rogue mercenaries, fascist aliens vs. democratic humanoids. What does it have to do with Camp?

Well, for one, Sontag says that Camp is dedicated to artifice and is anodyne to nature. Camp favors the products of society, such as clothing and furniture and décor. Indeed, nearly the entirety of *Killer Queens* takes place in an artificial environment. It moves from Stan's Diner, a restaurant in space, to the stolen spaceship, to the jail cell, to the jail complex, to the underground resistance movement's headquarters. Stan's Diner is a retro-style diner, harkening back to the 1950s (on Earth in the US). The black and white floor tiles and the shiny fixtures all code a particular architectural moment in time—highly anachronistic. The jail complex is another large, open space. It features a postmodern take on the panopticon, with cells arranged around the outside of a circular space, visible from a central point inside. As Sontag points out, Camp is obsessed with styles and technologies that are "démodé" (285).

The only scene that takes place out of doors are the several panels when Beiti is looking for his space ship. He struggles with the fauna; he trips over a root. "I hate this planet," he says (92), by which he means the moon's flora and fauna tripping him up. As he finally sees his ship, he takes off at a run, only to come under fire. We then see his ship head off into space while he is taken captive. Why are these scenes here? While Beiti appears to us to be a monkey (and Alex persistently calls him that), who knows what species he actually is. But the irony here is that this (apparent) monkey is so out of sorts *in* nature. But no, Beiti is as much a creature of artifice as any of the characters.

Sontag also says that Camp loves "exaggeration" (279) and "extravagance" (283). To be sure, *Killer Queens* revels in exaggeration. For one, the circumstances that the dynamic duo find themselves in are truly bigger than life. A reformed intergalactic assassin who won't kill children? An angry ship owner who remotely sabotages his own ship only to have it crash land (unscathed) next to the military base? On a planet far, far away, the kids of diplomats still post selfies on social media? It's all a little too much.

Second, the scenery and architecture are out of this world. The first page of the comic shows an exterior shot of Stan's Diner, a circular station orbiting in space. It is huge. The interior shots are even more amazing. Page 11 shows the floor space going on and on. Further, the space laser shoot-out has no effect whatsoever. The interior shots of the jail complex on Antigone are even more awe-inspiring. The two-page spread (37) shows vast areas of open space spreading out over multiple floors. Staircases wind their way to nowhere. It is probably not a coincidence that, even as we look at the ample space in the jail complex, Alex says she has run out of "jaw-droppingly clever" (37) escape plans.

Third, the comic does spend a lot of time on the characters' appearances. As noted above, Alex is the epitome of femininity, and quite a lot of the drawings of her make sure that we are aware of this. The frames draw our attention to her bodily attributes. The same is true for Max. From his fade haircut to his sleeveless shirt to his ripped pecs and abs, we are reminded of his physical masculinity. The authors take similar approaches with Callisto, Ballick, and Haws. All of them have exaggerated physical characteristics. None of Sontag's vaunted "androgyne" (279) here; the characters are all unabashedly sexed and sexual. Which leads, fourth, to their sexual behaviors and innuendos. The comic begins inside Stan's Diner. Max is in the bathroom, shirt nowhere to be found, making out with a being with purple skin. When they shift to Callisto, the all-female planet, Max finds himself in bed with three male concubines. After they are arrested, he makes a pass at his cellmate. And Max always has a sexual quip ready. When asked to shoot the cannons, he notes he's "handled *way* bigger guns than these" (59). As they escape down a tunnel, Alex asks how far it goes down. Max says "Not as far as I can go d—" (64). And so on, *ad astra, ad nauseam.*

In her "Notes," Sontag also points out the connection between Camp and "homosexuality" ("Notes," 290). She argues that "homosexual, by and large, constitutes the vanguard—and the most articulate audience—of Camp" ("Notes," 290). To her mind, Camp is a way for homosexuals to integrate into society by means of an aesthetic playfulness (290). And *Killer Queens* certainly does exhibit many of the aesthetic qualities of Camp.

And, yet, *Killer Queens* also *fails* as Camp. For one, Sontag says something cannot be—or at least should not be—self-consciously Camp. Rather, it should appear spontaneously, as a failure of art, or a failure of seriousness. More importantly, "It goes without saying that the Camp sensibility is disengaged, depoliticized—or at least apolitical" ("Notes," 277).

Can Camp be political? Can the political be Camp?

In an interview, writer Booher says, "I want to use the great big universe out there to explore issues we face in real life. That's what all good sci-fi is, right? A mirror we hold up to ourselves to expose our truth" (Cassandra Clarke, "Killer Queens"). What are the real-life, aka political, issues that *Killer Queens* tackles? For one, it takes on representation. It would seem that every character here (except Bieti, and there we're just not sure, but he does have a rainbow-colored ship) is queer. As I have said before, that matters. It also takes on gender norms. Booher also notes that Alex and Max are highly sexual, but not traditionally gendered. He notes that "both of them are vulnerable and insecure" (Clarke, "Killer Queens").

Perhaps most importantly, *Killer Queens* has something to say about capitalism and about fascism. The fact that the comic is written and published in 2022 cannot be overlooked. Although the artistic team here, Booher, Balboni, and Saxon, hail from the US, Italy, and Greece, respectively, they can hardly be unaware of global politics and the rise of fascism. After all, on the moon Antigone, the divide is explicitly between democracy and fascism.

In Sophocles's *Antigone*, Antigone disobeys the ruling of King Creon in order to mourn her brother, defying Creon's tyranny to follow divine law. After Creon orders her enclosed in the tomb, she hangs herself, once again defying the tyranny of Creon. The central conflict here is set on the moon Antigone where the humanoids battle the non-humanoid fascist dictator. The lines could not be clearer. Fascism and tyranny cannot win.

As such, *Killer Queens* makes an overtly political statement. In 2022, it takes a stand against fascism. I suggest that as readers we are meant to dislike Nastar (look at the connotations of his name), and we are meant to like Alex and Max. (I also readily concede that the author's intentions do not necessarily matter to readers.) They are guns for hire; they are capitalists. Ambassador Xixa hires their services; they collect their checks and go on their way. This is free enterprise at work.

Is this Camp? I think Sontag would say, "No." I also acknowledge that many reject Sontag's narrow definition of Camp. While *Killer Queens* does emphasize style and aesthetics, while it does foreground the playfulness of the plot and the characters, while it does call for the acceptance and inclusion of queerness, it ultimately makes a serious commentary on present day social issues and asks the readers to take a stand. Nastar begs for his life; Beiti is placed in a zoo (some questionable colonial implications there, to be sure!). Xixa's children sell their personal story for millions, and Alex and Max cash their chit.

Perhaps we can think of it as Camp 2.0, or 21st-century Camp, or my preferred choice: Post-Camp.

Shade 41 — *Youth* (2021)

Time Keeps on Slippin'

> "Oh the sky had been falling
> When I heard your voice callin' me by name
> Callin' me by my name"
> ("Shooting Star," Cris Williamson)

JUST HOW DO you experience time? Oh, I'm sure it's not always the same, is it? Some days, the time flies by. Some days, it drags on forever. Sometimes, the days of our youth seem like they were just yesterday. Sometimes, they seem a million years ago.

In many cultures throughout history, time has been considered as a repeating loop. In those societies, everything that happens has happened before. We are all headed toward a return to the beginning and the events of time will all happen again, although with some variations. The idea that time is ineluctable, well, that's fairly new. The notion that time travels in a straight line (yes, that was deliberate) is also kinda new. What are some other ways to look at it?

What would queer time look like?

J. Jack Halberstam writes, "If we try to think about queerness as an outcome of strange temporalities, imaginative life schedules, and eccentric economic practices, we detach queerness from sexual identity" (Halberstam, *In a Queer*, 1), then we might understand Michel Foucault's (he/him) vision of homosexuality not as sexual activity but, rather, as "a way of life" (Halberstam, *In a Queer*, 1). While Halberstam writes of altering the "typical" pattern of life—school, job, marriage, children—I would suggest that that queer notion of time can be applied in many areas, including comic books.

The comic series *Youth* appeared in 2021-2022. Each of the two Seasons contains four issues, for a total of eight issues. The series is a Comixology Original, written by Curt Pires (he/him) and illustrated by Alex Diotto (pronouns unknown). Pires and Diotto co-created the series along with colorist Dee Conniffe (he/him).

The series centers on five youths in California: Frank (he/him), River (he/him), Trixy (she/her), Kurt (he/him), and Jan (she/her). It begins with a parallel story line. Sometimes side-by-side, sometimes in parallel columns, Frank and River are having a bad day. The sequence ends with each of them punching an adult. Frank punches a customer at the burger joint where he works; River punches his stepfather. The two lovers then meet and decide to steal a car and leave town. As they drive, however, the car gets a flat tire. After they set the car on fire, they join up with three youths in a van. The van is struck by a meteorite and blows up, and all five acquire superpowers.

The origin story is familiar enough. Matthew Murdock (he/him), Bruce Banner (he/him), and Jonathan Osterman (he/him) were all exposed to radiation. They became, respectively, Daredevil, the Hulk, and Dr. Manhattan. Similarly, Peter Parker (he/him) was bitten by a radioactive spider and became Spiderman. Closer to the mark, Jefferson Reed (he/him) was struck by a green meteor and became, well, Meteor Man. Our five young friends are struck by a meteor and become something enhanced and connected.

Of course, the superhero character has long since been complicated. In the early days of superhero comics, the superhero and the villain were two-dimensional characters. Clark Kent (he/him) and Superman (he/him) were too-good-to-be-true; we could always count on them to make the right decision. Lux Luther (he/him) was similarly two-dimensional, but only ever had malicious thoughts. Born of the Romantic literary tradition, superhero comics and superheroes themselves were uncomplicated and not generally rooted in a real-life, three-dimensional society. The characters were motivated by simple thoughts, and they served as "types."

The Dark Knight Returns (1986) by Frank Miller (he/him) was one of the first superhero comics to really complicate the protagonist. Miller's Batman was darker, more mature, and more well-rounded than earlier versions. Was Miller's Batman queer? Certainly not if we center on the character's sexuality. But if we consider queer as process, then maybe. And if we take queer as "looking at something from an alternative perspective," then definitely.

In *Youth*, our five heroes have varying abilities. Some of them can fly. Some of them can repel bullets. Some of them revive the dead. One of them, Jan, is strongly connected to the other members of the group. In the second Season, Jan connects our group to other "posthumans" around the world. With these abilities, our superheroes fall into recognizable types. In what ways are they different? In what ways, then, do they queer the type?

For one, Frank and River are a gay couple. Granted, along the way Frank yields (with the help of some pharmaceuticals) to Trixy's temptations. When he believes that River is dead, Frank has sex with women, with men, and with nonbinary folx. Nevertheless, his connection and his heart belong to River. River is what brings Frank back from the edge of suicide. While the other transhumans seem to have same-sex desires and relationships, the lead couple is queer.

Which brings us back to the "posthumans." Jan suggests that all those who have been hit by and transformed by the meteor are no longer human. However, Jan does not use the word "superhuman." That word would be the root of our superheroes. Instead, she calls them posthumans. By extension, then, are they "postheroes?" Again, not a word used in *Youth*.

So, the comic can be read as a queering of the superhero tradition (seeing it differently; having superheroes behave differently). It can also be read as queer because the two leads are queer. But what else? What about queer time?

Halberstam talks about disrupting usual sequences, about taking things out of order. I would suggest that *Youth* does this in several ways. First, the narrative makes a number of pauses and backtracks. It's certainly not the first narrative to ever fill in information via a flashback. The narrative voiceover (small white letters on a full-page black screen) addresses us from some point in the future. The narrative then jumps back to "Once upon a time in the United States" (2). The narrator is looking back on "that summer." Late in Season 2, the narrator becomes clear to us. In the initial sequence with Frank and River, the first page shows three panels, top to bottom. The sequencing seems straightforward. The following page shifts to six panels—two columns, three panels each. The three on the left-hand side feature Frank at the burger joint. The three on the right-hand side feature River in his bedroom. How does one read these panels? In what order are we to take them? Typical order would read left to right, top to bottom, which would alternate Frank to River, three times. Might they also be read top to bottom on the left and top to bottom on the right, offering three Frank panels and three River panels? It is the only page in the opening sequence to use this form. It's a hitch in the order of things. It requires the reader to stop and ponder: how do I read this? How is it supposed to progress? What is the timing of this page?

Following another all-black page of narration, we shift to Frank and River sitting on a cliff overlooking the city in two pages of their making plans, followed by credits and a title page. Another hitch in the order of things, the creators make it clear, from the beginning, that things will not progress as expected.

Season One, Issue Two begins with the narrator pondering the start of everything. It ALL started with a bang. Pages 32-39 fill in the origin of the meteorite. The meeting of two beings, Infinity and Null (pronouns unknown), matter and anti-matter, cause the explosion of a planet, some of which lands on Earth.

In other examples of queered time, Season One, Issue Three begins with backstory on the two drivers of a Brinks Van. As they attend to their business, a man appears before them and destroys their van, killing them in the process. The narrator says, "Wait a minute. I think I fucked up. I jumped ahead…. Let's rewind a bit" (61). In Season One, Issue Four, the narrator backtracks again to relate how Frank and River met. The back story fills in the info of why the posthumans so frequently meet on the cliff.

What do all the shifts in chronology, the ruptures in temporality contribute? Do they produce Halberstam's disruption of "typical" time? Arguably, yes, they do.

The center of the series is the relationship between Frank and River. They are both disaffected youths. They are thrust into a world they do not fully understand and a world that does not really have a space for them as queer men. Then the meteorite complicates their lives further. They are forced into new circumstances that they do not understand: the superpowers, the military experiments, the transhuman networking. Here their lives have no chance to progress in any traditional way. The progression of youth, relationship, marriage, children, and career has been taken from them. Two queer boys don't have that future available. The transformation assures that.

Do our five youths reinvent the teenage superhero? Maybe not. I mean, they're quite different from the original Superman and Batman, but they are no more or less complicated than newer versions of the superhero. But the fact that Frank and River are queer does matter. It illustrates some of the ways in which time and progress function differently for them.

For Frank and River, time passes queerly.

Shade 42 — *A Man's Skin* (2021)

Body Swap

THE TIRESIAS MYTH takes many, many forms. In roughly 4CE, when Ovid (he/him) published the *Metamorphoses*, he wrote of the seer Tiresias (he/him), an aged and respected man. As Tiresias walked through the woods one day, he saw two snakes entwined, having sex. Either he was offended by this or he knew that something magical would happen (or it was a convenient plot point), but he struck the snakes with his wooden staff. The snakes were separated, and Tiresias suddenly found himself in a woman's body. Tiresias (she/her) lived that way for a few years. Conveniently, she found another pair of mating snakes and, when she hit them with the staff, Tiresias found himself back in his old man's body.

When Juno (she/her) and Jove (he/him) argue about who enjoys sex more, they ask the one person who has embodied both. Tiresias has had sex both as a man and as a woman, so they ask him to resolve their argument for them. The first moral of the story is that you should never get involved in the affairs of the gods. If you do, you will get smacked, just like those snakes. The second moral is that we have long had curiosity about what it would be like to be in a different body (and have sex while inhabiting that body). The third moral is that you should read your myths to find out who enjoys sex more.

Over time, countless versions and variations of Tiresias have appeared. Science fiction has offered a few versions, including John Varley's "Options" (1979) (cf. Shade 1 in *QSF*). In Varley's version, advanced technology provides consumers with a cheap and easy means of changing bodies. One simply grows a new body of a different sex and plops their old brain into their new body, creating a new technological version of Tiresias. Other science-fictional technologies produce similar effects. A transporter malfunction, for instance, might render a differently sexed body.

Hubert (Boulard) (he/him) and Zanzim (Frédéric Leutelier) (he/him) offer their own version of a sex change in their 2021 graphic novel *A Man's Skin* (*Peau d'homme*, 2020). Their story is set in a small, walled town in Renaissance Italy. Our protagonist is an 18-year-old woman named Bianca (she/her), who is about to be married off to an older man, Giovanni (he/him). Bianca really wishes that she had some means to get to know Giovanni before they marry. Luckily, the family has a secret. Bianca's godmother offers Bianca "a man's skin," which the family refers to as Lorenzo (he/him). When Bianca dons the skin, she transforms into Lorenzo, erection and all. (If you get hung up on the mechanics of it, it all falls apart.) As Lorenzo, she can now have those premarital experiences that men have long been able to have. However, when she enters the Cross Eyed Cat bar, she is appalled by the men's words and behaviors. More important, she hears at first hand Giovanni's attitudes about marriage and his preference for young men.

Over the next 150 pages or so, Bianca, Lorenzo, and Giovanni have a torrid sexual relationship, get married, have a child, and bring down the town's emerging religious zealot (Bianca's own brother, Angelo [he/him]). In doing so, the graphic novel tackles quite a number of issues: familial arrangements, gender roles, double standards, sexual identity, sexual desire, and religious zealotry.

Bianca comes from a relatively well-to-do family. Her sister is married, and her brother is a priest. The women in her life dismiss her concerns about arranged marriage. It's the way things are done. Her mother accuses Bianca of wanting to "revolutionize" marriage and marry for love (13). Bianca sees the infidelity within marriages. Her brother-in-law, Alessandro (he/him), quite publicly has many side women, and her sister takes a lover out of spite. Bianca would like a family—a husband and children—but she wants more equality and choice than offered to her. She goes to great lengths to make her marriage work with Giovanni, but they cannot maintain a normative, nuclear family. In the end, Bianca forms an "unusual" family. Under one roof, Giovanni has his young lover, Hans (he/him) and Bianca has her lover Tomaso (he/him), and they all care for the baby, Chiara (she/her)—one big, non-normative family, with one queer couple (Giovanni/Hans) and one straight couple (Bianca/Hans).

A Man's Skin assumes that (nearly) everyone has an active sex drive (if not sex life)—even the ironically named Angelo (he/him), who takes a vow of celibacy and tries to impose it onto everyone else. Bianca tells others that he is a hypocrite. When he was younger, she caught him, red in the face with his pants around his knees, watching the servants in their bath. But in this world, wives, old maids, maids, stable boys, husbands, all have sexual desires. In some cases, those desires fall into publicly sanctioned forms, and in others, they do not.

Bianca, which means "white" in Italian, is colored in the whitest of white tones. I mean, she looks like the newly fallen snow. But Bianca is not quite as pure as that snow. Wearing the Lorenzo suit, he is eager to have sex with Giovanni and poses for a nude portrait. As Lorenzo, he strips in the town square to confront and challenge Angelo's hypocrisy. Bianca never has sex with another woman. That's not who she is; that's not what she is interested in. She's not even curious about the experience. Instead, it's an exercise, at first to get to know Giovanni, and then to have the social experiences of a man, and finally, to challenge social mores.

Giovanni says that he has a little sexual experience with women. He wants to be able to perform in order to have children. But his desire has always been for younger men and boys (cf Shade 16). When drinking with Lorenzo, he tells Lorenzo that he will have sex with his wife (who is actually sitting across from him) in order to have children, but his pleasure will always come from outside. He believes that women should be kept locked away, virginal until marriage. He shares Nietzsche's (he/him) fear that the child will not be his own.

Gendered double standards are rife. Women must be virgins, but men must have sexual experience. Women must stay faithful (to ensure paternity), but men can have many, many partners. Women must maintain the honor of the family, while men can sully it at will. Giovanni argues that women were made inferior by God. Bianca/Lorenzo has little success in convincing him otherwise. The women in the town know that men have extramarital affairs. They know that sometimes those affairs are with women and that sometimes those affairs are with men. That's just men being men. Their only preference is that the men keep it out of the public eye and do not shame their wives.

In one scene, when Lorenzo and Giovanni are walking down the street together, two older men proposition them. Giovanni becomes incensed. He needs to be the older partner, and he sees the young boys as effeminate. When the older man hits on him, he feels emasculated. Bianca argues at several points that society needs to see women as equal, as capable, as autonomous. But Giovanni, like Angelo, cannot. For him, those roles are handed down from God.

What does all this switching of skins and sexes and sex partners mean? Is it a metaphor for trans individuals? Does it illustrate the fluidity of sexuality? Is it a corrective to history?

No and no and maybe.

While Bianca *does* experience herself as Lorenzo as something/someone different from Bianca, Lorenzo is not who she is. Arguably, Bianca is changed by the experiences of Lorenzo, and Bianca is a different person at the end than she was in the beginning (as also happens in Varley's "Options"). Yes, Bianca feels constrained by gender roles and wishes to have a fuller experience of life—which she is able to do as Lorenzo and later as Bianca. As with Tiresias, the changing of skins is a device to think about something else—gender roles and sexuality. Bianca's sexuality does not become more fluid, but her gender role becomes much expanded.

Does *A Man's Skin* answer Juno and Jove's question about sex? "No." For Bianca, anyway, sex is about love. She loves Giovanni and his body, and she wants him to love her *and* her body. Giovanni cannot. For him, love is about the body as well. Bianca has sex with Giovanni as Lorenzo and as Bianca. But she does not distinguish between the two experiences. Nor does she compare them (as Juno and Jove ask). When she takes Tomaso (he/him) as her lover, she wants to establish a relationship of equals—or as much as that is possible.

The story ends with Lorenzo taking on a life of his own. Graffiti appear in town: "Vive Lorenzo." Each year at Carnival, one person is elected "Lorenzo" and is an admired figure. What does it mean, then, that Lorenzo has taken on this role in the town? The townsfolk know nothing of Bianca's role as Lorenzo; nevertheless, they see a free spirit; they see someone invested in pleasure; they see someone willing to risk everything to remain who he is.

Now you know what to do the next time you see two snakes in the garden....

Shade 43 — *Rain* (2022)

A Stab to the Heart

WHO SAYS COMICS have to be fun?

My students sometimes complain that the texts I assign them to read are on the bleak side. That may be a fair observation. If you look at the canon (of whatever—English literature, Russian literature, PoMo literature, feminist literature), its texts tend to be dark, serious, and sometimes grim. Maybe writing "light" fiction is harder than it seems. Maybe the criteria are skewed for what we count as canonical (that is almost certainly true). But perhaps the feelings, the emotions, and the thoughts evoked by a dark text remain with us longer than those evoked by a light and funny text. Have you ever read a heart-wrenching book and then handed it to a friend and said, "You have to read this"? If so, then *Rain* is going to stick with you much longer than *Killer Queens* (Shade 40).

In January 2022, the first issue of a new series, *Rain,* from a new publishing venture, Syzygy Publishing, appeared. A new publishing venture is a dicey proposition at any time, but especially in the midst of a pandemic. In order to make a name for itself, in order to assure a readership, they turned to the work of the Joe Hill (he/him), whose first novel, *Heart-Shaped Box*, won the Bram Stoker Award in 2007. His third novel *NOS4A2* rose to fifth on the *New York Times* Best Seller list, and his next novel, *The Fireman* (2016), debuted at first on the list. Hill has also won an Eisner Award for his writing on the series *Locke & Key* (2008-2013). His name has drawing power.

In 2017, Hill released a collection of four novellas under the title *Strange Weather*, which included the story "Rain." After acquiring Hill's permission to adapt the story, publisher Chris Ryall (he/him) assembled a team, including David M. Booher (he/him) (*Killer Queens*) as lead writer, Zoe Thorogood (she/her) as artist, and Chris O'Halloran (he/him) for colors. Ryall details this process in the Editorial at the end of issue five.

The story is set in Boulder and Denver, Colorado. Because it is an adaptation of a short story, it takes a somewhat unusual approach to emphasize voice-over. A good deal of the story is told to the reader by the narrator, Honeysuckle Speck (she/her). That narrative choice has several consequences. As a reader, I was certain that Honeysuckle would survive all this because she is telling me the story in the past tense—she has lived through it and lived to tell the tale, which removes some of the narrative tension. How many times have you read a text or watched a film and felt the tension build, wondering if the heroine is going to make it? You can feel your pulse quicken and your nerves fray. The voiceover removes that kind of tension. This narrative choice also favors more interiority. Comics as a medium tend toward action, with no long expositions, no long descriptions, and no info dumps (though dialog does allow info dumps when needed). We see the visual setting, and we read the words in the speech bubbles. We gather *some* information from facial expressions and body language, but those are limited. In this graphic novel, we gain a great deal of insight into Honeysuckle through her narration. This strategy has the potential to heighten the emotional impact of the story.

At the beginning of issue one, Honeysuckle waits on a warm, sunny August day for her girlfriend to arrive. They will be moving in together. Visually, we see the two women lying together on a bed. Honeysuckle has short hair with a ski cap and torn jeans. Yolanda (she/her) has long dark hair with dreads and a long yellow patterned dress. They are surrounded by pictures, images, and phone screens that capture moments of their lives, but also convey something of their personalities.

Honeysuckle lives in a house across the street from her neighbors Ursula (she/her) and Ursula's son Templeton Blake (he/him). Ursula's husband died recently, though no one is quite sure if it was suicide or murder. In either case, Templeton is without a father and tends to reach out to other adults. Ursula is a mess, understandably. Ursula and Templeton love Honeysuckle and Yolanda, and they both seem stoked that Yolanda is moving in. But even as this move unfolds, even as we meet Honeysuckle's neighbors, the voice over tells us of the impending destruction.

Just as Yolanda's car pulls up, her mom (she/her) at the wheel and the back of the car piled comically high, the sky above cracks, and shards of crystals rain down, puncturing everyone and everything. Everyone outside at the time is killed by a thousand stab wounds. What was supposed to be the happiest day of her life quickly becomes the worst. Honeysuckle loses the person she loves most in the world. She also loses her "do-over" mom, the woman who accepted her for who she is and whom she loves. They are gone in a grotesque flash.

Acceptance and rejection are significant themes in *Rain*. Honeysuckle fled her own family because her parents refused to accept her when she came out to them. She no longer speaks with her father at all, and her mother refused to even acknowledge Yolanda's presence when they visited. Yolanda's parents, including her father the Reverend Doctor Rusted (he/him) took all of five minutes to fully embrace Yolanda and Honeysuckle. They said they were happy and proud to be her "do-over" parents. And then they put a Pride flag outside their house.

After Yolanda and her mother are killed, Honeysuckle cannot bear the thought that she might have lost her new father as well. She straps on her shit-kicking hiking boots and heads to Denver. Ursula reminds her that it's likely to be lawless out there. Honeysuckle responds, "I've spent my life avoiding people who'd rather see me dead than gay" (issue 2, 8). When she—eventually—arrives, she encounters a neighbor. She knows him by sight. Yolanda used to babysit his children. He's less than accepting, however. According to him, the rain is retribution for sinners like Yolanda and Honeysuckle. You've heard this rhetoric before: it's a new Flood in which God washes away the sinners and their sin. Honeysuckle finds Dr. Rusted, dead. She's received a third major kick in the gut—and she's not finished yet.

On the way to Denver, Honeysuckle befriends an MMA fighter named Marc DeSpot (he/him) (yes, there's a visual joke in there). He turns out to be a stand-up guy. No sooner does she meet Marc, than she realizes that the neighbor kid, Templeton, has followed her. Marc agrees to escort Templeton back home. Marc later helps Honeysuckle bury Yolanda and her mother. "I'll never forget him being out there with me, digging holes for people he never met…working between the raindrops" (issue 5, 6) He bonds with Templeton and plays endlessly with him, a new father figure for him.

It takes Honeysuckle a while, but she eventually puts all the pieces together. She figures out why the rain (which is now global) began in Boulder. She figures out the connection to Georgia (the country) and why Ursula took Templeton flying every night. Her husband committed suicide because the company he worked for stole his intellectual property and moved to Georgia. In retribution, Ursula seeded the sky with the chemicals that cause the rain. Her future and her family's future had been destroyed, and she wanted to destroy the future of everyone in that company. But as Honeysuckle points out, Ursula ended the future for everyone. When Honeysuckle figures it out, Ursula splits open Marc's head with a rusty machete and destroys another future. Another kick in the gut.

Young Templeton hears Honeysuckle's words. He sees his mother attack Marc—his own "do-over" parent. He runs outside, just as the rain begins. He falls to the ground as the crystals puncture his young skin. Ursula sees this, and she races outside and covers him with her own body. A final act of heroism? A final act of maternal love? A final act of selflessness (instead of her act of selfishness)? One person in Honeysuckle's life is spared the horrors of the rain.

Honeysuckle is queer. She loves Yolanda more than she has ever loved anyone in this world. She has lived her life as a queer person, and she has learned—and internalized at a gut level—survival strategies. She's learned to be careful; she's learned not to trust people easily; she's learned to be guarded with personal information; she's learned to be prepared for resistance, homophobia, and violence. Her queerness is a factor in the plot. Moving-in day is special for anyone, but it's especially poignant to Honeysuckle because of the rejection of her parents and the acceptance of her do-over parents. The loss of her do-over mom is especially hard because she knows it's a conscious choice for Mrs. Rusted. The fact that she tracks down Dr. Rusted is related to her queerness. Their relationship means that much more because of the circumstances. This man of the church (the church and religion run through the comic in several ways) proudly embraced her. The fact that she has had to be guarded and deliberate with relationships makes these relationships that much more meaningful.

Despite all the destruction, despite all the anger and hatred, despite all the deaths, *Rain* ends on a hopeful note. Honeysuckle and Templeton take the iPad with all the data, and they head to the University of Denver to find someone who can make the rain stop. If they cannot find anyone there, they will keep walking.

A stab to the heart and a kick in the gut, and one that I hope stays with you.

Shade 44 — *Pixels of You* (2022)
A Meeting of Minds and Bodies

IN HER (IN)FAMOUS "A Manifesto for Cyborgs" (1985),
the primatologist and theorist Donna Haraway maps out some
of the changes she sees in contemporary society. While she is,
ultimately, thinking of new metaphors for gender identities,
she also notes some changes in bodies and bodily relations.
For Haraway, the late 20th century brought about fundamental breakdowns in the demarcations between humans and
non-human animals, humans and machines, and the physical
and the non-physical. Although all three areas of demarcation
are interesting, let's focus on the second one. Haraway points
to some of the ways in which the distinction between humans
and machines are eroding, blurring. And, for her, that's something to celebrate. We incorporate machines into our bodies
all the time. We use pacemakers and stents. We use machines
to augment our physical strength and mental abilities (just
think of your smart phone). Conversely, we adapt ourselves to
machines. We wake up when our machines tell us (well, sometimes); we blindly follow the lead of our GPS instructions; we
watch programs the algorithms tell us to watch. Finally, we
construct machines to think, act, and move more like humans.
For Haraway, we are not the autonomous beings some of us
think we are. Instead, we are now shaped by the machines in
and around us. We are cyborgs. That's who we are at this moment in time.

The writing team of Ananth Hirsch (he/him) and Yuko
Ota (she/her) have been thinking about and writing about

these sorts of relations in *Pixels of You*. The two are married and live in Brooklyn. They—much like Haraway—are interested in human/animal relations. Their most recent book is all about their cats and how famous they are. Furthermore—like Haraway—they have been tracking some of the ways in which machines, in general, and Artificial Intelligence (AI), in particular, have developed. At irregular intervals in their graphic novel, they include factoids about recent AIs, computers, and machines in the news. For example, they note a report that suggests that AIs will "recreate and automate" the gender biases in evaluating résumés (13). They note that the global pandemic has only accelerated the deployment of AI surveillance systems (52). They note that tech companies and law enforcement agencies have created systems that identify individuals who might be at risk of committing crimes (think: *Minority Report* [2002]) (69). And they note studies that show some AI systems have a bias regarding skin complexion, such that they fail to even recognize some people (most commonly, Black people) as human beings (82). In other words, these factoids paint a less exuberant picture than does Haraway.

In early 2022, Hirsch and Ota published *Pixels of You*, which features one human woman, Indira Visariya (she/her), who was seriously injured in a car crash. As a result, she has an artificial eye that does not quite work the way it should. It causes near-constant pain. The other central character is a human-presenting AI (Fawn) (she/her) who is the child of two non-human-presenting AIs. Both of these women illustrate the collapsing of human/machine boundaries.

I have a few questions, though. At the beginning of the novel, Fawn is "grown" and works in a gallery. I wonder about Fawn's parents. Why would two AIs replicate the social norms of humans (they are humanoid, but not human-presenting)? One of the notes mentioned above says that AIs are created by humans and may well replicate human biases. So, by that logic, they might replicate human social norms and practices as well. I wonder about the house they live in. We see a few scenes inside Fawn's home. She comes home from work, takes off her shoes after a hard day, and sits in the living room with mom and dad. In other words, they live in a house that replicates the Western human home. Do the AIs have the need for a kitchen? For a dining room table? As far as we see, they do not eat, so what purpose does kitchens and dining rooms serve? As they sit in a living room, all three are connected to a wire. Perhaps they are collectively recharging, perhaps they are all uploading a firmware update. In either case, the function of the living room has been modified. Maybe the functions of the home have been adapted in certain ways. Maybe they simply copy humans. I also wonder about the process by which they have a child. They presumably jointly decided to have a child. They scrimped and "saved up" (31) so that their child could have a human-presenting form. The child (Fawn) was able to select her own body. They wanted her to have a "natural chassis" so that she could have "opportunities" they never had (30). Again, the human-produced AIs seem to replicate the desire for a nuclear family. Is this desire for offspring—for transcendence—inevitable given their programming? Is the desire for transcendence a function of any self-aware being?

I realize that these are not the central concerns of this graphic novel, but they are observations and questions it raises.

Fawn and Indira both intern at an art gallery. Indira's term is winding down and the gallery is showing her work, the theme of which is "The Unknown." At one moment, they are both looking at a piece when Indira asks Fawn for her thoughts on it. Fawn unloads on the piece, unaware that she is talking to the artist. "*How* is this about 'the unknown.' Maybe he thought the subject matter made it, like, bold or whatever…. It seems objectifying? Maybe I don't get it, but that frustrates me too. It's like it's *about* me, but it's not *for* me" (16). So, the AI does not know who the artist is; the AI makes gender assumptions about the artist based on the piece; and the AI, who is the subject of the piece, does not see herself in it. This exchange leads to a huge public argument in the gallery. Indira tries to brush off Fawn's comments because "there's nobody here," suggesting that the AI is not a person at all (41). Paloma, the gallery owner, "does not suffer brats" (47). She requires the two to work jointly on the end-of-season exhibition or lose their school credits for their internship.

What happens next is not exactly *unknown*. The two have a contentious beginning. They argue and bicker, and they eventually fall in love. The penultimate panel shows them warmly kissing. Even so, their pathway there is endearing.

Things begin poorly. Indira's eye is bothering her, and she has a less-than-satisfying appointment with her doctor. She then texts Fawn to meet her in SoHo. The meeting, however, is under false pretenses. It's not about their joint show at all; rather, Indira is scouting locations for a shoot for some clients. Through an internal app, Fawn is able to give Indira detailed weather and lighting information. As they continue to "scout," Indira photographs Fawn. Indira finds Fawn "intimidating" (58), but she also finds her photogenic and beautiful.

This moment leads to a discussion about cameras. Indira has inherited some hand-held digital cameras. Fawn's camera is hardwired. Her eye serves as the lens, and the data is stored in her brain. She tethers her phone to her brain "like everyone else" (64). Earlier, Indira told Fawn that she has a "fake" eye. Fawn's been thinking about that. She says to Indira that her eye takes in sensory data, transmits it to her brain for processing just like any eye. "Your eye's not fake" (65). The distinctions lie in the terminology. Fawn's parents called her body a "natural chassis," also addressing the natural/fake dichotomy. Fawn uses human-presenting as a way to avoid that judgmental binary. However, with Indira's eye, Fawn pushes the point even further. While Indira (and her doctors and much of the general public) sees Fawn's eye as mechanical, unnatural, and fake, Fawn (and it doesn't get much more natural than a fawn) asks her to rethink the classification. Does natural/fake derive from the means by which it is produced? By the materials from which it is made? Or from its function?

By focusing on the latter, Fawn shifts her own ontological status. Does the material of her body define her status, or her function? If someone focuses on the material construction of her body, then they would consider Fawn "fake." If someone focuses on her function, then they might consider her natural. If Fawn lives, loves, and produces art (like Indira), then is she not also human? Fawn is de facto queering the natural/unnatural distinction. Like Haraway, Fawn is asking Indira and the reader to think about fundamental definitions and boundaries in a new way.

As Indira makes her prop selections for the shoot, two non-human-presenting AIs are there to move the furniture. One of them makes a comment to Fawn: "You're not better than us" and calls Fawn a "rich brat" (67). The comments clearly upset Fawn (which Indira notices). But here, too, a distinction is being made. What is the source of the AI's malice? What distinction is it (I'm making a pronoun assumption here) making? This particular AI sees the human-presenting/non-human-presenting distinction as significant. It is assuming that either materials or appearance make the difference. Unlike Fawn, it does not seem to think that function is the key distinction—except when that distinction is in regard to manual/mental labor.

When Indira's eye continues to deteriorate, Fawn steps in to care for her when the system does not. Indira's parents are gone; the medical system treats her like an object. Fawn, however, treats her with care. The "nobody" from their first fight has actually become the one person who does care about

Indira. In other words, Fawn's function as caretaker confers upon her human status. (Consider the penultimate scene in the film *Blade Runner* [1986] when Roy's saving of Deckard's life confers human status on him.)

The events of *Pixels of You* are not far off. Its days—and its issues—will soon be upon us. The breakdown of human/machine status described by Haraway is accelerating. We will be more and more technologically enhanced until we become entirely technological. What will it mean to befriend a mechanical being? To have sex with one? To love one?

To paraphrase a line that runs throughout the graphic novel, "Shut up...and kiss me."

Shade 45 — *Slice of Life* (2021-2022) 2 vols.
Who's This Aristotle, Anyway?

AS ANYONE WHO follows science fiction knows, many casual fans associate science fiction with either large-budget summer blockbuster films (think *Star Wars* [1977], *Alien* [1979], or *Men in Black* [1997]) or with superheroes (think *Batman*, *Spiderman*, *Superman*, the MCU, etc.). The reality is much more complex.

A similar kind of reduction occurs with SF comics. While it is true that a sizable portion of comics published each month *are* superhero comics, they do not define the medium. So far in this volume, we have seen superhero comics, time travel comics, social justice comics, technological extrapolation comics, and more. Another popular, if less prominent, type of comic is the "slice of life."

In literary terms, the slice of life story/novel has abandoned Aristotle's (he/him) dictum on plot. For Aristotle, the plot is king. For traditionalists, the plot is a carefully crafted series of events that are interconnected and meaningful. Things unfold in a narrative for a reason. No extraneous thoughts are allowed. Every plot point leads to the climax and resolution. For a slice of life story, however, the author presents seemingly disconnected aspects of a character's life. The scenes and details do not necessarily add up to a whole. They do not necessarily cohere or resolve. No. The slice of life presents mundane acts of a person's daily existence. J. D. Salinger's (he/him) iconic *Cather in the Rye* (1951) relates several events of Holden Caulfield's (he/him) life. By the end, though, Holden is unchanged by those events. As another example, the TV series *Seinfeld* (1989-1998) often *claimed* to be a slice of life: "nothing happens!" though I'm not entirely convinced by that claim. More recently, Greta Gerwig's (she/her) movie *Lady Bird* (2017) could be thought of as a cinematic slice of life. The film has no villains or bullies, and no real resolution. No; instead, it's just a family trying to get by.

In June 2021, Brooklyn-based writer Kathryn "Kat" Calamia (she/her) and Phil Falco (he/him) began publishing their series *Slice of Life* via Webtoon. Following a Kickstarter campaign, the first eleven chapters have been published as collections (2021, 2022). (I was a financial backer of that Kickstarter campaign.) The webtoon continues to be updated on a weekly basis.

The series begins, as SF series often do, *en media res*. Ravyn (she/her) is all psyched to watch an episode of her favorite TV series, *The Sword of Lady Vengeance*. All of the memorabilia and paraphernalia strewn around her bedroom indicate her enthusiasm for the series. She has posters, action figures, DVDs, and a sword. Her sister Lucy (she/her) has *just* walked in the front door in time for the beginning of the episode. Although they are twin sisters and look a lot alike, they live very different lives. Ravyn is a nerd who is totally into fan culture; she has no friends at school. Lucy, on the other hand, is an academic and social overachiever, who is head cheerleader and in student government.

In turns out that Lucy doesn't really follow *The Sword of Lady Vengeance*, and she doesn't really get the appeal. She's also not up on the latest twists and turns. Consequently, she's a little dismissive when she learns that Lady Vengeance is going to—once again—have to kill off her arch-nemesis, the Demon Lord. The gall! Ah, but that's hardly the end of the indignities. They then argue over the ending of the series. Ravyn believes that Lady Vengeance, Yuriko (she/her), should have completed her life mission of remembering her dead boyfriend. Lucy, on the other hand, thinks that Yuriko was too young. She should have moved on with her life. Ravyn recoils in horror and throws her twin sister out of her bedroom.

Following a nightmare, the two sisters awaken to find themselves staring at Yuriko, in the flesh. Okay, Okay. That sounds like a lot of plot and not so much like a slice of life. But once Yuriko is in the Ravyn/Lucy world, it becomes much more mundane. They go to the mall to pick out clothing for the warrior princess. Ravyn wants to buy her nerdy clothing; Lucy wants to buy her trendy clothing. Yuriko finds her own look. Lucy's boyfriend drops by the mall to tell Lucy that he's actually gay. The three young women all have a very awkward dinner with Lucy and Ravyn's father. Ravyn and Lucy play softball at school. Ravyn and Lucy deal with the anniversary of their mother's death in very different ways. And so on….

Does it all add up? Well, sort of. Volume 1 collects the first four chapters from the webtoon, plus an additional "story" that is set in the future. In this future, we see Lucy and Yuriko together as a couple, hosting their first gathering in their apartment. Volume 2 ignores that future history and goes back to the early days of the two young women getting to know each other. Volume 2 ends with another future story. Those two future chapters effectively undo any narrative tension in the series. The reader does not need to wonder what it all adds up to—we know. The reader does not need to wonder whether they will get together—we already know. No, the point is not the development, tension, and resolution of a plot but the day-to-day lived experiences.

Slice of Life is a lovely, if uncomplicated, tale of two unlikely women meeting and falling in love. Yuriko and Lucy could not be any more different. One is a (fictional) medieval warrior-princess and the other is a 21st-century cheerleader. The whole how-can-they-possibly-even-communicate question aside, what would they have in common? What is the basis of their relationship? What would they talk about? Well, one night they do stay up all night talking, and they talk about ice machines, cheerleading, and meta-narrative questions about the TV show.

Were *Slice of Life* a typical comic series, we might get more back story on the characters. The comics might explain away linguistic differences and focus more on the battles (literal and metaphorical) that these two women fight. Villains might stand in the way of the lovers. Plot devices that separate the two (e.g., Yuriko's show could be revived and she would be pulled back into her own world, thus cruelly separating Yuriko and Lucy) might be deployed. But that is not the point here.

Slice of Life simply offers glimpses into the lives of these three women (and, to a lesser extent, the life of Dante [he/him], the gay boyfriend turned best friend). The comic does slide toward some stereotypes. The two twins are both white and blonde. They dress differently and have different personalities, but they both conform to cultural norms of body type and beauty. Yuriko is also slender and attractive. Although she says that the place she comes from does not have a name, her name and appearance suggest a Japanese background. When Yuriko appears, Ravyn yells, "Yurikosanisinmybedroom," or "Yurikosan is in my bedroom," which also suggests a Japanese background. In Shade 6, *Crossed Wires*, when Alan considers adding a kimono to his avatar, the author rejects that idea, noting that too much cultural appropriation already takes place in comics (and in cyberpunk, especially). Finally, Lucy's boyfriend is Dante, who is a Black football player. Although Dante defies cultural stereotypes in some ways, he still conforms in significant ways.

Slice of Life is a naive tale of two girls in love. It does not challenge the comic form, though it does borrow from fandom's penchant for shipping (the practice of putting fictional characters in relationships that are not always canon). In this case, though, the character appears in the real world and begins a relationship with the cheerleader. While the obvious choice would have been the fan girl, the choice to ship Yuriko with the cheerleader queers the cheerleader stereotype. (At the same time, it confirms the bias that the beautiful and popular cheerleader gets everything! (cf. Shade 39, *I Am Not Starfire*). The center of the series remains the relationship between Lucy and Yuriko and their everyday lives.

A real slice of life….

Primary Works Cited

Anderson, Ted (writer) and Jen Hickman (artist). *Moth and Whisper*. Issues. 1-5. Sherman Oaks, CA: Aftershock Comics, 2018-2019.

Ayala, Vita (writer), Emily Pearson (artist), and Marissa Louise (colors). *The Wilds*. Los Angeles: Black Mask Studios, 2018.

Bongiovanni, Archie (writer) and Tristan Jimerson (artist). *A Quick and Easy Guide to They/Them Pronouns*. Portland, OR: Limerance Press, 2018.

Booher, David (writer), Claudia Balboni (pencils and ink), and Harry Saxon (illustrator). *Killer Queens*. Milwaukie, OR: Dark Horse Comics, 2022.

Brombal, Tate (writer), Jeff Lemire (writer), and Gabriel Hernández Walta (artist). *Barbalien: Red Planet*. Milwaukie, OR: Dark Horse Comics, 2021.

Calamia, Kat (writer), Phil Falco (writer), and Valeria Peri (artist). *Slice of Life*. Vol. 1. No city: Phil Falco & Kathryn Calamia, 2021.

—.*Slice of Life*. Vol. 2. No city: Phil Falco & Kathryn Calamia, 2022.

Christmas, Johnnie (writer) and Dante Luiz (artist). *Crema*. Milwaukie, OR: Dark Horse Press, 2020.

Colinet, Pierrick (writer) and Elsa Charretier (artist). *The Infinite Loop*. San Diego, CA: IDW Publishing, 2015.

Dahliwal, Aminder (writer) and Nikolas Ilic (color artist). *Cyclopedia Exotica*. Montréal, Quebec: Drawn & Quarterly, 2021.

Eckert, Josh (writer) and James F. Wright (artist). *Contact High*. No city: F.I.M.C., 2017.

Fortson, Ashanti (writer and illustrator). *Galanthus*. (now dead). Archived at: https://web.archive.org/web/20201222011343/http://galanthuscomic.com/comic/book-one-cover.

Fraction, Matt (writer) and Christian Ward (artist). *ODY-C: Off to Far Ithicaa*. Berkeley, CA: Image Comics, 2015.

Gillen, Kieron (writer), Phil Jimenez (penciler), Tom Plamer le Beau (ink), and Scott Hanna (ink). *Angela: Asgard's Assassin*. New York: Marvel, 2014.

Glass, Joe (writer) and Gavin Mitchell (artist). *The Pride Season One: I Need a Hero*. Queer Comix, 2019.

Greenwood, Eve (writer and illustrator). *Inhibit: Book One*. UK: Comic Printing, 2019.

Hill, Joe (writer), David M. Booher (writer), and Zoe Thorogood (artist). *Rain*. Issues 1-5. Portland, OR: Syzygy, 2022.

Hirsh, Ananth (writer), Yuko Ota (writer), and Tess Stone (colors and letters). *Pixels of You*. New York: Amulet Books, 2021.

Horn, Tina (writer) and Jen Hickman (artist). *SfSx*. Portland, OR: Image Comics, 2020.

Hubert (writer) and Zanzim (illustrator). *A Man's Skin*. Portland, OR: Firebrand, 2021.

Jay, Iris. *Crossed Wires*. 1 May 2014 - 30 December 2021.

Lanzing, Jackson (writer), Collin Kelly (writer), Marcus To (artist), and Irma Kniivila (colors). *Joyride: Ignition*, Vol. 1. Los Angeles: BOOM! Studios, 2016.

—. *Joyride: Teenage Spaceland*, Vol. 2. Los Angeles: BOOM! Studios, 2018.

—. *Joyride: Maximum Velocity*, Vol. 3. Los Angeles: BOOM! Studios, 2016.

Mirk, Sarah (writer) and Eva Cabrera (illustrator). *Open Earth*. Portland, OR: Limerance Press, 2018.

Mulligan, Brennan Lee (writer) and Molly Ostertag (illustrator). *Strong Female Protagonist*. Marietta, GA: Top Shelf Productions, 2012.

Muró, Jennifer (writer), Thomas Krajewski (writer), and Gretel Lusky (illustrator). *Primer*. Burbank, CA: DC Graphic Novels for Kids, 2020.

North, Ari (writer and illustrator). *Always Human*. New York: Little Bee, 2021.

Ostertag, Molly Knox (writer and illustrator). *The Girl from the Sea*. New York: Scholastic Graphix, 2021.

Pires, Curt (writer), Alex Diotto (artist), and Dee Conniffe (colorist). *Youth, Season 1*. No city: Comixology, 2020.

—. *Youth, Season 2*. No city: Comixology, 2020.

Rodi, Robert (writer) and Jackie Lewis (illustrator). *Merry Men*. Portland, OR: Oni Press, 2018.

Sebela, Christopher (writer), Ro Stein (pencils), Ted Brandt (inks), and Tríona Farrell (colors). *Crowded: Soft Apocalypse*, Vol. 1. Portland, OR: Image Comics, 2019.

—. *Crowded: Glitter Dystopia*, Vol. 2. Portland, OR: Image Comics, 2020.

—. *Crowded: Cutting-Edge Desolation,* Vol. 3. Portland, OR: Image Comics, 2022.

Som, Bishakh (writer and illustrator). *Apsara Engine.* New York: Feminist Press, 2020.

Spurrier, Simon (writer) and Chris Wildgoose (illustrator). *Alienated.* Los Angeles: BOOM! Studios, 2020.

Stotts, Taneka (writer) and Genué Revuelta (illustrator). *Love Circuits.* Webcomic. 2017. https://www.lovecircuits.com/.

Tamaki, Mariko (writer) and Yoshi Yoshitani (artist). *I Am Not Starfire.* Burbank, CA: DC Comics, 2021.

Tobin, Paul (writer) and Colleen Coover (illustrator). *Gingerbread Girl.* Marietta, GA: Top Shelf Productions, 2011.

Trauth, Margaret (writer and illustrator). *Decrypting Rita.* Seattle, WA: Collapsar Press, 2016.

Trotman, C. Spike (editor) and Amanda Lafrenais (editor). *FTL, Y'All!: Tales from the Age of the $200 Warp Drive.* No city: Iron Circus Comics, 2018.

Valero-O'Connell, Rosemary (writer and illustrator). *Don't Go without Me.* No city: ShortBox, 2020.

Vaughan, Brian (writer) and Cliff Chiang (artist). *Paper Girls.* Portland, OR: Image Comics, 2016.

Vazquez, Kalinda (writer) and Carlos Gómez (artist). *America Chávez: Made in the USA.* New York: Marvel Comics, 2021.

Visaggio, Magdalene (writer), Eva Cabrera (pencils and inks), and Claudia Aguirre (colors). *Kim & Kim.* Los Angeles: Black Mask Studios, 2016.

—. (writer) and Claudia Aguirre (illustrator). *Lost on Planet Earth.* New York: Death Rattle, 2020.

Walker, Suzanne (writer) and Wendy Xu (illustrator). *Mooncakes*. Portland, OR: Lion Forge, 2020.

Weir, Ivy Noelle (writer) and Steenz (illustrator). *Archival Quality*. Portland, OR: Oni Press, 2018.

Yee, Reimena (writer and illustrator). *Séance Tea Party*. New York: RH Graphics, 2020.

Zdarsky, Chip (writer) and Kagan McLeod (illustrator). *Kaptara: Fear Not, Tiny Alien*. Berkeley, CA: Image Comics, 2015.

Secondary Works Cited

"Aldrif Odinsdottir (Earth-616)." *Fandom. com*. n.d. https://marvel.fandom.com/wiki/ Aldrif_Odinsdottir_(Earth-616).

"Angela." *Fandom.com*. n.d. https://imagecomics.fandom. com/wiki/Angela.

Atwood, Margaret. *The Penelopiad: The Myth of Penelope and Odysseus*. Toronto: Knopf Canada, 2005.

Ballard, Jamie. "Two in Five Americans Say Ghosts Exist—and One in Five say They've Encountered One." *YouGov.com*, 21 October 2021. https://today.yougov.com/entertainment/ articles/38919-americans-say-ghosts-exist-seen-a-ghost?

Bennington-Castro, Joseph. "How AIDS Remained an Unspoken—but Deadly—Epidemic for Years." *History,* 1 June 2020. https://www.history.com/news/ aids-epidemic-ronald-reagan.

Borges, Jorge Luis. "Pierre Menard, Author of *Don Quixote*." In *Ficciones*, trans. by Anthony Kerrigan, New York: Grove Press, 1962. 45-55.

Brown, Fredric. "Answer." In *Star Shine*. Montreal, Canada: Bantam Books, 1956. 15-16.

Calvin, Ritch. *Queering SF: Readings*. Seattle: Aqueduct Press, 2022.

—. "Queer SF." *Routledge Companion to Gender and Science Fiction*. Eds. Keren Omry, Lisa Yaszek, Sonja Fritszche, and Wendy Gay Pearson. Routledge. 2023, 49-56.

Christianson, Jon Erik. "Upgrading Cyberpunk in Iris Jay's *Crossed Wires* (Webcomic Q&A)." *Comics Alliance*, 7 November 2017. https://comicsalliance.com/crossed-wires-iris-jay-interview/.

Clarke, Cassandra. "*Killer Queens* Creators Tease How Their Queer Assassins Will Tackle Tyranny." *CBR*, 21 September 2021. https://www.cbr.com/killer-queens-creators-dark-horse-comic-lgbqt-interview/.

Clute, John and Peter Nicholls, Eds. *The Encyclopedia of Science Fiction*. London: Orbit, 1993.

Collins, Elle. "'I Wanted to Do a Buddy Story': Magdalene Visaggio Talks Friendship, Worldbuilding, and Identity in *Kim & Kim*." *Comics Alliance*, 7 June 2016. https://comicsalliance.com/magdalene-visaggio-kim-and-kim-interview/.

Conklin, Groff. *Omnibus of Science Fiction*. New York: Crown Publishers, 1952.

Dapul, Motzie. *The Pinoy Monster Boyfriend Anthology*. No city: no publisher, 2017.

"Death (personification)." *Wikipedia*. https://en.wikipedia.org/wiki/Death_(personification).

Durkee, Alison. "'The Very Hungry Caterpillar' Tops Amazon Bestseller List after Eric Carle's Death—but It's Been a Consistent Hit for Decades." Forbes, 27 May 20221. https://www.forbes.com/sites/alisondurkee/2021/05/27/the-very-hungry-caterpillar-tops-amazon-bestseller-list-after-eric-carles-death—but-its-been-a-consistent-hit-for-decades/?sh=59a7eb3c2260.

Eisner, Will. *Comics and Sequential Art*. Expanded edition. Tamarac, FL: Poorhouse Press, 1985.

Fortson, Ashanti. "About." *Ashanti Fortson*. n.d. https://ashantifortson.com/about.

—. "Artist Interview with Ashanti Fortson." Art-Res. n.d. https://artres.xyz/post/artist-interview-with-ashanti-fortson/.

Fransman, Karrie and Jonathan Plackett. *Gender Swapped Fairy Tales*. London: Faber & Faber, 2021.

—. *Gender Swapped Greek Myths*. London: Faber & Faber, 2022.

"Fred Phelps." *SPL Center*, no date. https://www.splcenter.org/fighting-hate/extremist-files/individual/fred-phelps/.

Gallagher, Ashley. "Wow! Webcomics! Review: *Love Circuits* by Taneka Stotts and Genué Revuelta." *POMEmag*, 22 September 2017. https://pome-mag.com/wow-webcomics-review-love-circuits-taneka-stotts-genue-revuelta/.

Gibson, William. *Neuromancer*. New York: Ace, 1984.

Gil, Joamette. *Power and Magic: The Queer Witch Comics Anthology*. No city: P+M Press, 2016.

—. *Immortal Souls: Power and Magic: The Queer Witch Comics Anthology*. No city: P+M Press, 2018.

Glass, Joe. "Who Is Joe Glass?" *Queer Comix*, no date. https://www.joeglasscomics.co.uk/about.

—. "The Grim Reaper Has Never Been So Cute: Interview with *Kim Reaper*'s Sarah Graley." *The AV Club*, 6 April 2017. https://bleedingcool.com/comics/grim-reaper-never-cute-interview-kim-reapers-sarah-graley/.

Golden, Audrey. "William Faulkner's *The Sound and the Fury* in Color." *Books Tell You Why*, 13

August 2016. https://blog.bookstellyouwhy.com/ william-faulkners-the-sound-and-the-fury-in-color.

Gottlieb, Jed. "Music Everywhere." *The Harvard Gazette*, 21 November 2021. https:// news.harvard.edu/gazette/story/2019/11/ new-harvard-study-establishes-music-is-universal/.

Halberstam, J. Jack. *In a Queer Time and Place: Transgender Bodies, Subcultural Lives*. New York: New York University Press, 2005.

Haraway, Donna. "A Manifesto for Cyborgs: Science, Technology, and Socialist Feminism in the 1980s." *Socialist Review*, Vol. 80, 1985. 65-107.

Horne, Karama. "Indie Comics Spotlight: Taneka Stotts Is Unapologetically Dedicated to Marginalized Creators." *Syfy*, 15 March 2019. https://www.syfy.com/ syfy-wire/indie-comics-spotlight-taneka-stotts-is-unapologetically-dedicated-to-marginalized-creators.

—. "Indie Comics Spotlight: Magdalene Visaggio Is Saving Lives One Weird Comic at a Time." *Syfy*, 15 July 2019. https://www.syfy.com/syfy-wire/indie-comics-spotlight-magdalene-visaggio-is-saving-lives-one-weird-comic-at-a-time.

Jagose, Annamarie. *Queer Theory: An Introduction*. New York: New York University Press, 1996.

Joyce, James. *Ulysses*. New York: Everyman's Library, 1997. First published in 1922 by Shakespeare and Company.

Kay, George. *Lupin*. Netflix. https://www.netflix.com/ title/80994082.

Kent, Beth. "2021-2022 California Environmental Legislation: What's Been Introduced?" *Legal Planet*. 2 March 2021. https://legal-planet.org/2021/03/02/2021-

2022-california-environmental-legislation-whats-been-introduced/.

Killermann, Sam. "The Gingerbread Person Version 4." *It's Pronounced Metrosexual*, 2017. https://www.itspronouncedmetrosexual.com/2018/10/the-genderbread-person-v4/.

King, Jack. "The Drama That Raged against Reagan's America." *BBC,* 19 October 2020. https://www.bbc.com/culture/article/20201019-the-drama-that-raged-against-reagans-america.

Kirby, Rob. "Introduction." In *QU33R: New Comics from 33 Creators*, Ed. Rob Kirby. No city: No publisher, 2014.

Knight, Damon. "The Dissecting Table." *Science Fiction Adventures*, November 1952.

Kubes, Tanja. "New Materialist Feminist Perspectives on Sex Robots." Conference Paper, Manchester, UK, August 2019.

Lang, Cady. "What Does Camp Mean Exactly? A Comprehensive Guide to the 2019 Met Gala Theme." *Time*, 2 May 2019. https://time.com/5581241/met-gala-2019-camp-theme-explained-photos/.

Le Guin, Ursula K. "Myth and Archetype in Science Fiction." In *The Language of the Night: Essays on Fantasy and Science Fiction.* New York: Harper Perennial, 1989. 68-77.

Leblanc, Maurice. *Arsène Lupin, Gentleman-Thief.* New York: Penguin Classics, 2007.

Lee, Tanith. *Don't Bite the Sun.* New York: DAW, 1976.

—. *Drinking Sapphire Wine.* New York: DAW, 1977.

—. *Electric Forest.* New York: DAW, 1979.

—. *Silver Metal Lover.* New York: DAW, 1982.

—. *Metallic Love*. New York: Bantam Spectra, 2005.

Lemire, Jeff (writer) and Dean Ormston (artist). *Black Hammer: Secret Origins. Black Hammer* #1-6). Milwaukie, OR: Dark Horse Comics, 2017.

Linke, Kai. *Good White Queers?: Racism and Whiteness in Queer U.S. Comics*. Wetzlar: Transcript, 2021.

Lorde, Audre. "The Master's Tools Will Never Dismantle the Master's House." In *Sister Outsider: Essays and Speeches*. Berkeley: Crossing Press, 2007. 110-113.

MacDonald, Heidi. "Interview—Spike Trotman on Self Crowdfunding: 'This is me getting out of the car.'" *The Beat*, 23 February 2022. https://www.comicsbeat.com/interview-spike-trotman-on-self-crowdfunding-kickstarter/.

McCloud, Scott. *Understanding Comics: The Invisible Art*. New York: Kitchen Sink Press, 1993.

McCarry, Sarah. *All Our Pretty Songs*. Book One: Metamorphoses Trilogy. New York: St. Martin's Griffin, 2014.

Meyer, Marissa. *Cinder*. Book One: The Lunar Chronicles. New York: Square Fish, 2013.

Morris, Steve. "Margaret Trauth on *Decrypting Rita*: 'I'm in an Intensely Experimental Phase Right Now." *The Beat: The Blog of Comics Culture*. 2 April 2014. https://www.comicsbeat.com/marrgaret-trauth-on-decrypting-rita-i-dont-want-to stagnate-interview/.

O'Brien, John A. *Fun with Dick and Jane*. Chicago: Scott, Foresman, and Co., 1947.

O'Leary, Shannon and Joan Reilly. *Big Feminist BUT: Comics about Women, Men, and the Ifs, ANDs, and BUTs of Feminism*. No city: Alternative Comics, 2014.

Ortner, Sherry. "Is Female to Male As Nature Is to Culture?" *Feminist Studies*, Vol. 1, No. 2, Autumn 1972. 5-31.

Ovid. *Metamorphoses. Project Gutenberg*, 2007. https://www.gutenberg.org/files/21765/21765-h/21765-h.htm.

Pearson, Wendy. "Alien Cryptographies: The View from the Queer." *Science Fiction Studies*, Vol. 26, Iss. 1, March 1999. 1-22.

Redpath, Audrey. *Oath: Anthology of New (Queer) Heroes.* Canada: Mary's Monster, 2016.

Rich, Adrienne. "Compulsory Heterosexuality and Lesbian Existence." *Feminist Frontiers III*. Eds. Laurel Richardson and Verta Taylor. New York: McGraw-Hill, 1993. 158-79.

Rodi, Robert. "Home." *Robert Rodi*, 2017. http://www.robertrodi.com/index.html.

Santoni, Matt. "Review: *The Pride* #1-6." *Comicosity*, 29 November 2015. http://www.comicosity.com/review-the-pride-1-6/.

Sappho. "He Is More Than a Hero." In *Sappho: A New Translation*. Trans. Mary Barnard. Berkeley, CA, University of California Press, 1958, 39.

Scott, Darrieck and Ramzi Fawaz. "Introduction: Queer about Comics." *American Literature*, Vol. 90, Iss. 2, June 2018. 197-219.

Shadel, J. D. "This Long-Awaited Graphic Novel Explores Surreal Femme Futures." *Them,* 14 April 2020. https://www.them.us/story/aspara-engine-bishakh-som-graphic-novel.

Shakespeare, William. *Macbeth. The Complete Works of Shakespeare*, 3rd edition, Ed. David Bevington, Glenview, IL, Scott, Foresman and Comapny, 1980.

Sontag, Susan. "Notes on 'Camp.'" In *Against Interpretation and Other Essays*. New York: Delta, 1966. 275-292.

Stein, Daniel and Jan-Noël Thon. *From Comic Strips to Graphic Novels: Contributions to the Theory and History of Graphic Narrative*. Berlin: De Gruyter, 2013.

Stone, Sam. "Vita Ayala Wants to Keep Comics Fun—and Shatter Barriers." *CBR.com*, 12 June 2020. https://www.cbr.com/. vita-ayala-interview-keep-comics-fun-shatter-barriers/.

Stone, Tucker. "'It's Not a Slam-Bang-Action-So-Quiet': An Interview with Cliff Chiang and Brian K. Vaughn. *The Comics Journal*, 19 December 2019. https://www.tcj.com/ its-not-a-slam-bang-action-so-quiet-an-interview-with-brian-k-vaughan-and-cliff-chiang/.

Sullivan, Caitlin and Kate Bornstein. *Nearly Roadkill: An Erotic Infobahn Adventure*, New York: High Risk, 1996.

Tiptree, James, Jr. "The Women Men Don't See." In *Warm Worlds and Otherwise*. New York: Del Rey, 1975. 131-64.

Topel, Fred. "Exclusive Interview: George Takei on 'Takei's Take.'" *Mandatory*, 13 December 2013. https://www. mandatory.com/fun/619943-exclusive-interview-george-takei-on-takeis-take/.

Trotman, C. Spike. *Poorcraft: The Funnybook Fundamentals of Living Well on Less*. No city: Iron City, 2012.

Varley, John. "Options," In *Universe 9*, Ed. Terry Carr. New York: Doubleday, 1979.

Vedder, Leslie. *The Bone Spindle*. London: Hodder Children's Books, 2022.

Vogel, David. "Why the Golden State Became Green: The Geographic Origins of Environmental Protection in California." *Institute of Governmental Studies* 2003.

https://www.igs.berkeley.edu/sites/default/files/files/
events/vogel-paper-3-5-15.pdf.

Whitbrook, James. "Trans Comic Heroes Matter, and *Kim
& Kim*'s Magdalene Visaggio Knows Why." *Gizmodo*, 16
May 2016. https://gizmodo.com/trans-comic-heroes-
matter-and-kim-kims-magdalene-vis-1776899454.

Williamson, Cris. "Shooting Star." *The Changer and the
Changed.* Wolf Moon Records, 1975.

Wertham, Frederic. *Seduction of the Innocent.* New York:
Rinehart, 1954.

Wilson, Emily (translator). Homer, *The Odyssey.* New York:
W. W. Norton, 2018.

Wisp. "*Decrypting Rita*: A Comic by Margaret Trauth." *Yes
Homo: A Queer Review Wbecomics.* 6 September 2015.
https://yeshomo.net/decrypting-rita/.

Woolf, Virginia. *Mrs. Dalloway.* New York: Harcourt, Inc.,
1981. First published 1925.

@zoewhittall. "A thing I wish I knew about Thoreau as a
teenager was that his mother brought him sandwiches
and Walden Pond was on her property. I think I might
have made some different life choices had I understood
that." X, 28 August 2019, 12:54 p.m., twitter.com/
zoewhittall/status/1166755931847311361.

About the Author

Ritch Calvin (he/him) was born and raised in a small farming town in northwest Ohio. Don't let the picture books fool you. It wasn't all that bucolic. Science fiction was a way out. After he had exhausted the entire SF collection at the local library, he discovered (his mother was a librarian) the wonders of interlibrary loan. Although he spent many years working in a local factory, he also co-owned and ran a bookstore. While listening to a shortwave radio in that bookstore, he heard an interview with Carlos Fuentes, and that opened up a whole other world.

He obtained a BA and MA in English from Bowling Green State University and a PhD in Comparative Literature from SUNY Stony Brook. He is now an Associate Professor of Women's, Gender, and Sexuality Studies.

He served on the Executive Committee of the Science Fiction Research Association (SFRA) for six years (two as VP, two as President, and two as Past President). He was also the media reviews editor for the SFRA Review for six years. He was the Conference Director for the SFRA's 2015 annual conference (Vandana Singh, Alexis Lothian, and M. Asli Dukan were the Guests of Honor).

He has published essays in *Extrapolation*, *Femspec*, *Science Fiction Film and Television*, *Science Fiction Studies*, *New York Review of Science Fiction*, *SFRA Review*. His bibliography of the works of Octavia E. Butler appeared in *Utopian Studies* in 2008. His first edited collection, on *Gilmore Girls*, appeared in 2007. In 2014, he edited (with Doug Davis, Karen Hellekson, and Craig Jacobsen) a volume of essays titled *SF 101: An Introduction to Teaching and Studying Science Fiction*. In 2016, he published *Feminist Epistemology and Feminist Science Fiction: Four Modes* (Palgrave). In 2022, his *Queering SF: Readings* was published by Aqueduct Press. He is currently working on a book on C. J. Cherryh and another book on Queer YA SF.